WE ARE EACH OTHER'S BUSINESS

WE ARE
EACH OTHER'S
BUSINESS

WE ARE
EACH OTHER'S
BUSINESS

BLACK WOMEN'S
INTERSECTIONAL POLITICAL
CONSUMERISM DURING
THE CHICAGO WELFARE
RIGHTS MOVEMENT

NICOLE M. BROWN

Columbia University Press   *New York*

Columbia University Press
Publishers Since 1893
New York   Chichester, West Sussex
cup.columbia.edu

Copyright © 2024 Nicole Marie Brown
All rights reserved

Library of Congress Cataloging-in-Publication Data
Names: Brown, Nicole M. (Sociologist), author.
Title: We are each other's business : Black women's intersectional consumerism during the Chicago welfare rights movement / Nicole M. Brown.
Description: New York : Columbia University Press, [2024] | Includes bibliographical references and index.
Identifiers: LCCN 2024001469 (print) | LCCN 2024001470 (ebook) | ISBN 9780231205221 (hardback) | ISBN 9780231205238 (trade paperback) | ISBN 9780231555906 (ebook)
Subjects: LCSH: Poor African Americans—Services for—Illinois—Chicago—History—20th century. | Poor women—Services for—Illinois—Chicago—History—20th century. | African American women—Political activity—Illinois—Chicago—History—20th century. | Consumers—Political activity—Illinois—Chicago—History—20th century. | Consumer behavior—Political aspects—Illinois—Chicago—History—20th century. | Welfare rights movement—Illinois—Chicago.
Classification: LCC HV1447.C55 B76 2024 (print) | LCC HV1447.C55 (ebook) | DDC 362.83/8089960730773711—dc23/eng/20240221
LC record available at https://lccn.loc.gov/2024001469
LC ebook record available at https://lccn.loc.gov/2024001470

Printed and bound by CPI Group (UK) Ltd, Croydon, CR0 4YY

Cover design: Julia Kushnirsky
Cover image: Shutterstock

CONTENTS

Acknowledgments *vii*
Preface *xi*

Introduction 1

1 Harvest 20

2 Business 49

3 Magnitude 88

4 Bond 124

Conclusion 155

Appendix A *165*
Appendix B *167*
Notes *169*
References *205*
Index *213*

ACKNOWLEDGMENTS

Here I humbly offer expressions of gratitude to those who helped usher this book into being, with the full understanding that this list is incomplete. To each person who has encouraged me to finish what I started, I thank you.

Thank you to my intellectual mentors, Bernice McNair Barnett, Moon-Kie Jung, Clarence Lang, and Ruby Mendenhall. Thank you to Joellen El-Bashir and Ida Jones, curator and assistant curator, respectively, at the Moorland-Springarn Research Center at Howard University for their support and kindness. I'd also like to thank Beverly Cook and Denise English at the Carter G. Woodson Regional Library. Thank you to Janis Jones and Gretchen Neidhart at the Daley Library and Lee Grady and his staff at the Wisconsin Historical Society. Tremendous gratitude goes to Lauren Trimble and the team of analysts at JSTOR for providing me with the data set to conduct my computational research.

I'm also grateful for the support and encouragement I received at Saint Mary's College of California; my Sociology Department colleagues, Zeynep Atalay, Robert Bulman, John Ely, Ynez Wilson Hirst, and Ana Ramirez; as well as my colleagues in Ethnic Studies, including Loan Dao, Emily Klein, Michael Viola, and

Skye Ward. I'm indebted to the members of my summer writing circle—Teresa Kramer, Karen Ruff, Sarah Vital, and Joseph Zeccardi—who provided helpful feedback on early drafts of the manuscript. I would also like to thank the inaugural faculty cohort of the Radical Imagination Laboratory (RIL), who helped me stay grounded, focused and joyful: Zahra Ahmed, Anna Corwin, Jason Jakaitis, Monique Lane, Amissa Miller, Scott Schönfeldt-Aultman, Tangela Blakely Reavis, and Nekesha Williams.

I am also grateful to Spencer Keralis and Glen Layne-Worthey at the University of Illinois at Urbana-Champaign and Jamila Moore Pewu at California State University, Fullerton, for inviting me into their scholarly communities and encouraging me to share various rearticulations of this work. Their generosity knows no bounds.

I'd like to thank everyone at Columbia University Press, including the faculty board and Lowell Frye, associate editor. Special recognition is due to editorial director Eric Schwartz for his patience and kindness throughout the process as he answered my many questions with care and reassurance. Thanks also to the readers of my manuscript. Many thoughtful and generous comments were provided, which served well in making the final product better.

I would not have finished this book without the assistance of Natasha Gordon-Chipembere. To her I express heartfelt gratitude for her feedback, guidance, and encouragement in responding to reviewer comments, and the same goes to Durell Callier and Dominique Hill for sharing their networks and making this introduction.

I am forever grateful to my family for their support, encouragement, and love through this project's ups and downs. Special thanks to Sheri-Lynn Kurisu and family and to the Deloatch family for being the best cheerleaders I could ever ask for.

I will be forever grateful for the love and support of my children, Derek and Daniel, and my husband, Robert Deloatch. They truly represent the best of us, with their integrity, thoughtfulness, humor, and determination. They have fiercely protected my heart and mind throughout this process.

Finally, this book is dedicated to my grandmother, Conswella Gouch, who loved me to life.

PREFACE

Being from Chicago, I have a special affection for the incomparable Pulitzer Prize–winning poet laureate, Gwendolyn Brooks. For a young Black girl growing up on the Southside, Brooks served as a role model and tremendous source of pride for me and my community. Brooks wrote about the experiences of Black folk with an authenticity and care that resonated with many Blacks up north who had deep connections to the South and southern sensibilities.

Brooks wrote the poem "Paul Robeson" in 1971, during the height of the welfare rights movement. The last stanza reads "We are each other's harvest. We are each other's business. We are each other's magnitude and bond." The subjects of Brooks's writings were the types of people who made up the welfare rights movement. In addition to speaking and seeing Black folks in the fullness of our humanity, "Paul Robeson" also illustrates the need for scholars to pull from various disciplines within the arts and sciences to more robustly articulate the lives and contributions of Black women. In this poem, she speaks directly to a simple truth: that we are literally each other's business. In her homage to Paul Robeson, Brooks speaks to the power and responsibility we have to one another.

XII • PREFACE

As such, *We Are Each Other's Business* speaks to the responsibility we have to one another to share the everyday experiences and contributions of our communities. Using the last stanza of Gwendolyn Brooks's poem "Paul Robeson" as a guide, the book's title and structure are a nod to my deep admiration and appreciation for Brooks and the city of Chicago.

WE ARE
EACH OTHER'S
BUSINESS

WE ARE
EACH OTHER'S
BUSINESS

INTRODUCTION

Chicago was founded in the late 1700s by Jean Baptiste Point Du Sable, a Haitian fur trader who was the first of the city's nonindigenous permanent settlers (Dickerson 2005). Migration of Blacks to Chicago from the South began in the early 1900s. Discriminatory Jim Crow laws, racial segregation of public facilities and schools, lynchings, and the collapse of the cotton industry all contributed to Blacks' migration to the north (Spear 1967; Wilkenson 2011). Between the first great migration to the second, the African American population in Chicago grew by nearly 25 percent to make up well over 10 percent of Chicago's overall population (U.S. Census Bureau 2012).

The promise of Black middle-class prosperity also spurred the exodus from south to north (Frazier 1957), and Chicago's Southside became known as a major hub, called the "Black Metropolis" (Drake and Cayton 1993). With such a heavy concentration of Blacks in Chicago, a distinctive consumer market developed. Yet, for many African Americans, the north was not the land of milk and honey. Due to housing segregation, much of the African American population became concentrated in the city's Southside "black belt." Exploitation of Black residents by

2 • INTRODUCTION

white landlords was common. With cramped living conditions and a decline in industrial jobs came exacerbation of social problems such as poverty and crime (Massey and Denton 1993; Wilson 1987, 1997).

Post–World War II Chicago is the site of the study described in this book, which explores intersectional issues of race, class, and gender. While the National Welfare Rights Organization (NWRO) and the overall movement have been well researched (Naples 1998; Hancock 2004; Nadasen 2005; Orleck 2005; Kornbluh 2007), little research has been done on the affiliated groups of the Chicago Welfare Rights Organization (CWRO), many of whose histories and community relations predated the formal creation of both the CWRO and NWRO. These neighborhood organizations addressed many of the social issues that plagued Black communities in Chicago. The organizations were both religious and secular, and many were either formally or informally led by African American women.

We Are Each Other's Business examines the political activities of welfare rights organizations and the Black women who served as the lifeblood of these groups at the convergence of the consumer, welfare, and women's rights movements.[1] Focusing on the very point at which these political movements' aligned, this book analyzes the political consumerist activities of welfare rights organizations in Chicago during the 1960s and 1970s. I argue that Black women of the Chicago welfare rights movement deployed sophisticated strategies of political consumerism that are most effectively appreciated via an intersectional analysis. Contrary to assertions that Black people's practices in consumer spaces are conspicuous or excessive, I demonstrate how the women involved in the movement viewed consumerism within the context of citizenry rights. Further, the consumer market was used as a vehicle for critique of the state and its treatment of poor Black women.

INTRODUCTION • 3

The book's argument reimagines the struggle between Black women and the state during the welfare rights movement as a battle of technologies. It reframes Black women's political consumerist strategies as sophisticated technology and elucidates the challenges of Black women's relationships to and with various economic and education systems. Specifically, Black women's attempts during the welfare rights movement to secure consumer credit from the Sears Corporation demonstrate a use of what I call a "Black feminist technology" deployed for making radical demands around poor people's access to new consumer credit tools, not for the purposes of conspicuous consumption but, rather, as a budgetary tool with a recognition that poor people can effectively govern themselves. By reframing Black women's political consumerist activities within the context of technology, we are able to better appreciate the forward-thinking activism and contributions of these women.

I also highlight the impact of what I call "algorithmic assemblages of race, class, and gender" that shape the strategies and effectiveness of Black women's activism.[2] More importantly, this work centers Black women's desires and contradictions to expose how power operated through various systems and how people were able to resist and fight back.

The book also reframes government poverty policies as "analog algorithms of poverty." These are policies and procedures of the state that construct poverty to the detriment of those living under such conditions. I argue that these rigid policies based on consumption patterns served to institutionalize beliefs around what the poor deserved. This deconstruction of the poor served the state, through its welfare policies, to commodify and reconstruct or distort the lives of poor people. As such, when referencing the "poor" in this text, I am referring to the women and families who found it impossible to sustain themselves given their

4 • INTRODUCTION

economic constraints. Sometimes those women and families fell within the government's definition of eligibility for state benefits. Sometimes they did not. The poor in this context are those Black women who fought for welfare rights out of necessity.

We Are Each Other's Business begins in Chicago during the welfare rights movement (spanning 1965 to 1975) and utilizes a series of case studies to illustrate the political consumerist strategies, practices, and meaning-making of welfare organization leadership and membership. Specifically, I consider how members of the CWRO-affiliated organizations made political meaning of and strategized through consumer activities, which economic and social conditions led to targeted consumer activism and the social and economic structures that promoted and inhibited the use of consumerism as a politicized project, and how forms of political consumerism identified during the Chicago welfare rights era were successful (or unsuccessful) as a democratizing tool for poor Black women and, by extension, poor people's movements across the nation.

Why focus on organizations rather than individuals? In addition to resisting the dominance of white middle-class individualist narratives that dominate postmodern, economic, and cultural studies of consumerism, this project takes up a Black feminist epistemology based in community. Focusing on community organizations as a unit of analysis allows individuals such as Dovie Coleman and Dorothy Shavers to be highlighted while also centering communal ontologies that were dominant within Black women's movements. The women of the movement often met with state officials in groups of three or four because the Black women leading these WROs were often collaborative, supportive, and protective of one another. I argue that this communal focus on the consumer advocacy of organizations is an underappreciated aspect of the Chicago welfare rights movement and comes in direct tension with neoliberal, individualistic consumerist research as well as the charismatic narratives of male leaders. Black women working collectively is a recognized tradition within African-centered communal work. Within the Chicago welfare rights movement and WROs, community was where true power resided, and "without community, there is no liberation" (Lorde 1979). In an effort to resist erasures of the political work of communities of poor Black women in Chicago WROs and the consumer movement, I focus on the organizations these women created, toiled in, influenced, and fought to preserve and protect.

Though I ground my research in archival methods, I quickly discovered that the erasures evident in the archives were reified in my supplemental efforts to computationally recover Black women's experiences and contributions from complimentary academic discourses. The book takes, in one hand, the epistemic violence of the archives and, in the other, the epistemic violence of academic discourses and computational methods and turns them on each other to expose the continual missteps within academic research about Black women's lives. Scholars such as Saidiya Hartman (2008), Marisa Fuentes (2016), and Christina Sharpe (2016) have provided roadmaps for how to call out such archival violence. This calling out is also relevant as it relates to methods within research and scholars' overreliance on preserved archives, and it is another example of how these archives bring with them the social, political, and cultural values and limitations of their time. Those limitations can lead to erasures that impede our ability to understand data in a different way. Thus, we can learn from and deploy the strategies of scholars like Sharpe (2016) to contend with the "fiction of the archives."

I contend that intersectional analytics and methodologies expose how systems and structures serve to erase and obscure

6 • INTRODUCTION

Black women ontologies. This work offers another iteration of a disruptive path that I hope more social science scholars will follow and, with continued use, deepen to become well worn, and more firmly defined, specifically as it relates to Black women's visionary roles and their deployment of justice technologies.

INTERSECTIONAL POLITICAL CONSUMERISM DEFINED

I define "intersectional political consumerism" as consumer activities motivated by one's intersecting social locations (race, class, and gender). For intersectional political consumerism to occur, there must be a desire to influence some political condition (of one's social locations) and evidence that marketplace sites of consumerism are used or targeted for some political purpose designed to influence how resources are allocated (toward a specific group). Intersectional political consumerism is not limited to subaltern groups, as groups with power can exercise intersectional political consumerism just as can groups that are marginalized.[3] The latter groups, though, will come into intersectional political consumerism and make meaning of their experiences with consumerism differently as a political project. In terms of indicators of intersectional political consumerism, this project looks specifically at the welfare rights era for the presence of a political agenda, engagement of the marketplace via consumerism, and intersectional social locations serving as the primary motivation for mobilization. The presence of intersectional political consumerism was measured via both computational analysis of writings covering the historical period and a content analysis of archival data describing contextual historical events within the welfare rights era that engage race, class, gender, access to resources, and consumerism.

Of key importance to the analysis is the uncovering of how African Americans made political meaning of consumer activities and consumer spaces, the economic and social conditions that led to the implementation of consumerist activities as an act of protest, and the political and economic structures that promoted and inhibited this form of political activism in the historical periods before, during, and after the welfare rights era. By understanding the circumstances within which political consumer activism was deployed and identifying the reasons for its decline as a political project, we may glean transferable knowledge to illuminate the conditions of today and how mass political economic action might be harnessed to improve these conditions.

In the illustration exploring race, gender, and class, each social location is represented by a plane and shares a point of intersection with the others. With an infinite number of potential identities, we could in theory have so many intersecting planes that the result would appear to be a solid sphere filled by these

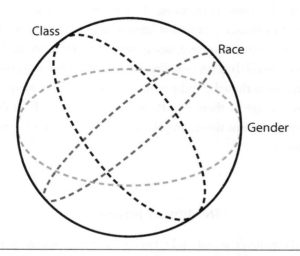

FIGURE 0.1 Assemblages of social location

social locations. Zygmunt Bauman (1998) explores domains through which power plays out via one plane, class; his "flawed consumer" theory relates to identity reconstruction of the poor (Marotta 2000). But intersectionality offers a complexity to Bauman's model by using as a point of analysis the intersection of multiple planes—in this case, race, gender, and class. This dynamic assemblage of social locations uncovers another dimension of how power operates as a result of race, gender, and class identity construction.

Bauman (2002) describes power as a battle for legitimacy, the ability to define what is legitimate and to exact or impose one's will, agenda, beliefs, politics, and so on on another. Through consumerism, we can illuminate one battle for legitimacy. We can explore who defines legitimacy, how these definitions are resisted, and, since this study is historical, the outcome of the battle. The intersectional political consumerism model reveals that it is not just class that delegitimizes some subjects as flawed; it is not just class that causes some subjects to be viewed as incapable of adequately performing their societal roles to be consumers or to engage a capitalist "democracy" as consumers; it is not one plane but a convergence of several social locations illuminated through intersectionality. Despite the tensions between Black feminist thought and postmodernism (Collins 1999)—or perhaps because of them—I attempt to apply a Black feminist lens to postmodern theorizing about consumerism via intersectional analysis.

"Realms of Power"

Pierre Bourdieu's social field (1993) examines where people negotiate various forms of power. The social field is described

INTRODUCTION • 9

as "a social arena within which struggles or maneuvers take place over specific resources or stakes and access to them" (Jenkins 2002, 84).[4] Patricia Hill Collins's domains of power (2000) explain how the matrix of domination, which is the social organization of intersecting oppressions, is organized. The realms of power within intersectional political consumerism are a marrying of the concepts of social field and domains of power, in that they describe the ways in which power is negotiated and influenced by intersecting social locations within the consumerist setting. Within the realm of the social—specifically consumerism—there is a struggle over how power is organized through intersecting social locations and how that organizing is used to gain access to resources for political purposes (which influence how power manipulates or distorts intersecting oppressions and transforms to achieve intersecting justices). In this way, power is multidirectional; its organization is changing as it is being constructed. These realms are moving power in multiple directions at once and are capable of having multiple, simultaneous interpretations and consequences. These realms of power represent social, political, and economic phenomena that are legitimized and include historical remnants, traces, and legacies that persist.

For African Americans, one historical legacy represented by the sociopolitical phenomenon of consumerism would be the unyielding historical denial of access to full citizenship in a consumerist society through access to consumer products, services, and spaces. For a realm of power to exist, there must be (a) the presence of a struggle over who is viewed as legitimate within the consumer space, (b) a connection with historical context that influences current conditions, and (c) a connection to the site of power and a specific ideology[5] seeking promotion.

Realms of power in this study include governance (i.e., local, state, and federal government), business/industry (defined here as African American consumerism), economic policy (e.g., neoliberalism), and condition (e.g., poverty). The governance realm of power focuses specifically on the role of the state in facilitating and hindering the process of the political transition of citizens from customers to consumers during the 1960s. To promote capitalist engagement, the state helped shape consumer identity not only via government protection policies but also through the education system. African American consumerism as a realm of power refers to the growing acknowledgment of the Black consumer market and African American consumerism as political entities in the welfare rights era. I examine neoliberalism as a realm of power to explore this economic policy and its ideological infiltration and influence during the period of study. The condition of poverty as a realm of power refers specifically to the feminization and "Blackening" of poverty that took place during the 1960s. Governance, African American consumerism, neoliberalism, and poverty are all realms through which power played out in Chicago during the 1960s and 1970s. In this study, intersectional political consumerism is a tool by which to consider these realms of power and how they work to organize through social locations for political purposes.

Realms of power are the instruments of structures and ideologies in that the state, industry (consumerism), and economic policy (neoliberalism) are all instruments of capitalism, while the feminization of poverty is an instrument of patriarchy and the Blackening of poverty is an instrument of racism. These structures and ideologies (capitalism, patriarchy, and racism) have historical legacies whose remnants are detected in the instrument. Like a magic wand, a realm of power moves and manipulates intersecting social locations within its sphere and contorts them to serve the purposes of that ideology. Yet, the exposing of these oppressions can also uncover corresponding resistance (attempts at correction) through the actions of political actors embodying these intersecting social positions. Realms of power serve to push, pull, distort, shape, and manipulate intersecting social locations depending on context. I explore realms of power as instruments of capitalist technology. Governance, industry, economic policy, and conditions of poverty all work to push forward capitalist technologies.

To understand how governance was used as an instrument of capitalist technology, I looked at the state's actions in pushing consumer credit on the citizenry. To understand how industry was used in service to capitalism, I looked at consumerism and the ways in which it perpetuated and fought against capitalism via commercial and community-based intersectional political consumerism. To understand how economic policy played a role in the perpetuation of capitalism in consumerist society in the 1960s and '70s, I explored the ways in which neoliberal policies infiltrated consumerism imaginaries as well as the ways these ideas were turned inward by welfare rights organizations to achieve material gains for poor people. I also considered the specific ways in which the Blackening and feminization of poverty, as well as the measuring and defining of who was counted among the poor, perpetuated capitalism while also frustrating WRO members' efforts to democratize choice and win an adequate guaranteed income.

In considering the unique challenges facing the poor as consumers and addressing the types of consumerism employed for political purposes, I argue that intersectional social locations shape the consumer strategies chosen by various welfare organizations that advocated on behalf of poor people. In addition to the national organization's efforts to initiate credit campaigns, the local welfare rights organizations attempted to engage consumerism through buying clubs, rent strikes, co-ops, and credit

12 • INTRODUCTION

unions. Still, rather than organizing a national campaign around increasing the number of minority-owned businesses, community control over businesses serving Black communities, or securing jobs for Blacks in those stores (as many of the local organizations had done), the NWRO pursued securing credit from department stores that sold quality products (such as furniture, appliances, and clothing).[6] While the former examples appealed to more of a Black nationalist approach, the latter was more consistent with an integrationist-type capitalism, which sought to include poor African American people.

On May 21, 1966, following the University of Chicago's Ad Hoc Committee conference on guaranteed annual income, George Wiley's Poverty Rights/Action Center (PRAC) sponsored a strategic planning meeting to discuss organizing what later became the National Welfare Rights Organization.[7] The formal welfare rights movement began in June 1966 with welfare recipients marching from Cleveland to the Ohio state capitol to demand higher benefits.[8] Hearing of the march, Wiley[9] decided to help coordinate welfare rights rallies in other cities across the nation, later known as the "June 30 demonstrations." On August 6, 1966, the first national meeting was held and the National Coordinating Committee of welfare rights groups was formed,[10] along with the formal organization of the NWRO.[11]

NWRO members launched a national boycott of Sears in 1969 in an effort to secure credit for welfare recipients. Interestingly, several decades prior, President Theodore Roosevelt proclaimed that the one book he would give the Soviets to teach them about America would be the Sears catalog, implying that the vast opportunities available to capitalist Americans was evident in their ability to engage as consumers. It seemed fitting that some twenty-plus years later, Chicago mothers receiving welfare would focus their attention on this company as a way of securing what they felt were their citizen rights under capitalism.

The boycott of Sears, which began in Philadelphia, was very much linked to the citizen entitlements of welfare recipients, who purported that they were discriminated against by product companies like Sears specifically because they were poor. That the extension of credit was viewed as a fundamental right rather than a privilege reserved for the white middle class was a core tenet of the NWRO campaign. The organization targeted Sears because of its dominance in the consumer market and because of the likelihood that it would be unyielding, which would draw attention to NWRO's cause as well as apply pressure on Sears's competitors to yield to avoid similar attention. NWRO fought to secure credit rights for its members and made itself central within the consumer credit chain, requesting that welfare recipients receiving credit prove their affiliation with NWRO via a reference letter.

The national boycott was somewhat successful in that although the Sears Corporation did not relent, several individual stores did yield to the NWRO demands and extended limited credit to welfare recipients. Cincinnati stores agreed to the NWRO plan in its entirety. Still, there were inherent contradictions of the NWRO movement in terms of seeking liberation and full citizenship through access to credit while also reifying traditional gender roles related to womanhood, motherhood (including women's roles in the labor market), and materialism (Boris 2002; Piven and Cloward 1977).

The NWRO's focus on credit illustrated the first national concerted effort to actively acknowledge the poor as consumers. Prior to this time, the poor were not viewed by large retailers as relevant, and aside from the unscrupulous neighborhood

14 • INTRODUCTION

businesses that sought to exploit them, the poor were mostly ignored in the larger realm of consumerism.

During the welfare rights era, women and men were demanding that they be given the opportunity to engage as "citizen-consumers" (Cohen 2003), whether unemployed or underemployed. This connection of citizenry and consumerism is key as we discuss the Chicago WROs and their efforts to secure consumer entitlements for the poor. For members of these organizations, navigating the world as consumers was viewed as a right of every U.S. citizen, and any barrier between poor people and their right to engage as consumers was considered a threat to their ability to create, maintain, and enjoy social relationships.

We Are Each Other's Business challenges us to consider what it means to recognize poor Black women as sophisticated strategists who understood and engaged the powers and contradictions of consumerism. The book also fills in some gaps when we consider only class or individual micro-level analysis to understand how consumption and consumer spaces are politicized. This book is timely given renewed discussions related to universal basic income programs in the wake of the COVID-19 pandemic, efforts to dismantle welfare assistance (with cuts to the SNAP program and the push for additional work requirements), and the continued attacks on the poor by the state and in the public sphere. This book also emerges during a time when algorithms are driving poverty and consumer policies and having disproportionately negative effects on poor consumers (Eubanks 2019; O'Neil 2017; Benjamin 2019). In addition, little research has been done on the groups affiliated with the Chicago Welfare Rights Organization, many of which, as I noted earlier, had histories and community relations that predated the formal creation of the NWRO. Post–World War II Chicago, as a major destination for African Americans during the great migration, offers a unique and complicated terrain in which to explore algorithmic assemblages of race, class, and gender.

The CWRO and its advocacy efforts for poor people was situated during a time when a larger consumer rights movement was taking place, and as a result, it employed specific strategies that demonstrated the overlapping of welfare rights, women's rights, and consumer rights. *We Are Each Other's Business* amplifies the political consumerist work of poor Black women in these welfare rights organizations. More broadly, the book combats the ahistorical contemporary calls for political consumer activism, which also serve to erase Black women, particularly poor Black women. This book contains lessons on how Black women are ignored in their movement work and movement messages can get co-opted by those in power. In addition, the book shows how middle-class capitalist strategies as tools of liberation are flawed and that there must be a critique of capitalism. Finally, the book considers how social class allegiance can trip up Black people because of its connections to whiteness, and political consumerism can take many forms besides boycotts.

CHAPTER SUMMARIES

Chapter 1, "Harvest," explains my use of intersectional archival research to reframe Black women's innovation during this time as a form of technology. Similar to processes of parallel computing, the consumer, women's, and welfare rights movements overlapped (proceeding relatively simultaneously), sharing some similarities in language (code), goals (tasks), and actors (end users). A unique combination of racism, sexism, and classism blocked poor Black women's access to other programs (consumer and women's rights) and served to stifle all three movements.

16 • INTRODUCTION

Yet, Black women made tremendous strides in navigating their own program (welfare rights) despite the missed opportunities and efficiencies of other programs to partner. Since historical sociology often relies heavily on archival research, an intersectional analysis allows for a defense against the epistemic violence of the archives toward Black women. Chapter 1 also foreshadows the shortcomings of methods not grounded in intersectional analytics as social sciences become increasingly enchanted by computational approaches to inquiry.

Chapter 2, "Business," contextualizes various welfare organization landscapes shaped and maneuvered by Black women during the 1960s–1970s. This chapter shows the similarities and differences between two welfare organizations, The Woodlawn Organization (TWO) and Jobs or Income Now (JOIN), and their relationship to capitalism. The comparison allows for a distinguishing of two dimensions of intersectional political consumerism, both commercially and community based, and explains how these dimensions manifest as either capitalist or socialist within these welfare organizations. The chapter highlights the impact of what I call algorithmic assemblages of race, class, and gender, which affect the strategies and effectiveness of TWO and JOIN.

Comparing the histories and political consumerist strategies of these community organizations during the 1960s, the chapter covers how these organizations' ideologies influenced the types of intersectional political consumerism they chose to employ in their efforts to win rights for poor people. The analysis finds that while TWO, a predominantly Black and formally male-headed organization serving Chicago's Southside Woodlawn neighborhood, employed a commercially based intersectional political consumerism to achieve its goals, JOIN, an interracial and women-led Northside Uptown neighborhood organization, utilized a community-based form of intersectional political consumerism. To be clear, Black women were present, visible, and vocal within both organizations. Their navigation of these organizations and battles for influence were shaped differently depending on the membership and formal leaderships' gender and racial makeup. In other words, the algorithmic assemblages of race, class, and gender helped determine organizational strategies and goals.

Chapter 2 also details the various ways in which whiteness gets centered as communities of color attempt to engage intersectional political consumerism, while also considering the types of social relationships that are forged across consumer spaces when community organizations are ideologically capitalist or socialist. I conclude that TWO's and JOIN's political activism around access to consumerism for their neighborhoods was essentially a battle for their communities' legitimacy as consumers.

Chapter 3, "Magnitude," continues the discussion in chapter 2 about how consumer spaces are a site of struggle for legitimacy and how Black consumers' aspirations tied to white middle-class values leave space for neoliberal ideas to creep into Black consumer imaginings while masking structural inequities. I argue that the construction of middle-class neoliberal identities through consumerism aided the welfare apparatus in deconstructing the poor. However, Black women's organizing around consumer credit served to repurpose these financial tools to benefit poor people. As evidence, the chapter looks specifically at the deployment of Black women's sophisticated understanding of the connection between consumer credit and citizenry rights as a Black feminist technology. The chapter considers the contradictory roles of consumer credit as both a liberatory (middle-class) tool utilized by the poor and a neoliberal mechanism serving to mask growing gaps in income and social deprivation.

18 • INTRODUCTION

Despite the radical approach to consumer advocacy, the NWRO's Sears Credit Campaign failed to engage capitalist mechanisms such as retail credit to secure socialist outcomes. The chapter argues that even as the NWRO's entrenchment in freedom from poverty through liberalism (choice), capitalism (retail credit), and proximity to white middle-class materiality did not lead to success with the Sears campaign, the pursuit of consumer credit as a Black feminist technology of access pushed the boundaries and imaginaries of what Black women demanded and deserved. While chapter 2 shows how ideology influences political consumerist strategies, chapter 3 demonstrates that intersectional political consumerism was unsuccessful because there was an ideological disconnect between strategy and desired results.

Chapter 4, "Bond," builds on chapter 3 by addressing the state and various mechanisms it uses to institutionalize neoliberal values through consumption. These mechanisms, which I call "analog algorithms of poverty," serve to institutionalize beliefs around poor people's "deserved materiality." The chapter argues that the analog algorithms of poverty engaged during the 1970s, along with the relationship between the state and private industry, led to a specific type of commodification of poor people's lives. As evidenced by the welfare policies introduced during the Nixon administration and, in response, the fight for a guaranteed annual income for the poor, consumption measures served to catalyze the organization and mobilization of the poor. I further argue that the poor became pawns in the neoliberal consumerist exchanges between the state and private businesses by exposing the dysfunctional and symbiotic bond or relationship between the state, private businesses, and funding funneled through the poor to businesses. Since analog algorithms of poverty were based on consumption patterns, beliefs around what the poor deserved greatly influenced opinions and policy regarding appropriate minimum income levels.

The Black women of the Chicago welfare rights movement fought bravely for the dignity of their families and communities. They defined themselves as consumers before industry would come to accept and monopolize on their existence as a consumer bloc. Though the outcomes of their movement strategies were varied and sporadic, their legacies lived on in their communities and beyond. This book is dedicated to their efforts.

1

HARVEST

We are a harvest of survivors. But then,
that's what we've always been.

—Octavia Butler, *Parable of the Sower*

Often, when teaching sociological theory, I incorporate speculative fiction as a way for students to differently understand and identify various approaches used to help explain the world around us. In addition to W. E. B. Du Bois's "The Comet," I include poetry readings by June Jordan, Audre Lorde, and the science fiction of Octavia Butler. I particularly enjoy incorporating Butler because her speculative Afrofuturist work exploring themes related to race, politics, and humanity are still relevant today. Her work is also indicative of Black women's abilities not only to be forward-thinking but also to radically imagine possibilities beyond current circumstances, to project ourselves into alternative futures. It is precisely this world-making ability of Black women that shapes my perspective as a historical sociologist to see Black women's work and contributions to the welfare rights movement as analogous to technology, and specifically to concepts in computer science.

Particularly as technology has become synonymous with algorithms and digital environments,[1] the relationship between Black women's advocacy and activism must be recognized for the sophisticated, forward-thinking, and deliberate technology it is. Like algorithms, historical archives are grounded in a particular past—the one preserved (and shared). Both algorithms and archives can be used to project into particular futures. However, without a robust record of historical data to access and rely on, we ultimately reify existing structures and limit the number of models we can explore.

Piecing together the stories of Black women in a historical record dominated by male voices and experiences is particularly challenging. Decisions around whose perspectives are worthy of documenting and preserving, whose contributions are valued and deserving of being brought into the future are often made by those who do not recognize Black women as essential to humanity's survival. This reality can make the archives a treacherous place.

During my research, a major frustration with some of the archival sources available to me, such as the Industrial Areas Foundation (IAF) and local affiliates of the Chicago Welfare Rights Organization, was an erasure of Black women in the collections. Attempting to undo the erasures in those archives and preserving Black women's contributions became a priority over the course of writing this book. Though my research was limited to the availability and accessibility of the historical record, I recognize that my use of the historical record, including how I interpret it, engages a politics of research. As Julia Jordan-Zachery (2013) notes, "Research is a political act and intersectional research is no exception. Researchers make decisions, which have political consequences, when they decide who can speak, whom they speak to, what they can speak about, what questions are asked, how we observe behaviors, and also how we measure such behaviors" (102).

Most algorithms and archives have a common characteristic in that they rely on historical data and the accompanying historical assumptions. The archives are a series of political decisions related to what is deemed worthy of curation and survival. Historical assumptions provide and preserve context. In some cases, I found myself researching activities of people who were not my original intended foci of research in order to understand the social context in which Black women attempted to do their advocacy work. In many ways, this highlights not just the epistemic violence against Black women that is present and activated in many archives but also how important it is for Black women to preserve our own stories.

Since historical sociology often relies heavily on archival research, an intersectional analysis allows for a partial defense against the epistemic violence of the archives toward Black women.[2] This violence also provides space to emphasize the necessity to interrogate, critique, and contextualize the ratification of particular ideologies within the consumerism scholarship—the same ideologies that often render Black women invisible and/or irrelevant in archives that center male stories and histories, such as IAF. An intersectional analysis that includes an interrogation of historical assumptions provides some defense to encoded ideologies that reside in the archives.

This violence extends also to the use of computational tools in service to social science research. Just as archives are subjective, so, too, are computational approaches to textual analysis. There are linguistic limitations to many of these tools, and those that were created to analyze English focus on standard white English usage (Bolukbasi et al. 2016; David 2016). That is why these tools should not be adopted wholesale, particularly when engaging work intended to recognize Black women. Computational tools are to be used in concert with qualitative reflexive processes that serve to complement, not supplement, projects of rescue and recovery (Brown et al. 2016).

Topic modeling was one method that allowed for the surveying of large amounts of data related to governance, industry, economic policy, and conditions of poverty. Topic modeling is a form of computational analysis that uses statistical modeling to discover abstract themes in a collection of documents, also known as a "corpus" (Blei 2012). The documents are presented as a sort of bag of words, and the emerging statistically correlated themes across documents have corresponding probabilities of occurrence in the corpus. Themes are grouped as "topics" based on their pattern of distribution, and the topic output consists of a word list, which provides context for the topic. See table 1.1 for an example of a word list. The topics are given a numeric indicator (e.g., topic 12), which, after reflecting on the theme that emerged from the words that make up a topic, I renamed "Labor and Employment."

In the JSTOR database, I identified more than 1.5 million results of interest to the study.[3] I identified search criteria that corresponded with various "realms of power," searching for publications that referenced poor Black women, neoliberalism, consumerism, welfare rights, the U.S. government, and U.S. citizenship. The search parameters included works published between 1965 and 2014.

The output identifies the general themes emerging from the corpus, insight that would have been impossible to uncover by attempting a traditional close reading of 1.5 million texts. The topic modeling results[4] revealed several relevant themes related to the study for the 1.5 million publications identified in the corpus, including topic 12—Labor and Employment, topic

20—Schools and Formal Education, and topic 30—Markets and Economies. The "consumerism" search terms yielded topic 12, a theme related to labor and employment. The topic word list is in table 1.1, which shows the specific words in the topic as well as the number of times each is presented.

TABLE 1.1 TOPIC 12 WORD LIST: LABOR AND EMPLOYMENT

Word	No. of occurrences
Labor	1,334,173
Workers	1,219,894
Work	842,151
Employment	770,232
Wage	569,000
Job	425,504
Union	399,519
Wages	338,461
Employees	320,979
Working	320,745
Jobs	277,464
Industrial	264,284
Unemployment	244,806
Economic	226,993
Unions	218,373
Force	206,832
Time	205,052

For topic 12, we see that the word "labor" is present 1.3 million times. However, the value of the model's output is not just that it determines word frequencies; the model is able to identify all the words in the list that have a statistically significant probability of being represented together in the subcorpus.[5] Therefore, the context of these words reveals their relation to one another, as they are grounded in word frequencies.

In the historical and archival record of the welfare rights movement, there was evidence that welfare recipients wanted access to consumer rights, activities, spaces, and relationships that were independent of their employment status. During that time, there was significant debate around whether the poor had rights to be consumers if they were not engaged in the formal workplace. The presence of this theme in a corpus query on "consumerism" shows that in academic discourse, there is a subset of literature that considers consumerism and its relationship to workers and employment.

The themes generated from the topic modeling on the "race/class/gender" query also allowed me to see, among other things, whether JSTOR authors and researchers discussed the realms of power engaged in my study and whether discussions of race, class, and gender were present. Similar to the Markets and Economies topic found in the consumerism query, the race/class/gender search terms yielded topic 17, a theme related to the economy, industry, and consumer market. Here we see a theme emerge that encompasses several realms of power in a query for documents related to poor Black women: namely, business/industry and (condition of) poverty. The topic word list is shown in table 1.2.

Next, I used a technique called "intermediate reading" to better understand the context of topic 17 (Brown et al. 2016).[6] Interestingly, the most representative documents that make up the

TABLE 1.2 TOPIC 17 WORD LIST: ECONOMY, INDUSTRY, AND CONSUMER MARKET

Economic	555,016
Market	329,573
Business	252,545
Tax	213,041
Policy	199,513
Income	179,205
Trade	170,663
Price	169,891
Economy	168,881
Capital	160,261
Growth	148,667
Financial	137,753
Bank	135,428
Consumer	130,804
Investment	122,619
Industry	122,165
Development	121,137

topic appear not to discuss poor Black women at all.[7] Though there were limitations to the search terms used to identify documents that discuss poor Black women specifically, we see that in the economic literature from which this topic is heavily based, there is an absence of discussion around intersectionality (race, class, and gender) in the context of economy, industry, and the consumer market. In this way, even as we "search" for poor Black women in the digital record, there remains a segment of the data that erases them.

When incorporating computational analysis into my historical content analysis, I was reminded of the importance of using these two approaches as complementing rather than competing with one another to understand if and how the academic discourse engaged topics that were found in the historical record. Another benefit to engaging big data in concert with close readings of the archival record was the potential to identify gaps in the research, not just in topics and themes themselves but also in the ways these themes may have been analyzed, interpreted, and discussed. Computational analysis allows for an omnipresent perspective on research, connecting the distant reading with the close reading, connecting the historical data with more recent research, while exploring multiple dimensions of research at the same time.

Black feminist theorizing encourages an appropriate reflexivity via its insistence on the acknowledgment of subjectivities, its recognition of our interconnectedness—that of persons/end users, language/code, and goals/tasks—and its persistence in knowing that the personal is political. This work is an epistemological project, and therefore it is as political as it is personal. Sociologists' focus or obsession on or with generalizability in the social sciences is partly responsible for its sprint toward computational methods. I believe this obsession is a trap!

That said, this book is an explicitly political and epistemological project, in that I recognize the terrain of previous political scholarship that served to reify particular one-dimensional hegemonic notions about Black women. These hegemonic notions include inaccurate assumptions that Black people generally and Black women in particular are culturally deficient and also inept at technology. Those who define concepts such as "technology" and who define Black women without our input or consent fall into analytical, methodological, and theoretical trappings that misrecognize Black women's activities. Methods that equate quantity with universality ignore the deliberate ways in which Black women's preservations are hindered. Quantification brings with it a false sense of objectivity, which is then used to produce false generalities. Assertions based on the presence of many narratives in the archives can serve to reinforce "misogynoir,"[8] in much the same way that state welfare policies used quantitative technologies to assert "objectivism" over Black women's lives. This reframing is but one intervention, one that aims to correct emerging scholarship on Black women's everyday resistance and engagement with technology to combat the political effects of previous theorizing about Black women.[9] With this in mind, before talking about Black women's political consumerism in the welfare rights movement, it is important that we historicize consumerism.

HISTORICIZING CONSUMERISM

Historicizing consumerism serves to uncover structural relationships between the material and the ideological. The relationship between African Americans and consumerism has often fused the desire for access to material goods and services and acknowledgment as first-class citizens in U.S. capitalist society (which has embedded meaning in the context of access to consumer spaces).[10] These desires and acknowledgments are further entangled with the historical legacy of slavery, which complicates efforts to distance African Americans from a shared identity as commodities to recognition that they are human beings worthy of consumer rights. We are no more separated from our histories than we can be separated from our social location assemblages. Social locations such as race, class, and gender are interconnected with experiences of the past. Any attempt to artificially dissociate these assemblages from their historical context—a context that persists into the present and future—dismisses their constitutive relationships, thus ignoring a critical component that influences, among other things, how power plays out.

A lack of acknowledgment of Black people's complicated historical relationship with consumerism causes these discussions to fall short when scholarship about white consumer patterns attempt to generalize and assign meaning by imposing an ahistorical logic on African American experiences. Some scholars have focused specifically on African Americans. Historians such as Traci Parker (2019), Robert Weems (1998), Cheryl Greenberg (1997), and Jason Chambers (2009) have done admirable work related to Black consumers, consumerism, and consumer culture. Unfortunately, not all consumer-focused scholarship considers Black people's historical relationship to consumerism in relation to what occurs today. My issue is that consumerism, as a mechanism that was once oppressive to African Americans because of a status as commodity, is now being used, at best, as a tool of resistance and change and, at worst, as a mechanism to mask the system of oppression that persists through the minimizing of indicators of material deprivation. The ways in which commodification influences how power flows have changed for African Americans. Though commodification is no longer literal, the battle still wages, evidenced by historical legacies related to how consumerism is engaged and through which social positions are empowered and disempowered.

Currently, political strategies to maintain systems of oppression are more covert and masked by a coupling of consumerism and neoliberal values that suggests that democracy may be achieved in the marketplace. The interrogation of consumerism provides a space for the exploration of power (agency and oppression), desire, and history. A lack of willingness to wrestle with the connectedness of historical legacies and realms of power is a main reason that much of the mainstream scholarship on consumerism (read "white consumerism") has failed to thoroughly explain the nuanced relationship African Americans have with consumerism, which is distinct from white middle-class experiences. Scholars have imposed the meaning-making of white consumerism on the experiences of African Americans by focusing on the outcomes of the relationships of consumerism. But too few have explored the relationship between historical legacies and consumerism, or between materiality and ideology. The lack of recognition of historical legacy makes it difficult to fully appreciate the activism of Black women. There are exceptions, including the work of Cassi Pittman Claytor (2020), Matthew Countryman (2007), and Mary Pattillo-McCoy (2000), who engage Black selective patronage as well as middle-class Black consumerism specifically. But not much work looks specifically at poor Black women and consumerism engaged for explicit political purposes.

The Black women of the welfare rights movement would eventually expose the hypocrisy of the citizen-consumer coupling simply by leaning into it and audaciously demanding access to consumer spaces and white middle-class consumer experiences. That the women advocated for this access and insisted that their rights as consumers were independent of their employment and class status placed them in a precarious position, as it activated among opponents the historical residual resentments of Black people's existence in consumer spaces. That poor Black women demanded the same treatment as middle-class white women in a consumer space was particularly radical because historically, Black women had been excluded and told by mainstream consumer spaces that they served no purpose in this sphere, aside from being used as commodity or in service to the white middle class's acquiring and maintaining their commodities. When we bring the full weight of the historical legacies of consumerism to bear in understanding Black women's position in society, we are able to better appreciate their activism for what it truly was: unapologetic, unwavering, and bold in its attempts to create alternative futures that were disconnected from the historical legacies that would disempower them.

WADING THROUGH PARALLEL MOVEMENTS

Understanding Black women's consumer activism during the Chicago welfare rights movement also means contextualizing CWRO-affiliated organizations' consumerist activities within the larger welfare, women's, civil, and consumer rights movements, which occurred during overlapping periods. The consumer movement began in the early twentieth century with legislation designed to protect (white) consumers. Also during that time, Black people were mobilizing around consumer-focused issues, with the "Don't Buy" campaigns that flourished throughout the country in the 1920s and 1930s. These campaigns focused on fostering reciprocal relationships between Black patrons and the white establishments that conducted business in Black communities. Ensuring that Black people were employed at the establishments they patronized was a primary goal of the Don't Buy movement, to ensure that the communities were not exploited by white businesses through the extraction of Black dollars from the community.

Though the civil rights movement has an expansive arc that extends from the first acts of resistance to the institution of enslavement to today, the periodization of this movement primarily focuses on the legislation of the 1960s. The Civil Rights Act of 1964 and the Voting Rights Act of 1965 were sandwiched between national and Illinois state consumer rights legislation. During this time, the intersecting of the consumer movement and the civil rights movement became more difficult to ignore. In 1966, the Southern Christian Leadership Conference's Operation Breadbasket threatened to employ boycotts as a strategy for securing fair hiring practices from local companies. Operation Breadbasket was launched in Atlanta after Leon Sullivan shared the lessons from the Philadelphia selective patronage campaigns. Access to credit and freedom from exploitive credit practices were also key areas of concern for civil rights leaders as well as Black Power proponents. In addition, civil rights organizations such as the Student Nonviolent Coordinating Committee prepared leaders who would later serve as women's rights advocates. Many of these organizations were interconnected.

The National Welfare Rights Organization's political agenda would soon converge with the civil rights and women's rights movements and also play out in the realm of consumerism. The NWRO has been credited with formally organizing the first and largest movement on behalf of welfare recipients. The scholarship of Felicia Kornbluh (1997) has helped historians understand the organization's role in advocating for consumer rights for the poor. The NWRO's Sears Credit Campaign is an exemplar of these efforts to combine the multiple agendas of the women's, welfare rights, consumer, and civil rights movements.

For me, a helpful analogy is to consider these movements in the context of parallel computing. Parallel computing uses multiple processors simultaneously to solve a particular problem.

The problem is broken into smaller tasks so it can be solved more quickly and efficiently. If we think of inequality as the problem to be solved and each of the major movements (civil, consumer, women's, and welfare rights) as parts of a program executed in service of solving this inequality problem, we can begin to see some of the potential advantages of parallel activism. Similar to processes of parallel computing, the consumer, women's, and welfare rights movements overlapped (proceeding relatively simultaneously), sharing some similarities in language (code), goals (tasks), and actors (end users). The convergence of these movements demonstrated how the unique combination of racism, sexism, and classism blocked poor Black women's access to other programs (such as the consumer and women's rights movements) and interfered with their ability to work together, thus hindering the progress of all three movements.

Part of the criticism related to theorizing the women's movement using a wave theory model of feminism is that it condenses the long history of Black feminist activism as a response to the middle-class white women's movement of the 1960s when, in fact, Black women's advocacy can be traced back much further, to Amy Garvey, Ida Wells-Barnett, and Sojourner Truth. At any rate, Black women in the welfare rights movement made tremendous strides in navigating their own program (welfare rights) despite the missed opportunities.

This convergence provided a unique opportunity for Black women to assert themselves as advocates for poor people's consumer rights. Unfortunately, that opportunity was hampered by the inability and unwillingness of the consumer and women's rights movements to see poor Black women as fellow political actors. With the consumer and women's movements of the time actively ignoring and/or distancing from Black women, those movements persisted, while the welfare rights movement was decimated.

I look specifically to technological analogies to differently describe and acknowledge the vision and skill of poor Black women's consumer activism during the welfare rights movement because through their activism, these women were demanding specific futures for themselves and their children. Within this movement, we get a glimpse of the intersections of race, class, and gender that Black women had to navigate.

This project is a reframing and retelling of histories with a specific positioning of Black women as sophisticated creators and users of technologies. The power of this positioning for poor Black women (and the organizations they maintained), not as other but as central, is a representation that belongs as much to the future as to the past. This positioning makes possible a new meaning of Black women's activism during the welfare rights movement. Black women of the welfare rights movement were not supplemental, not an appendage to consumer technologies; rather, they existed as integral innovators, innovation being part of their identities. Here I am connecting Stuart Hall's (1990) encoding/decoding theory with my interpretation of these movements' source code. In the case of the welfare rights movement, the algorithmic assemblages of race, class, and gender provided the "source code" for how to delegitimize poor Black women as consumers. This reframing of Black women's political identities in the context of technology leans into the power of Black subjectivity, turning Foucault's (1998) power/knowledge entanglement on its head.[11]

This text does not expand the work of historians who engage mainstream consumerism broadly or even Black consumerism specifically. Instead, it invites intersectional and postmodern theory into the conversation to consider how Black subjectivity directly relates to the material conditions that are impacted in the realm of consumerism.

Neoliberalism's Ideological Stealth

Neoliberalism is an important realm of power in which to understand poor African American's intersectional political consumerism, because within it are embedded several ideologies that are best understood in the larger context of welfare rights. It is important to draw out the various historical specificities (Mohanty 1984) that shape how the Black women of the welfare rights movement were characterized. The movement ended just prior to Ronald Reagan's formal adoption of neoliberalism as economic policy in the United States.

Neoliberalism is defined as the belief that human well-being is best advanced through individual freedom, free markets, free trade, and strong private property rights (Harvey 2005). Under neoliberalism, the role of the state is to secure an institutional framework that allows for these things. Neoliberalism calls for maintaining a hands-off approach, giving tax cuts to the rich, and letting the economy regulate itself. Neoliberal policies contributed to a deep concentration of wealth among a relatively small percentage of the population, a trend that has persisted since its introduction.

Neoliberalism led to sweeping economic reform that caused irreparable harm to poor people.[12] In many ways, the treatment and outside opinions about the people of the welfare rights movement—particularly African American women—foreshadowed the ushering in of neoliberal policies that would become an unexamined and widely accepted cultural narrative pathologizing impoverished Black people.

One appeal of neoliberalism is its claim that democracy can be reached through unencumbered free (consumer) markets. Baudrillard (1998) explored economic pushes and pulls by describing democracy through consumerism as myth; that, structurally, it is impossible for growth (often read through various indicators of levels of consumption) to promote democracy. Instead, growth through consumption contributes to the perpetuation of poverty, which is masked by a consumerist society. In response to the protests and uprisings occurring across the nation, the Kerner Commission report of 1968 spoke to the promotion of democracy by calling for, among other things, an end to discriminatory consumer and credit practices. The report specifically addressed the poverty conditions faced by African Americans, which, it determined, were caused and perpetuated by white racism that was deeply embedded in the neoliberal discourse.[13] So, as U.S. society began to adopt neoliberal economic policies promoting market-based consumerism, poverty conditions were exacerbated, particularly among African Americans.

Ideology holds society together and therefore can affect social relationships and distort our understanding of them. In a similar way, the market serves as a way of explaining social relationships. For example, globalization connects our consumption practices to other parts of the world (products are less expensive to make in developing countries) while masking and distorting the exploitive nature of the relationship between capitalism's labor and production. Stuart Hall, David Morley, and Kuan-Hsing Chen (1996) suggested that the way to make the distortions more apparent was to determine their underlying ideology. These authors made the case, borrowing from Gramsci, that what we understand as "common sense" is actually distorted ideology with a historical imprint that is accepted uncritically. So, common sense really doesn't help one understand social relations as much as how what is happening fits into an accepted ideology with a historical legacy. Hall et al. were calling on us to read the source code.

In thinking about the impact of neoliberalism and how it informed WRO members' actions and intentions and our understanding of how their social relations might be distorted by neoliberal common sense, this deeper search for hidden ideology and historical imprinting serves as a reminder of the challenges of dealing with such distortions (of a group of people and a movement). In *Sister Citizen*, Melissa Harris-Perry (2011) advances the theory of the crooked room. According to this concept, since Black women are assaulted with distorted representations of their humanity, they are constantly maneuvering and contorting in attempts to stand upright in this crooked room. To understand the actions of Black women, we must therefore understand the ways in which these rooms are crooked and the biased systems that design them this way. In understanding political consumerist activities of marginalized groups in the context of race, class, and gender, one must be mindful of the ways in which the crooked room of neoliberalism forces actors to contort in ways that may not ultimately serve them. An example might be the perpetuation of credit purchasing. I ponder what these crooked rooms looked like for those engaging in intersectional political consumerism, including how the realms of power and various assemblages were arranged and how Black women attempted to resist and rearrange the room as well as themselves.

Despite the obligatory contortions, the women and men of the local welfare organizations insisted that they be engaged as consumers, even those who resisted or were denied access as wage-earners.[14] The view was that citizens engaged society as consumers and that the poor should have a right to engage just as any other American (Bauman 1998). This line of thinking was out of step with neoliberalism, which attempted to regulate away the condition of being poor by punishing those who operated under the conditions and system of poverty. And neoliberalism

38 • HARVEST

intended to make clear the consequences of citizens attempting to reject this ideology of common sense.

Another way in which neoliberalism masked its aversion for certain segments of the population was through what is termed "abstract liberalism." This is described as a strategy of whites that resists institutional changes by invoking liberalist ideas of equal opportunity, choice, and individualism to vaguely explain issues around race (Bonilla-Silva and Dietrich 2011). Neoliberalism as a realm of power has characteristics that overlap with those of other realms of power, including conditions of poverty—specifically, the feminization and "Blackening" of poverty. By framing race-related issues in the language of liberalism, whites could appear "reasonable" and even "moral" while opposing almost all practical approaches to deal with de facto patriarchy and racial inequity (Bonilla-Silva 2003).

Postmodern critiques of consumerism reject the idea of a so-called rational stance of neoliberalism as equalizing within a consumerism framework while supporting the idea that it has the potential to expand access for marginalized people to realms of power previously denied. This acknowledgment of tensions between strategy and goals is demonstrated by the welfare rights movement's stance that consumerism is a vehicle by which the needs of the poor could be met.

The Feminization and "Blackening" of Poverty

Neoliberal capitalism, racism, and patriarchy persist as interconnected structures. Inclusive capitalism (Prahalad 2009) attempts to detach the problematic by suggesting that there exists an opportunity for inclusion of the poor as consumers and markets while also alleviating poverty as a form of development. While the poor are "benefited" through increased access to goods and services, it is uncertain whether their political position significantly changes. One way to test this possibility is to identify, within a neoliberal frame, the political activities of the poor that seem to alleviate poverty. Perhaps there is something to be learned from the concept of "quiet encroachment of the ordinary" (Bayat 2009). The concept focuses on everyday practices of the poor that diminish the state's governing power and results in sociopolitical changes to their communities and government. Included in the ordinary are signals of strategies employed by marginalized groups—particularly poor Black women—to resist disparaging narratives thrust on them in a consumer activist context.

The feminization and Blackening of poverty are important to acknowledge in the larger discourse around poverty. These are subrealms of the condition of poverty realm of power and help provide a more nuanced understanding of which ideologies were legitimizing and influencing the intersectional political consumerism of WRO members. In the early 1960s, the United States saw substantial gains in civil rights and antidiscrimination legislation. During this time, the country also saw the "face" of poverty change, as the poor increasingly shifted from concentrated rural areas to urban areas (Mingione 1996). Prior to this shift, there was a disproportionate focus on whites in Appalachia. This awareness of a different type of poverty was beginning to emerge in the late 1950s and early 1960s with John Kenneth Galbraith's 1958 work, *The Affluent Society*, and Michael Harrington's 1962 book, *The Other America*. These pieces, among others, were the budding fruit of what the anthropologist Oscar Lewis would later coin as a "culture of poverty," which is described as maladaptive behavior demonstrated by the poor as a result of their marginalized positions in a capitalist society. The new face affixed to poverty was unmistakably urban and Black.

In these poverty studies, Galbraith and Harrington argued that a lack of opportunity led to maladaptive behavior in urban Black poor people. Studying behaviors of the poor, these authors determined that in order to change these cultural behaviors of the poor, structural changes must be made that allow for increased opportunities. Around this time, Daniel Patrick Moynihan released a report in 1965 related to the Black family.[15] Moynihan argued that the Black community essentially consisted of a stable middle class and an unstable, maladaptive lower class consisting of "broken" homes, female-headed households with "illegitimate" children, and rampant welfare dependency. This disorder was caused in large part, according to Moynihan, by slavery's disruption of the family structure and previous discrimination. The solution to resolving this "pathological" behavior was not so much about government interventions to provide more opportunities for Blacks as it was about restoring the Black male as patriarch and bringing stability back to the Black family.

Ultimately, Moynihan's perspective would be rebuked (temporarily) in favor of those of Galbraith and Harrington, whose work made a significant impact on John F. Kennedy's poverty policy perspective (Wilson 1987; Murray 1984; Mead 1986). As problematic as Harrington's (1962) thesis may have been as it relates to identifying maladaptive behaviors of poor Blacks, in comparison with that of Moynihan, this vantage point did allow space for empathy. The culture-of-poverty thesis emerged during the peak of the civil rights movement and during a time of increased legislation around consumer protection issues. With such intense perspectives swarming around Blacks and equal rights at the time, it is not difficult to imagine the impact such a contentious environment would have in shaping and directing discourse (not only around the poor but also around the poor's characterization as consumers). In an environment in which people were attempting to appeal to whites' sense of individual equity, the culture-of-poverty thesis had useful (and also deeply problematic) consequences as it related to policy development and antidiscrimination legislation to address the issue of limited opportunities for poor Blacks. Again, the way to make distortions more apparent is to interrogate the underlying ideologies and historical imprints. Ideologies of racism, sexism, and classism serve to shape figurative and material narratives around Black women's activities, which included their consumer activities.

While the early 1960s saw promise in legislation, the late 1960s saw tremendous turmoil with the assassinations of major civil rights leaders and explosive protests across many urban cities. What we also saw after 1965 was a proliferation of research on poverty. During the 1960s, policy makers were compelled to do something about perceived poverty, because people were afraid of the frustrated poor and the related social unrest (Murray 1984). There was urgency in dealing with structural elements that limited opportunities and manifested in behaviors specific to those in a culture of poverty. During the late 1960s, Black culture was associated as much with political protest (Smethurst 2005; Gans 1974) as with social unrest and maladaptive poverty culture.

By the 1980s, the transition from a culture of protest to the coupling of Black culture with a culture of poverty was complete. The ideologies of patriarchy, racism, and neoliberal capitalism came to the forefront of the culture-of-poverty discourse. This transition caused irreparable damage to welfare rights. The New York City–wide coordinating committee of welfare groups, which later became the National Welfare Rights Organization, demanded decent shelter, adequate food and clothing, and human dignity for the nation's poor. The main goal of the

NWRO was winning a federal guaranteed income (Kornbluh 2007). The welfare rights movement, made up mostly of poor women of color, had among its primary goals securing what it considered citizenry rights to participate in the economic system and making available government benefits that allow the poor to more equally engage as consumers.

In *The Feminization of Poverty*, Gertrude Goldberg and Eleanor Kremen (1990) suggested that social welfare advocacy should focus on facilitating women's participation in the workforce by supplementing low wages to offset the high financial costs of parenting or provide support for those women who, for whatever reason, were not in the workforce but caring for children. The view that women should be able to choose to rear their children rather than being forced into the workforce disrupted capitalism but also reinforced and sustained patriarchy. In "Subversive Potential, Coercive Intent: Women, Work, and Welfare in the 1990s," Kornbluh (1991) described the government's role in prescribing the basic needs of the poor. Welfare was described as giving "material aid to poor people while denying the minimum necessary for dignity and decency. It establishes unmarried women as social pariahs while providing the financial resources that allow women with children to make it alone" (23). The dichotomy of the so-called deserving and undeserving poor was invoked.

The welfare agencies provided itemized lists of what they felt the poor deserved and, by omission, made commentary on what they did not. This effort to regulate the budgets and choices of the poor (poor Black women in particular) was resisted by the welfare rights organizations' efforts to show which needs were not being met through this regulation. WRO members asked welfare recipients which items were excluded that they considered essential to survival.[16] WROs' focus was on welfare recipients' right to choose consumer purchases for themselves. This was a major point of conflict between the state and protestors in the welfare rights movement.

Ellen Reese and Garnett Newcombe (2003), in their comparison of NWRO and the Association of Community Organizations for Reform Now (ACORN),[17] make the point that although the two organizations worked with the same constituency, NWRO's focus was related to fighting for a certain standard of living for the poor that more closely resembled that of middle-class whites. The authors further noted that NWRO's agenda was not to mobilize the poor beyond obtaining these consumer rights (which would have led to a substantial change in their political position) and suggest that this focus may have led to the organization's descent.

Historians of welfare rights such as Nancy Naples (1998), Ange-Marie Hancock (2004), Mary Eleanor Triece (2013), Premilla Nadasen (2005) and Annelise Orleck (2005) discuss the rise and fall of the welfare rights movement from myriad perspectives, including situated knowledges, agency, Black feminist frameworks, and the framing of policies. Frances Fox Piven and Richard Cloward (1998) make the distinction between mobilizing and organizing. They also state that the decline of NWRO was due to its focus on mobilization to the detriment of organizing and this lack of affiliation prevented the poor from gaining political influence. Piven and Cloward note that the collective political power of unions to influence was not available to the poor and African Americans, so those groups had to look to other forms of collective political action. They looked to consumer spaces.

Activists as well as welfare recipients were demonized for their tactics to secure more rights, particularly consumer rights, as well as for their use of those rights. Poor women were accused of getting a free ride or undermining the role of the father by no longer depending on him for a wage. The welfare rights movement crumbled under the weight of this backlash. According to Kornbluh (2007), it was not the mistakes of the movement that led to its demise but overwhelming structural forces, including Nixon's neoliberal Family Assistance Plan, which limited poor women's agency and ensured that full citizenship would be forever married to work (regardless of whether or not employment could get one out of poverty). This marriage would become cemented in the wake of the Reagan administration's neoliberal policies concerning social welfare programs.

The Reagan administration immediately followed the welfare rights movement and continued Richard Nixon's work in conducting an all-out war on the poor. This administration's policies were particularly hostile toward poor Black people, specifically with the passing of reforms that gave significant tax advantages to the wealthiest of the population (known as Reagan's "trickle-down economics") and punished the poor, through programmatic cuts, for their economic status. The administration epitomized neoliberal conservatism of the 1980s and was perhaps most damaging with its cuts to major social support programs, extensive increases in defense spending, increases in Black community policing, weakening of affirmative action programs, and inaction regarding civil rights violations. Specific assaults on social support programs included significant cuts to welfare and food stamp programs. As social relief programs of the New Deal and Great Society initiatives such as affordable housing, urban development grants, food stamps, and employment and job training programs were gutted, homelessness skyrocketed, and unemployment among African Americans continued to increase, even as aggregate numbers decreased (Caraley 1996).

HARVEST • 45

Indeed, the 1980s proved to be a particularly hostile time with regard to policies affecting the poor and signaled a sharp shift in thought on how poverty and the poor should be controlled (Murray 1984).[18] In this environment, the culture-of-poverty literature and cultural analysis of the poor reemerged. On the conservative side of the discussion, Murray took a quantitative approach to understanding the lack of progress toward alleviating poverty. His focus was on government-administered programs. His view was that social welfare programs, instead of reducing poverty, actually contributed to its perpetuation. In the process, Murray devotes an entire section of *Losing Ground* to looking specifically at Black poverty over a thirty-year period (1950–1980) and provides statistics consistent with culture-of-poverty narratives, including unemployment rates, education levels, crime rates, out-of-wedlock birth rates, and female-headed households. The analysis concluded that policies of Lyndon B. Johnson's Great Society were deeply flawed and dichotomized the poor—the "most industrious, most responsible" versus the "least industrious, least responsible"—and reproduced the deserving/undeserving narrative. The "race issue" was to be settled by administering equal treatment for all by "making the nation colorblind," eliminating affirmative action programs, and implementing voucher programs for education (Murray 1984). Finally, Murray proposed eliminating welfare completely and replacing it with nothing.[19] The implication was that people would be forced into the job market, suggesting that the poor were impoverished by choice and needed to be penalized so they would make different choices.

For better or worse, Murray's *Losing Ground* embodied the tone of policy makers, politicians, and the general public during the 1980s and foreshadowed a future direction of work-based assistance. Murray's approach is but one example of the

46 • HARVEST

methodological failings of quantification in policy spaces. With numbers, it solidified hegemonic views of poor people that were expressed, reproduced, and constructed by scholarship of the time. This type of scholarship, which was personal, racist, and political, had significant welfare policy implications. So, as the state contributed to the feminization and Blackening of poverty, it did so in the context of neoliberalism and the associated promotion of market-based consumerism, which left little room for the poor. The culture-of-poverty narratives and the flawed consumer concept were related in that they were class based, though the culture-of-poverty narrative presented in the neoliberalism and poverty realms of power masked the ways in which poverty was feminized, sexualized and Blackened/racialized. This masking is a compelling reason that neoliberalism and the feminization and Blackening of poverty are identified as realms of power that should be taken into account as we seek to understand the environment in which Black women battled for rights.

Black women's advocacy and activism are and have been a form of technology. Both algorithms and archives rely on historical assumptions. In the archives, assumptions about whose perspectives deserve to be preserved have political consequences that can lead to the erasure of Black women's voices and perspectives. Algorithms also have encoded ideologies that can render Black women invisible. Part of our responsibility as intellectually curious beings is to look for what's present as well as what is absent and ask why. Using ahistorical logics to understand commodification and consumerism distorts our understanding of the relationships between African Americans and consumerism.

The implication of this parallel computing demonstrates how the unique combination of racism, sexism, and classism impacting Black women of the welfare rights movement affected their ability to access other programs with similar tasks and end users. The rise of neoliberalism as economic policy played a major role in Black women's inability to access the momentum of other programs during that time. Neoliberalism served not only as economic policy but also a mechanism by which misogynoir as ideology was hidden, and the hidden ideology and historical imprint of Black women's marginalized relationship with the state was distorted as neoliberal common sense. Neoliberal capitalism, racism, and patriarchalism persisted as interconnected structures that cemented the feminization and Blackening of poverty. This environment made for hostile terrain for Black women of the welfare rights movement, particularly as they used consumer credit technology as a vehicle for achieving their goals.

While postmodernism criticizes neoliberalism's ability to equalize access within a consumer framework, it also recognizes the potential to expand access by reducing material deprivation. That is why the realm of power is so intriguing. Black women's use of consumerism broadly, and consumer credit specifically, as a Black feminist technology in service of meeting the material, social, and political needs of other Black women in their community illustrates how consumerism is no trifling matter. It's serious business. The next chapter expands on this business of Black women who engage a unique type of intersectional political consumerism that attempts to blur the boundaries between capital and community.

Bauman's (2007) theory of the flawed consumer is helpful in understanding how class impacts one's ability to engage in a consumerist society, but it falls short in explaining how intersecting social locations such as class, race, and gender can influence how power operates in the consumer marketplace. Intersectional political consumerism provides researchers with a theory that engages structures and ideologies while acknowledging that social identities are interconnected and both influence and are being influenced by these structures. The incorporation of intersectionality in the analysis of political consumerism allows researchers to more thoroughly understand how the activists of the welfare rights movement experienced consumer resistance and power. As these social identities converge, the struggle and negotiation over who is deemed legitimate as consumers becomes more apparent. The social relationships forged through the consumer marketplace and understood in their historical contexts provide meaning for these activists' intersectional political consumerism. The following chapters engage these social relationships, tracing the steps of the actors of the movement as they fight for poor people's rights to be consumers.

2

BUSINESS

The first annual Temporary Woodlawn Organization (TWO) fashion show, "The Cavalcade of Fashions," was held on December 3, 1961. It was one of the few TWO public events where women were showcased as formal leaders and organizers. Interestingly, in the description of the Temporary Woodlawn Organization[1] given by the *Chicago Defender* newspaper article publicizing the event, TWO was described as a "non-sectarian, non-political and interracial" organization. From its inception, TWO was a Black neighborhood organization with a clear political stance related to "self-determination" for its community. Yet, in the context of a woman-led fashion show event, which promoted and raised funds for the organization, an apolitical positioning was evident, which diluted and downplayed these women's work. That Black women's participation in TWO was highlighted in the press for their "non-political display of fashions" speaks to the level of dismissiveness that existed within and outside the organization as it related to the permissible leadership spaces and contributions of women.

TWO hosted its second annual fashion show on December 9, 1962. It consisted of "high fashion glamour" hairstyles and clothing. A small number of young girls and men also participated

50 • BUSINESS

in the show. The fashions displayed, including an "elaborate beaver collared jacket" and a "gown from far-off Hong Kong, a beautiful vibrant blue woolen topped by a cashmere jacket covered in iridescent sequins," were examples of luxury, elegance, and expensive "high quality" that occupied the same Woodlawn community space as slumlord-controlled rentals, dilapidated schools, and eroding merchant-consumer spaces.[2] The runway's backdrop of "baby skid row" illustrates the extreme class border-crossing that these annual fashion shows represented. The shows provided a way for Black women to be visible within the organization, even if it was through emulating European conventions of beauty and patriarchal notions of women's apolitical and docile domains of influence in the organization's work. The Black women of TWO were not apolitical public event coordinators and participants, as the fashion show may suggest. They were integral community leaders concerned with political issues related to the poor, and those issues included consumerism. TWO's inaugural fashion show would also foreshadow an NWRO public action to engage politically via consumerism (which I discuss in more detail in chapter 3).

The reality is that local welfare organizations positioned consumerism squarely in the political arena. Roughly a decade after TWO's first fashion show, we see an uptick in both consumer protection legislation and major welfare reform.[3] Other organizations connected with welfare rights, such as the Welfare Council of Metropolitan Chicago, were also concerned with consumer issues. The Welfare Council wrote several position statements related to consumer credit issues and welfare, and, in its newsletter, NOW (News of Welfare), made many references to the "consumer bill of rights" package as major consumer protection legislation.[4] Harlem Consumer Education, Inc., held annual conferences. During its sixth consumer education conference in

October 1968, consumer co-ops, consumer legislation, economic boycotts,[5] and communication with consumers were discussed.[6] In its first semiannual report, written in December 1972, the Public Interest Economic Center (PIE-C) made the connection between the poor, women, minorities, and consumers—citing their common interests and shared a lack of power and resources to fight against political and judicial injustices.[7] Though these connections were made in the hopes of nurturing alliances among these groups, the appeals lacked explicit recognition of the impact of many of these identities, particularly poor Black women as consumers. More explicitly, though organizations were discussing various identities, they were not adequately attending to the algorithmic assemblages of race, class, and gender that would come to dictate strategy choices and effectiveness.

Rent strikes were organized by several NWRO organizations during various periods, including Jobs or Income Now (JOIN) and TWO. Tenants were regularly referred to as "consumers" as these groups attempted to draw attention to the exploitation of renters by slumlords.[8] The Lawndale Tenants Union held regular rent strikes in Chicago as a way of fighting absentee landlords and forced evictions of neighbors, stating "the only way to stop the man is to stop his money."[9] The Near North WRO, another CWRO-affiliated group, was also heavily involved in actions on behalf of renters as consumers. In fact, before Marion Stamps joined the Black Panther Party and led efforts to get Harold Washington elected as the first Black mayor of Chicago, she was a member of the Near North WRO, fighting for public housing rights and later founding the Chicago Housing Tenant Organization (CHTO) in the Cabrini-Green housing project. During her time as chair of the Near North WRO, Stamps pushed back against not only the state and its repressive welfare programs but also NWRO's leadership, calling for more accountability, involvement, and support for the regional organizations. Stamps did not bite her tongue; she was extremely direct in her verbal communication, had little tolerance for bureaucratic structures, and stated in one meeting with NWRO representatives that she had issue with "black men who go around talking black and sleep white," referring to NWRO leader George Wiley. Still, she was willing to work with anyone who had solid programs that could potentially lead to positive change for Black people.

Given this persistent interest in consumer rights by welfare organizations, particularly credit for the poor, one question I considered was how local community organizations affiliated with NWRO came to understand their groups' roles in these efforts. In comparing two NWRO-affiliated organizations in Chicago, JOIN and TWO, I sought to understand how these organizations came to very different conclusions regarding the role of consumerism in the larger poor people's movement and the invoking of various types of intersectional political consumerism. How is it that these organizations seemed to enthusiastically adopt some forms of intersectional political consumerism and incorporate its strategies in its efforts to obtain rights for poor people while openly criticizing and/or resisting other NWROs' strategies around intersectional political consumerism?[10] The histories of these organizations should be considered when addressing this question. This chapter describes the histories of JOIN and TWO, as well as the communities they represented, and identifies the specific types of intersectional political consumerism representative of their ideological influences.

CHICAGO: SOUTH VERSUS NORTH

The Woodlawn area,[11] which extended from 60th to 67th Streets and South Park–Stoney Island Ave,[12] became predominantly

BUSINESS • 53

Black following the major outmigration of whites to the suburbs after World War II. By the mid-1950s, Woodlawn had attracted stable "middle-class" Black families seeking improved living conditions not limited to affordable housing.[13] It was not long before the community began to feel the effects of discrimination and exploitation in the form of white flight[14] of businesses (particularly impactful because much of the area was commercially zoned[15]); conversions of larger residences into smaller, cheaper, and poorer-quality dwellings; and development of transient hotels and taverns. By the 1960s, Woodlawn had become 89 percent Black, with an equal minority of Puerto Rican and white people in the community.[16] With the creation of expressways to annex the Black-concentrated area, and as property deteriorated and crime increased, the area was quickly classified as a ghetto, vulnerable to unscrupulous business opportunists, politicians, and white institutions.

The local community group TWO began as the Temporary Woodlawn Organization and was a collaboration between clergy, local businessmen, and representatives from various block clubs in the community. On January 5, 1961, representatives from the Woodlawn Pastor's Alliance, the Woodlawn Business Men's Association (WBMA), the United Woodlawn Conference, the Block Club Council, and the Knights of St. John held a meeting to discuss the forming of this independent, temporary organization, which would be charged with "carrying out the will of the people."[17] This multiracial, primarily male group sought the assistance of Saul Alinsky and the Industrial Areas Foundation (IAF) for organizational and administrative resources.[18] Alinsky (and a conglomeration of churches), however, had shown an interest in Woodlawn as a potential project several years prior to the Temporary Organization's request for assistance. Following the failure of an IAF organizing attempt in 1954,[19] in December 1958, representatives from the Catholic, Lutheran, and

Presbyterian churches held a number of conferences discussing what they believed to be pressing issues of Woodlawn.[20] The Roman Catholic Archdiocese,[21] in which Alinsky was heavily involved, suggested that the group facilitate forming a large community organization, similar to Alinsky's strategy with the Back of the Yards neighborhood.[22] The Catholic Church's interest was actually in securing West Woodlawn, stopping white flight and saving the neighborhood from the fate of the neighboring deteriorating East Woodlawn, which had more Black residents and suffered a "pattern of demoralization."[23] The church's efforts were clearly an attempt to preserve West Woodlawn's existing white congregation.

For Alinsky, the fractured and highly dispersed and decentralized leadership in the community made it an attractive target for organizing.[24] Black residents of both East and West Woodlawn were caught in the crosshairs, as anti-Blackness was embedded in the (West Woodlawn) Catholic Church's desire to not "end up like" East Woodlawn, because it believed Black to be synonymous with dilapidated, beyond repair, something to be halted, and thus requiring its immediate intervention. This is a familiar source code. By August 1961, the IAF began formally funding The Temporary Organization.[25] Here we can begin to understand how algorithmic assemblages of race, class, and gender served to focus and shape organizational strategies being imposed on Woodlawn.

First, the creation of TWO provided the entry of white religious institutions into the discourse of Black community development and self-determination. The changing racial demographics of their congregations, coupled with the deterioration of the communities in which their churches resided gave, in their view, "legitimate" claim to take institutional actions to "assist" Black neighborhoods.[26] One problematic aspect of this discourse was the privileging of whiteness as religious leaders considered the ways in which they might assist the community in avoiding or preventing the complete disappearance or absence of white people as they abandoned the area. Under the banner of integration, the organized churches' efforts hoped to improve conditions in Woodlawn so that it could again be an attractive space for white people to live.

Rather than directly address issues of Black disenfranchisement and racially motivated divestment and economic exploitation of the community by government and businesses alike, or the impact institutions such as University of Chicago had in targeting vulnerable sectors of the community that were predominantly Black and economically fragile, the churches chose instead to center the presence of whites and whiteness as an indicator of the neighborhood's health and potential for renewal. It thereby completely sidestepped any real discussion around how racism operated in the city and impacted its community members. The churches' strategies—or, rather, set of instructions that were shaped by their raced, classed, and gendered positions as white organizers—identified the presence of Blackness as a problem to be managed. By engaging and centering Saul Alinsky and the IAF during their discussions about "what to do about Woodlawn,"[27] the church leaders essentially conceded to the notion that white men must be brought into Black communities to assist in their organization. White men just as easily could have been used to organize efforts to combat the racist practices of other white men that stifled the viability of communities such as Woodlawn. However, that strategy was not a consideration for the clergy. They instead opted for an organization whose program solutions did little to disrupt the status quo.[28]

56 • BUSINESS

North of Woodlawn, another Chicago neighborhood, Uptown,[29] was described as one of the toughest communities in the United States.

> More street fights and bar fights and back-alley fights than in all the other Chicago precincts put together. First in wife-beatings . . . second in Chicago robberies . . . second in knifings and among the worst in the world for "just plain senseless vandalism. . . . More American Indians live here than anywhere else outside the reservations. East Indians are here, blacks, the Spanish-speaking, Orientals. . . . But it's the white southern migrants—mountain folk from eastern Kentucky, East Tennessee, and North Carolina—that make Uptown what it is. More of them set down here than anywhere in the country. One out of every three men, women, and children that walk Uptown streets is originally from Appalachia.[30]

Institutions such as the press and police defined the area by its crime and poverty rather than identifying root causes of these community issues, thus ignoring efforts of the people living in the community and describing them as helpless and needing to be saved from themselves.

Many of the estimated ten thousand former coalminers of Appalachia and their families who migrated to Chicago moved to the Uptown neighborhood.[31] In 1967, Uptown was estimated to have approximately fifty thousand residents, with the majority being poor Southern-Appalachian whites.[32] The Uptown area was frequently referred to by those outside the community as a white hillbilly ghetto.[33] Yet, JOIN, a community union in Uptown, described the community as a multiracial area many of whose community members were Puerto Rican, Indian, and Black as well as white.[34] In speeches

BUSINESS • 57

and written communications regarding Uptown, JOIN frequently noted the attempts of institutions in power to divide poor people along racial lines as they fought and struggled for rights to quality welfare, employment, and housing.[35] The algorithmic assemblages of race, class, and gender in the Uptown community forced it to define itself very differently from how the media and local government defined it. What outsiders saw as innate racial and classed detriments Uptown residents viewed as unifying assets. They identified the underlying causes of their community issues as failings of the government, not the people.

JOIN was formed in fall 1964[36] (three years after the Temporary Woodlawn Organization) as one of a dozen Students for a Democratic Society (SDS) projects in northern cities that came out of the 1963 March on Washington for Jobs and Freedom.[37] The SDS projects were originally administered by the Economic Research and Action Project (ERAP) sponsored by the United Auto Workers union (UAW; Frost 2001).[38] After spending time in the community and surveying its problems and needs (by having the people come to them for help with their problems), the SDS began to focus on housing conditions, police harassment, and quality of welfare programs.[39] The group believed that if people received help with their specific issues, they would come to trust and accept the organization, which would then connect their specific issues with structural issues around which actions could be organized.[40] With twelve hundred members, JOIN had twenty-one full-time staff (eleven of whom were from the community, the remaining ren being college graduates). During the 1960s, JOIN was the largest organization in Chicago that was organizing poor (Southern-Appalachian) whites in an urban area.[41]

58 • BUSINESS

Peggy Terry, a white woman born in Oklahoma,[42] moved from Alabama to Uptown Chicago in 1964.[43] She was an active member of the Congress of Racial Equality (CORE); became active in local welfare rights as a key leader of JOIN and the editor of its newsletter, *The Firing Line*;[44] and later united the local group with the NWRO. Terry was also vocal about the need for JOIN to break away from SDS people in the organization and for the poor and working poor to begin to speak and lead themselves. She wrote to JOIN members, "We believe that the time has come for us to turn to our own people, poor and working-class Whites, for direction, support and inspiration, to organize around our own identity, our own interests."[45] Eventually, JOIN would separate itself from SDS's influence.[46] Unlike the Temporary Woodlawn Organization's founders, JOIN members were interested in disrupting status quo inequalities related to class, politics, and people's relationships with the state (see table 2.1). JOIN was also outspoken in its desire to organize itself from within rather than be organized by outside influences.

ALGORITHMIC ASSEMBLAGES OF RACE, CLASS, AND GENDER

Ideologically, those from SDS who later formed JOIN took to heart Huey Newton's call for whites to organize their own communities.[47] The organization was interested in cultivating "radical opposition and consciousness among whites." Recall that the UAW was the original sponsor of this project, feeling that automation was a threat to workers. To prepare for this threat, the union believed that poor whites needed to organize around issues such as guaranteed annual income.[48] JOIN's ideological lineage points to organized labor influenced by

TABLE 2.1 CHICAGO WELFARE RIGHTS ORGANIZATIONS

	The Woodlawn Organization (TWO)	Jobs or Income Now (JOIN)
Community makeup		
Year created	1961	1964
Location	Woodlawn—South side of city	Uptown—North side of city
Reason for creation	Short-term response to urban renewal and University of Chicago encroachment on neighborhood	Long-term response to job creation and other issues of poor stemming from SDS Project following March on Washington
Intersectional identities		
Membership makeup	Predominantly poor and working-class African American women and men	Predominantly poor and working-class white women and men
Leadership makeup	Predominantly church-affiliated men-led, with majority women taking organizational and protest roles	Predominantly women-led, with majority of women taking organizational and protest roles
Power navigation		
Major campaigns	"Square Deal Campaign," rent strikes	Welfare programs, rent strikes, ending police brutality
Alliances/affiliations	Industrial Area Foundation (IAF), Woodlawn Business Men's Association (WBMA)	Students for a Democratic Society (SDS), Kenwood-Oakland Community Organization (KOCO)
Leading ideologies/ structures	Patriarchal, capitalist, anticommunist	Feminist, anticapitalist, socialist
Primary realms of power engaged	African American consumerism	(Condition of) poverty
Types of intersectional political consumerism employed and major successes	Commercially centered Successfully negotiated with landlords for rental housing improvements; lobbied major retail chain stores for employment for Blacks; managed and rented community housing; opened local supermarket and employed 50+ community members	Community-centered Successfully organized 1,200 poor (primarily white) people within the community; successfully negotiated with landlords for rental housing improvements; started community buying clubs and food co-ops; lobbied welfare offices on behalf of uptown residents, securing benefits for them

Marxism as a movement compass. Socialism was embedded in JOIN's source code.

The group strongly objected to the city's urban renewal plans, stating, "the institutions of housing and urban renewal is a dominant manifestation of capitalism at the local level."[49] JOIN also housed former members of the Student Nonviolent Coordinating Committee (SNCC), CORE, and the Southern Christian Leadership Conference (SCLC) who had become disillusioned by the hierarchical nature and tactics of those organizations.[50] In addition, within JOIN were members who recognized that the whites in organizations like SNCC and CORE had middle-class backgrounds and were more interested in trying to organize Black people than their own people. Further, these members felt that middle-class whites needed to come to terms with the idea that working-class and poor whites were "their own people."[51]

JOIN viewed itself as a "conflict organization" aimed at resistance and revolution rather than a resolution-focused community organization aimed at compliance and reform. It explicitly rejected the so-called Saul Alinsky model of community organization, stating, "JOIN's approach to the community is to involve the poor *first*, to build a union that the non-aligned, non-established, low-income people control and which brings ministers, social workers and progressive shop owners into support at a second stage on the terms of the poor."[52] This is in direct contrast to TWO, which not only focused on working within the confines of systems and government (in some cases) but was also an IAF–supported organization and project of Alinsky. This approach was undoubtedly related to TWO's overwhelmingly male formal leadership, further indicated by the extreme prejudice and hostility of IAF to women-led community groups.

JOIN's female leadership was visible and critical in the organization centering of women's concerns. During her time with

BUSINESS • 61

JOIN, Terry was invited in 1968 by Martin Luther King Jr. to be a part of the steering committee for the Poor People's Campaign.[53] and to speak on Solidarity Day on June 19, 1968.[54] In her speech, Terry stated,

> Poor whites are here today because we found out that 65 percent of the poor in these United States are white. We are here today united with other races of poor people, Puerto Ricans, Mexican-Americans, Indians, and Black people, in a common cause. That COMMON CAUSE is FREEDOM!. . . . We hereby serve notice that poor whites are beginning to understand that black and white in this country are pitted against each other for no other reason than that it is profitable for the rich white folks to do so.[55]

Though much attention and preservation of JOIN's historical record focuses on Peggy Terry, Black women were active in this predominantly white organization and made significant contributions. Dovie Coleman,[56] a Black Uptown resident who was chair of the organizing committee for JOIN,[57] was also on the steering committee of the Poor People's Campaign with Terry.[58] Coleman, considered a "founding mother" of NWRO, was originally from St. Louis and came to Chicago in 1948. She worked as a hairdresser for several years before becoming temporarily paralyzed from an auto accident. Unable to find adequate work following the accident, Coleman applied for public assistance. The Chicago Friends Welfare Rights Organization, a group of middle-class allies, described Coleman's journey into the welfare system and advocacy in this way: "After several months of paralysis, during which Dovie feared she might never walk again, and several unsuccessful attempts to return to work, she was forced to apply for public assistance. Dovie often uses her

62 • BUSINESS

own experience to show how easily any working person can be forced to accept welfare."[59]

Coleman worked with JOIN until May 1967 when, along with niece Dovie Thurman ('Little Dovie'), broke from JOIN to form an independent organization in Uptown, Welfare Recipients Demand Action (WRDA). Thurman was raised by her grandmother in St. Louis after her father died. At the age of nineteen, while her husband was in Vietnam, Dovie moved to Chicago near her aunt, "Big Dovie." WRDA operated out of Coleman's apartment, and she endured tremendous personal sacrifices to conduct her community organizing work. The office was underfunded and struggled to stay afloat. (Many of the WROs struggled for funding, holding raffles and chicken dinners to raise money for their organizations.)

Nicknamed the "human tornado," Coleman was a fierce and highly effective advocate for welfare recipients, often leading marches, protesting and (tirelessly), meeting with appointed officials and calling them to task. In comments to a reporter, Coleman stated, "They have taken away everything from the poor. . . . Now with this new welfare legislation they are even trying to take away our children. That's too much. I guess that's why we're all here. We've never had much, but we intend to change things so at least our children will have a chance."[60] Coleman used her extensive knowledge of the state's disciplining technologies (in the form of welfare policies) to help others address issues with the welfare department and then enlisted the ranks of WROs.

According to a May 23, 1966, JOIN news release, Dovie Coleman, Dovie Thurman, and Harriet Stulman (who was white) were arrested for remaining in the Cook County welfare office building after officials refused to meet their demands.[61] Little Dovie[62] explained that she was arrested while protesting

BUSINESS • 63

inhumane treatment in the welfare system. She stated in a *JOIN Community Union* newsletter,

> My reasons for going to jail was to prove that welfare recipients should have a union that's able to demand collective bargaining and to be able to approve any welfare laws that are passed by the legislature. I feel the only way people are going to know how bad conditions are for recipients are for recipients to stand up and protest for their rights, even if it means going to jail. I'll tell you one thing, the matrons in prison treat you better than some of the caseworkers. And they see to it that you get baloney sandwiches which welfare sometimes doesn't allow.[63]

Thurman wanted others to know that dealing with the Cook County welfare department was so difficult and inhumane that women were willing to endure jail to change it. "My husband's fighting for this country over in Vietnam and I can't even get the welfare department to pay the $6 a month they owe me."[64] Thurman was angry about not just the indignities suffered under the state welfare system but also the country's hypocrisy.[65]

In July 1966, JOIN, along with members of Kenwood Oakland Community Organization (KOCO), marched and picketed the downtown welfare office to protest welfare conditions and to get a meeting with the director of public aid. Coleman and Thurman were among the JOIN representatives who secured a meeting as a result of the demonstration and spoke with then director Raymond Hilliard regarding welfare conditions. It was the first time such a meeting had taken place.[66] Hilliard agreed to regular meetings with JOIN and KOCO to discuss these issues but died shortly after.[67]

In 1967, Thurman, who would later serve as one of the regional delegates for the Poor People's Organizing Convention in June 1968[68] and assisted JOIN's theater initiative,[69] met with the new director of public aid, William Robinson (who replaced Hilliard after his death) at the beginning of his tenure. They met to discuss the Welfare Rehabilitation Service Center and the department's policies and treatment of the poor. In the "Welfare Rights" column of *The Firing Line*, Thurman stated, "I told him that Springfield should mail out all checks in advance of holidays like Thanksgiving and Christmas so welfare people could enjoy a little of this middle-class season of fun."[70]

On February 4, 1969, after they had broken off from JOIN, Coleman, Thurman, and Catherine Dandridge of the Westside Recipients Action Group (WRAGS) met with David Daniel, newly appointed director of Cook County's Department of Public Aid, to advocate for poor people's rights (including food, clothing, and rent allowances; housing; day care centers; furniture allowances; transportation; job training programs; medical aid; and assistance with getting children to college). The women of the movement often met with officials in groups of three to four because the Black women leading these WROs were often collaborative, supportive, and protective of one another.

Coleman and Thurman, in their leadership roles in JOIN, reflected and centered the issues affecting the people of Uptown. That these women served in a predominantly white community union in visible leadership positions, protested, and were arrested for their resistance spoke to the integral role that Black women played in influencing the direction of these organizations.

TWO, in contrast to JOIN, was a strongly patriarchal organization. The president was Pastor Arthur Brazier, a prominent Black community leader, and most of TWOs formal leadership positions were held by Black men. Despite the fact that 60 percent of the organization's inaugural delegates were women[71] and that women were highly visible as foot soldiers on picket lines for rent strikes, TWO—as well as its primary sponsor,

BUSINESS • 65

IAF—remained openly hostile toward the community's Black women leaders.[72] While doing due diligence to determine if Woodlawn was a viable project, Nicholas von Hoffman, who was a leading field representative for the white male–led IAF, said in a memo to Alinsky, "The West Woodlawn area has long been dominated by a clique of formidable matriarchs who have been running their husbands and the show for years. Without a doubt one of the important organizational tasks that would confront us in West Woodlawn would be gathering the men and putting some spine into them."[73]

This hostility toward Black female leadership persisted as the Woodlawn organization grew. For example, in a memo to Alinsky, IAF Woodlawn field representative Leon Finney referred to TWO member Rosa Pitts (who was also area vice president of the South Shore organization) as "an ungrateful bitch."[74] In the same memo, Finney also stated that TWO should "get a strong man" in the area of Parkside where Ada Moore was acting as vice president after Lorraine Johnson (another woman) had been removed.[75]

Rather than find ways to incorporate indigenous leadership in the area, part of IAF's strategy was to remove Black women's leadership and influence. What's more, TWO's formal Black male leadership did not insist Black women be equitably represented at the leadership table as the IAF was working to organize West Woodlawn and create TWO. This helps explain how the assemblages operated to embed unequal gender dynamics and apparent sexism in TWO, particularly in contrast to practices in JOIN.

One of TWO's more vocal critics was the West Woodlawn Woman's Community Club (WWWCC).[76] WWWCC had extensive roots in the Woodlawn neighborhood, dating from as early as 1954; it concerned itself with such varying issues as holding garden parties, keeping the community clean and well kept, discussing the fluoride that was being added to the city's drinking water, and addressing illnesses of residents.[77] Dedicating a full page of the club's newsletter to address the creation of The Temporary Organization, the writer encourages the club members not to be "unthinkables." The newsletter states that WWWCC had worked tirelessly to address issues of the community and criticized the presence of "outsiders" who were attempting to speak on their behalf: "Why should strange people who have never lived among you come to you as 'paid workers' (by whom?) and be so eager to 'organize you' and then move out? Why follow any group that tells you in the front they are 'Temporary?'"[78] The primary issue WWWCC had with TWO was its focus on West Woodlawn, and the former questioned what efforts the latter was making to improve East Woodlawn. WWWCC was also critical of efforts being led by church leaders in TWO that they felt were already being done by block clubs (headed by women), and that TWO's motivations rested in grandstanding rather than making decisions that improved the community and used the resources it already had.[79]

TWO also received harsh criticism in the local Black paper, *The Crusader*. The publication was clear in its stance that the first aim of the community should be economic control. Invoking an internal colonialism narrative, the paper pointed to non-Black-owned businesses of all types (from supermarkets to filling stations) for examples of exploitation of the community (e.g., refusal to hire Black employees and sale of inferior goods).

While TWO's call for self-determination appeared on the surface to be very much in line with the Black nationalist paper's insistence that "NEGROES MUST CONTROL THEIR OWN COMMUNITY,"[80] the paper named outsider

BUSINESS • 67

organizational involvement as deliberately interfering with and manipulating the initial intent of TWO (and the Pastor's Alliance) in developing a community betterment program to oppose the University of Chicago's south campus project.[81] The paper stated, "IAF operators Mitch Von Hoffman, boss of the setup; Walter Schaibel of the Steelworkers Union AFL-CIO, and Arthur Carlson, Future Outlook League promoters, have already been accused of fomenting strife in the mixed religious leadership of TWO."[82] According to the paper, the interracial Pastor's Alliance was splintered over a financing issue instigated by Von Hoffman, Schaibel, and Carlson in which the Protestants were told that the Catholic Archdiocese had given $64,000 to finance IAF's Woodlawn program.[83] The paper asserted that this money was nothing more than a "slush fund" for the IAF to push forward its objectives to allow exploitation through "stores, apartments and other places made 'available' by crooked real estate operations now reportedly busily 'scaring' white home owners and tenants out of the district and throwing open homes and apartments at five times the rentals paid by whites to the oncoming Negro home seekers."[84] Here the consumer market is viewed as a battleground for the claiming and reclaiming of the Woodlawn community's economic liberation, and Black consumer exploitation is laid out as the collateral damage.

TWO's affiliation with IAF made it susceptible to this type of criticism because IAF was often credited as an entity that organized "the unorganized, the powerless and propertyless so that they can possess both the opportunity and the power to act on all affairs."[85] Presenting Alinsky and the IAF as white saviors of the Woodlawn community,[86] this type of narrative served to show how much of the community work done by organizations such as WWWCC and the Woodlawn Conference was ignored.

68 • BUSINESS

This erasure of local groups' efforts and labor was dangerous to the community because it devalued (some of) the indigenous leadership within it, specifically that of Black women. And much of the resistance to TWO's affiliation with IAF stemmed from the weight of this white savior narrative of the organization and the concern that issues of the community might become white-male-centered as a result of IAF's presence.

The privileging of patriarchal and white-centered forms of organizing communities provides insight into which intersectional political consumerism strategies were chosen and how they were employed. For TWO, there is a correlation between the patriarchal power structure of the organization and its desire to replicate forms of (white) capitalism for the purposes of community uplift. In contrast, JOIN, whose leadership was not patriarchal but still embedded in and centered whiteness, sought more communal forms of intersectional political consumerism.[87] In some ways, JOIN explicitly rejected (white) capitalism (as was the case with its criticism of seeking credit as a viable strategy for transformative intersectional political consumerism), while in other ways, it proved susceptible to capitalism's allure through promises of middle-class materiality.

What precipitated the creation of the Temporary Woodlawn Organization was an urban planning initiative by the Land Clearance Commission and City Plan Commission that was drafted without the consultation of community members and excluded the community from decision-making.[88] The plan, which was drawn up by the South East Commission,[89] was heavily influenced by the interests of the University of Chicago,[90] which was in need of cleared ground for its south campus expansion plans.[91] This prompted a reactionary measure: the Woodlawn Community Rehabilitation Plan, an interracial initiative, was created by leaders in the community who felt there should be a response and resistance to the initial city plan, which excluded input and oversight from the Woodlawn community. Essentially, community members were attempting to thwart a land grab by the University of Chicago.

The demands of the Temporary Woodlawn Organization's rehabilitation plan spoke to the interest of (mostly white) Woodlawn business owners,[92] various Black community groups and clubs, and religious institutions. Its plan included a demand for a more comprehensive community plan and a call for respect for the rights of Woodlawn residents. Specifically, the plan called for a guarantee that (a) the area would remain a neighborhood that included affordable low- and middle-income housing, (b) the people of Woodlawn would be represented and heard in all planning discussions, (c) priority be given to first rehabilitating nonresidential properties so that new affordable housing may be built for current Woodlawn residents living in dangerous conditions, (d) small neighborhood retail businesses be provided with additional incentives that would facilitate their viability, and special aid be provided to (primarily white) property owners to rehabilitate their dwellings.[93]

Uptown would also become vulnerable to city planning several years after the Temporary Woodlawn Organization's founding. Addressing issues of decent housing for low-income families, Uptown residents were concerned that they would be displaced or relocated by City Hall.[94] The community felt the Lakeview-Uptown Community Council, which was responsible for drafting plans for the neighborhood, was seated by Mayor Richard J. Daley's supporters, who remained complicit in the neighborhood's demolition and poor people's displacement in the name of urban renewal.[95]

Renters as Consumers

During the 1960s, landlords of low-income properties began to see an increase in tenant demands for accountability related to the condition of their properties. Renters began seeing themselves as consumers—and as such, they had expectations as well as rights.[96] Recognizing their right to decent housing afforded through their rent payments, they used rent strikes—similar to boycotts—as a common strategy for fighting back against slumlords. To hold successful rent strikes, tenants needed to be organized and unified.

TWO began organizing pickets, rent strikes, and sit-in demonstrations in efforts to force unscrupulous landlords to improve tenant conditions. In May 1961, TWO took action on behalf of the residents of 6244 South Greenwood Avenue to get the landlord to make major repairs to the building, including fixing the heat, leaky ceilings, and walls; having garbage removed from the basement; fixing rotten windowsills and frames; and fixing chipped paint and plaster.[97]

TWO continued its advocacy work with the first in what became a series of rent strikes that took place during December 1961,[98] which included a picket line of thirty-three TWO members targeting the home of Julius Mark, who was the landlord of 6434–36 South Kimbark Avenue. TWO had organized rent strikes against Mark because of his refusal to address rat and roach infestation, falling plaster, hazardous electrical outlets,[99] and a broken water pipe, which resulted in tenants having no water and coal for heating stored in the basement being ruined.[100] TWO later purchased and delivered four tons of coal so striking residents would have heat (the landlord had not replenished the supply after the rent strike began).[101]

In February 1962, another demonstration (held in building owner Millard Brown's office) on behalf of the residents of the buildings at 6110–12 South Woodlawn Avenue and 6338 Harper Avenue focused on restoring heat and electricity to the building after Brown refused to pay or to allow Commonwealth Edison access to the basements to read the meters.[102] Thirty members of TWO's Housing and Planning Committee picketed Brown's office,[103] and TWO assisted the tenants in getting an injunction to order Brown to allow Edison access to the basement to read the meters and have the power restored.[104] Five months later, TWO claimed a rent strike victory after Victory Mutual Life Insurance took over the building from Brown and agreed to make repairs.[105]

TWO's rent strikes were successful because the organization mobilized notable numbers of people who were willing to picket and strike and because it had resources to assist rental customers as they weathered the storm of the strikes.[106] It is important to note that though TWO's formal leadership was male, the rank-and-file membership—including those on the picket lines—were overwhelmingly Black and female. Black women were sacrificing their bodies and their time to implement the direct-action strategies of TWO. Not only were they actively fighting for their rights as consumers, they were also inspiring their contemporaries. JOIN would take on TWOs successful rent strike strategy as its own several years later.

JOIN organized multiple rent strikes, which served to improve conditions for Uptown residents. In May 1966, JOIN assisted the tenants of 4107–15 North Broadway Street by organizing a rent strike and picketing in front of the building to discourage the landlord from collecting the rent. The organization also aimed to get the landlord to sign its contract to make various repairs to the building and exterminate rats and roaches.[107] JOIN also organized the tenants of the 1128–38 Sunnyside Avenue building; that rent strike resulted in a contract signed by the landlord to fix broken toilets and water system, hire a janitor to maintain the building, put lights in the hallways, and exterminate rats and roaches.[108] The rent strikes were a good organizing strategy for getting neighborhood people involved with JOIN by addressing some immediate issues.

Despite several successes with rent strikes and obtaining collective bargaining contracts with landlords as a strategy, the larger housing goal for JOIN was to eliminate slums in the Uptown area. JOIN recognized that rent strikes led to the improvement of conditions for the tenants in those buildings, but for the poor to have decent housing, politicians needed to be held accountable, and the poor needed to resist the city's efforts to push them out through urban planning.[109] In 1967, JOIN embarked on a more aggressive effort targeting Mayor Daley's urban renewal plan, collecting signatures and calling for the city to provide decent housing and schools for the poor and to "Stop Urban Renewal. Start Poor People's Power."[110]

A key aspect of JOIN's organizing strategies was studying the histories and strategies of other Chicago organizations—specifically Black organizations—and included holding workshops related to the histories and strategies of TWO, the West Side Organization (WSO), the Coordinating Committee of Community Organizations (CCCO), and the Southern Christian Leadership Conference.[111] JOIN was heavily influenced by the efforts of the SCLC and the Black freedom movement, which resulted in improved race relations (and more connectedness) between Black people and southern white people participating in JOIN.[112] The group even modeled the phrase "People's Power" and "Hillbilly Power" after the "Black Power" rallying cry.[113]

In October 1965, inspired by Dr. Martin Luther King Jr.'s SCLC staff, which also overwhelmingly consisted of Black women, JOIN became active in a citywide movement to

BUSINESS • 73

eliminate slums.[114] Here we see explicit evidence of the influence of Black people—specifically Black women—on the organizing actions of JOIN. The organization also worked collaboratively with TWO, participating in a joint demonstration against Mayor Daley and the director of the Office of Economic Opportunity, R. Sargent Shriver (whom JOIN referred to as "Poverty Director Shriver" in its December 16, 1965, progress report) after they excluded poor people from a poverty conference and banquet held in December.[115] JOIN would later build formal coalitions with Black organizations that it had previously studied. In 1966, for example, the City-Wide Welfare Union (CWWU) was created through joint organizing by JOIN, WSO, and the Kenwood Oakland Community Organization.[116] The groups offered a joint statement of support for the candidacy of William Robinson as the new director of the welfare department, to succeed then recently deceased Raymond Hilliard.[117]

Common themes emerged in JOIN's community organizing training materials, such as the need for political and economic power for the poor, the impact of urban renewal for the poor, and the creation of new and strengthening of existing independent grassroots organizations of poor Black, Brown, and white people.[118] Community organizers presented a history of the role of the organizer in U.S. history, the history of the Chicago political machine; the role of the Democratic Party in Chicago; the various ethnic blocs represented; the structure, policies, and common practices and operations of the city government; illegal activities in politics; and the independent organizations that function outside the political machine. Other parts of this training focused on the different types of community organizations and which decision-making and financial structures worked best for organizations based on their constituencies and their community's needs.[119]

74 • BUSINESS

Here a recognition that because JOIN's and TWO's communities had different constituencies and varying needs, it was possible—and likely expected—that they would be structured differently. Still, the ideological differences and histories that became embedded in these organizations as a result of their leaderships' assemblages of race, class, and gender may have focused and limited the strategies employed to meet the organizations' goals.

Visions of Self-Determination

Fifteen months after its creation, the Temporary Woodlawn Organization became a permanent entity and was renamed The Woodlawn Organization. TWO's goals were to work toward the integration of housing, schools, and jobs to ensure that the Woodlawn area received city services and preserve the existing housing in the neighborhood.[120] TWO's first convention was held in March 1962, with delegates representing over one hundred organizations from the Woodlawn area. The group elected as president Reverend Arthur Brazier, pastor of the predominantly Black Apostolic Church of God.[121] The convention's theme was "Self-Determination," and the delegates voted in favor of community self-governance and planning related to housing, jobs, and schools in the area.[122] Like JOIN, TWO had connections with SCLC. Reverend Ralph Abernathy of the SCLC was the keynote speaker for the inaugural convention. SCLC's influence, which included Abernathy and C. T. Vivian as keynote speakers during multiple conventions[123] and their messages of nonviolence, which echoed SCLC's efforts to promote civil disobedience and demonstrations in the north, deeply resonated with TWO. The group committed itself to conducting mass demonstrations addressing job discrimination and rent strikes to stop slum housing and, unlike JOIN, explicitly stated a commitment to fighting communism.[124] Also, unlike JOIN and its female leadership, TWO received early positive attention from Mayor Daley and began with a less antagonistic relationship.[125]

Daley, speaking at the convention, assured the membership that no final plans related to Woodlawn would be made without first consulting with and gaining approval from the people of Woodlawn.[126] These comments came after the mayor released the city's proposal for the new "Woodlawn Plan," which was sharply criticized as a plan to remove Black people from the area.[127] One Woodlawn resident stated in a *New Crusader* article, "We have come to realize that all Negro-owned property, however new, modern or well-kept, is 'slum' or 'deteriorated.' We have come to realize that white-owned property 'Back-of-the-Yards' (where the mayor lives) is, however old and decrepit, worthy of preservation and is not to be rehabilitated."[128] The resident's comment spoke to what was believed to be anti-Black sentiment among city officials that labeled Black neighborhoods as inferior and white neighborhoods as ideal, regardless of the physical condition of the area. The residents were explicitly calling out the source code. Interestingly, the Back of the Yards neighborhood referenced by the Woodlawn resident was the same Back of the Yards neighborhood previously organized by Alinsky.

A year later, Daley announced a plan for the city to buy commercial property from 61st to 63rd Streets on Cottage Grove (part of which had been considered previously for the University of Chicago's south campus) to build low-cost relocation housing.[129] By its third convention in 1964, TWO had counted among the organization's accomplishments the cleaning up of two hundred slum buildings in Woodlawn and the securing of over four hundred area jobs for Black people.[130]

In 1965, TWO issued a working paper related to poverty and race in Chicago. It discussed the people's fight for self-determination through representation and voice related to urban renewal plans initiated by the city and the University of Chicago, as well as poverty initiatives controlled by the Office of Economic Opportunity and Chicago Committee on Urban Opportunity.[131] The paper laid out how, on an institutional level, Black people were being disenfranchised, pointing to the segregated housing market, segregated schools, and lack of employment opportunities and union representation as but a few examples. The call for self-determination was a call for local and national government officials to get out of the way and allow the community to decide how to allocate resources earmarked to combat poverty.[132]

Early on, TWO incorporated anticommunist rhetoric into its goals and vision statements. Invoking communism was often used as a weapon against Black militant groups, so the organization's efforts to distance itself from communism was understandable. Plus, TWO was clearly capitalist in its economic ideology, as evidenced by its particular brand of engagement with intersectional political consumerism; it opted for community and racial uplift by way of business ventures and commercially centered political consumerism that sought to engage merchants.

The Future Outlook League (FOL) was a fledgling Black capitalist organization in the area that had a healthy presence in Woodlawn, with ten squad leaders in the area.[133] FOL, formed in 1935 in Ohio and influenced by the Chicago boycotts, was a direct-action organization whose goal was to target white-owned stores "that depended on African-American customers but barred them from employment" (Phillips 1999, 190). Arthur B. Carlson, who was the president of the Future Outlook League in Woodlawn, worked collaboratively with George

BUSINESS • 77

Kyros, president of the Woodlawn Business Men's Association and owner of Alexander's Restaurant, on a program to integrate the service staff.[134] Carlson later briefly became directly affiliated with TWO (as an acting temporary vice president[135]), but by October 1961, FOL had withdrawn from the organization.[136]

While Carlson and the FOL were initially drawn to TWO because its calls for self-determination and engagement with a form of political consumerism related to the "Square Deal" campaign (discussed later),[137] which seemed to be consistent with the goals of FOL,[138] ultimately the groups diverged over strategy. Still, TWO would later take on strategies reminiscent of FOL's goals around employing Blacks at white-owned businesses. For example, in July 1963, TWO representatives approached Marshall Field's demanding that at least twenty Black people be hired immediately, stating that the retailer had held long-standing discriminatory hiring practices against Black people while benefiting from Black patronage.[139] Several months later (bargaining began on September 24, 1963), after threatening a boycott and picket, TWO negotiated with High-Low Foods Inc., a local grocery chain store, to hire twelve Black employees, including a Black manager.[140]

Here lies another distinction between JOIN and TWO. TWO employed its intersectional political consumerism as a strategy to secure employment (in white businesses) for its community members. This quid pro quo follows a line of thinking that suggests that merchants who benefit from the money of Black patrons have a responsibility to the community to employ some of its members. In essence, TWO attempted, through intersectional political consumerism, to alter the social contract between Black residents and white businesses. However, the assemblages of race, class, and gender often complicated TWO's attempts to amend this contract.

DIFFERING STRATEGIES AND IDEOLOGIES

During the mid-1960s, TWO began to engage in more financial ventures,[141] including managing and renting a six-hundred-unit housing project,[142] operating a bus company,[143] and opening a supermarket employing fifty-six Black people in the TWO-Hillmans shopping complex, with two-thirds of the board members of the shopping center belonging to TWO.[144] For TWO, self-determination included being directly engaged in capitalism and helping start several Black-operated businesses in the community. One such business, Observer Printing and Publishing, was responsible for publishing TWO's newsletter, *The Woodlawn Observer*, as well as a the publications of a dozen other community organizations and commercial businesses,[145] including a weekly publication for Students for a Democratic Society.[146] Whereas JOIN clearly expressed disdain for capitalism, TWO used its capitalist ventures to promote its political agenda. *The Woodlawn Observer*'s tagline was "Craftsmanship for Self-Determination."[147]

In contrast, JOIN's focus was on community-centered forms of intersectional political consumerism. On March 1, 1967, during a welfare committee meeting, JOIN first discussed starting a buyers' club food co-op for the poor and working poor of Uptown. The co-op would allow members to pool their money or food stamps to buy from wholesalers rather than large chain stores. In its newsletter, *The Firing Line*, JOIN makes reference to the "big chain stores who charge us much too much for low grade food, and who would see us die of starvation rather than lower their prices."[148] Within a month, JOIN was encouraging people to join the new Leland Food Buying Club and expected more buying clubs to be formed in the Kenmore, Clifton, and Lakeland areas.[149]

BUSINESS • 79

Here we see a clear sentiment that big capitalist corporations care more about profit than the welfare of people. The comments signal a history of exploitation and distrust of chain stores and corporations and a preference for wholesalers, which were perceived to be less interested in raising prices for profit. With this suggestion of a food co-op, the members of JOIN legitimized themselves as consumers and, through this process, were relieved of the stigma attached to using food stamps in stores,[150] and they were empowered to choose the items they wanted to purchase. Twenty-five families participated.[151]

JOIN saw a clear link between the realm of consumerism and political protest. In the JOIN newsletter, Peggy Terry wrote, "Poor people are fighting back. They are setting up Food Co-ops, forming their own Credit Unions."[152] But tools such as co-ops and credit unions are community-centered mechanisms that harness the collective power of individuals without the incentive of profit. This is not a support of capitalism in the context of consumer activities; rather, it is a call for poor people to work collaboratively without the influence or surveillance of the private sector.[153] This is a very different political consumer strategy than TWO's, whose ideological roots embraced capitalism.[154]

The residents of Uptown and Woodlawn experienced both discriminatory price gouging and unfair treatment from store merchants. JOIN was aware of the retail practices in their community stores that negatively impacted the poor, such as false packaging to conceal contents and mislabeling packaging so items would appear to be cheaper (or have reduced prices) without actually lowering prices. Despite federal legislation prohibiting such deceptive practices, there were no federal penalties for breaking those laws.[155] JOIN organized the boycott and picketing of Price Rite repair shop after a local woman brought in two radios and a phonograph to have them repaired, only to have the

80 • BUSINESS

radios sold without her permission and the phonograph returned with the arm missing.[156] JOIN drafted a consumer and business agreement with the sentiment that the agreement might expand to include other businesses.[157] This was a strategy TWO had used several years prior. Still, JOIN employed these strategies far less frequently than more community-centered forms of inter-sectional political consumerism.

Woodlawn residents made efforts to work collaboratively with local business owners to ensure its residents were treated fairly and dealt with respectfully. The community's relationship with the Woodlawn Businessmen's Association was but one dem-onstration of how the Woodlawn residents went about holding merchants accountable to the community.[158] TWOs Resolution on Retail Trade spoke directly to the community's desire for neighborhood businesses that provided important goods and ser-vices to do so at low cost, and demonstrated the organization's promotion of shopping in the Woodlawn area (and supporting efforts that would facilitate shopping such as parking lots) as well as its insistence that these businesses exhibit fair retail practices.[159]

The WBMA, which was all white and started in 1955 when the University of Chicago launched its land clearance deal,[160] joined TWO in hopes of remaining viable in Woodlawn. WBMA president George Kyros was a strong advocate/spokesman of TWO, stating, "We must each support the other if we are going to have economic security, social equality and business prosper-ity. That is why the business men are such vigorous supporters of our new Temporary Woodlawn Organization. This is a single, unified effort from which everyone will benefit. We business men know that we cannot prosper unless all the people prosper with us."[161] In March 1963, WBMA gave TWO a $600 check as membership dues. Kyros, who presented the check to TWO president Arthur Brazier during a photo op for the *Woodlawn*

BUSINESS • 81

Booster, said that the WBMA "appreciates TWO support of the businessmen's desire to develop in Woodlawn shopping facilities second to none in the neighborhoods of Chicago."[162]

Even as WBMA expressed connection and solidarity with the predominantly Black Woodlawn community, local businessmen had a clear financial interest convergence[163] in supporting TWO and its efforts to resist the University of Chicago's encroachment, as well as its continued efforts to conserve the area of Woodlawn. Having seen the effects of urban renewal in other parts of the city lead to the removal of small businesses with the insertion of large chain stores into commercially zoned spaces, local white business owners were afraid of being pushed out of the Woodlawn area and losing their investments.[164] Still, not all the business owners were eager to support TWO. A good portion of Kyros's efforts went toward halting white flight by easing the minds of his fellow white business owners that Woodlawn and their business investments in the area should not be abandoned and that support of TWO would be the best vehicle through which to secure their futures.

Picketing and boycotting as a strategy for fighting discriminatory hiring practices and unfair treatment of customers were staples among TWO's tactics.[165] TWO's most public and scrutinized operation was called the "Square Deal" campaign, which included a march on businesses believed to have unfairly treated its customers. TWO continued these employment efforts, targeting not only businesses but also their suppliers. In 1966, CCCO and SCLC sponsored an "Operation Breadbasket" initiative to push for jobs for Black people with companies that were suppliers for various Chicago supermarkets. The company Certified was one of the targets of this campaign, and its board chairman, DaVinci, was also president of the company's milk supplier, Country Delight. Country Delight was known in the community for hiring practices that discriminated against Black people. DaVinci himself confirmed this during a meeting with several CCCO representatives, calling Black people lazy. CCCO was getting nowhere with DaVinci, so TWO decided to intervene and was able to broker a deal with forty-three owners of Certified stores in the Woodlawn area to pull Country Delight products from their stores.[166]

This supplier boycott of Country Delight was a clear example that companies perpetuating anti-Black sentiment and hiring practices would not be tolerated, nor would they benefit from Black patronage. Worth noting is the contrast in dominant strategies of the predominantly white and poor JOIN organization and the predominantly Black and poor TWO organization.

JOIN and its members were privileged in their choosing of community-centered forms of intersectional political consumerism, such as food co-ops and credit unions, and in their criticism of the CWRO's efforts to obtain credit from merchants because their access to whiteness did not prevent them from being identified in the role of consumer.[167] The algorithmic assemblages of race and class help in understanding how even as class could have prohibited these white community members from being seen as legitimate, their race did not disqualify them; rather, it validated them as consumers. The consumer rights movement and the legislation that followed was unquestionably tied to whiteness, as whites remained the standard bearers while African Americans protested in consumer spaces for access to equal treatment as consumers.

In contrast to JOIN's efforts, for TWO members to take up commercially centered forms of intersectional political consumerism meant continuing a long tradition of resistance to a system that refused to acknowledge them as legitimate consumers precisely because of race, regardless of class. So, the distinction

BUSINESS • 83

between community-centered versus commercially centered forms of intersectional political consumerism is influenced by a long history of these people's relationships with consumerism and capitalism, relationships heavily influenced by race, gender, and class. JOIN's stance centered on the anticapitalist, procommunal poor and working poor as it related to its engagement with intersectional political consumerism is not without inconsistencies. One JOIN flier stated,

> How long will welfare recipients have to wait to enjoy Christmas?? Forever???. . . . As long as Americans think poor people should be punished for being poor. Illinois welfare recipients will get over 30 percent below the government's minimum income for survival. Their children will grow up hungry and cold, poorly dressed and poorly educated and without anything in their Christmas stockings. Christmas is just like any other day for public aid recipients except their kids will look a little hungrier and sadder knowing other Americans are enjoying their Christmas.[168]

Here, JOIN is acknowledging the discrepancies between the poor and others and the material deprivation of the poor that is amplified during holiday seasons. However, in their effort to demand additional allowances for such holidays and that these allowances be expedited so the poor may have some of what others have,[169] JOIN acknowledges that this engagement will be with a marketplace that supports and perpetuates capitalism and big business. And this message is a different kind of political engagement compared with rent strikes, co-ops, and credit unions,[170] as it is wrapped in a holiday that is cemented in (white) middle-class consumerism.

When JOIN says "Hilliard is no Santa Claus" and "Christmas is like any day on welfare—terrible"[171] and implores shoppers to "consider what it would mean to have no money for toys, food or clothes this Christmas,"[172] it is calling on (white) middle-class values of materiality. In this way, though JOIN is privileged in its position to choose and more forcefully advocate community-centered intersectional political consumerism (because denial of access is not based on race), that position is not completely divorced from capitalism precisely because JOIN uses both mechanisms of political consumer activism, community centered and commercially centered.

What all these protests come to represent is a desire for closer proximity to middle-class symbolism and materiality. Ultimately, this proximity does nothing to dismantle systemic oppression of the poor, white or Black. Still, that the poor should be expected to go without in a society that couples materiality with citizenship is equally problematic.[173] Oscar Wilde said, "to recommend thrift to the poor is both grotesque and insulting. It is like advising a man who is starving to eat less." It is disingenuous of society to promote a narrative that marries democracy and citizenship with middle-class consumerism and then deny the poor access to that role and chastise them when they demand it as a right. That is a by-product of algorithmic assemblages of race, class, and gender. It was the very contradiction JOIN routinely pointed out.

Terry said, "what we have to do is tear this system down and build it back to suit ourselves. The reason we believe that JOIN is a success is because it produced a core of strong, serious working-class whites who are willing to help them tear it down and rebuild it for the benefit of both races."[174] Here, she is speaking of the capitalism that is implicated in much of JOIN's multiracial organizing and protesting, yet calls on the same system to improve the material position of the poor. Given the societal contradictions, this is both understandable and deliberate. What

BUSINESS • 85

is less understandable, and likely unintentional, is that Terry's statement also erases the presence of nonwhites—specifically Black women—in the leadership of JOIN. Though the Uptown neighborhood did consist of primarily poor white residents, Black women served in leadership roles, provided skillful organizing, and took up bold, direct actions that included, but were not limited to, being arrested.

For both JOIN and TWO, battles for legitimacy around access to consumerism for the poor were priorities in their communities. The ways in which strategy influenced the types of intersectional political consumerism employed relied heavily on the raced, classed, and gendered assemblages of both organizations' leadership. For TWO, patriarchal ideologies that focused on capitalism resulted in an affinity for commercially centered intersectional political consumerism. JOIN, a female-led organization with a privileged racial and social location among its primary membership and a generally anticapitalist stance, preferred community-centered forms of intersectional political consumerism. Neither dimension of intersectional political consumerism was fully exhibited in its purest form, nor were the algorithmic assemblages of race, class, and gender uniform across members. However, the assemblages of the organizations' formal leadership demonstrate their relationship to and subsequent influence on these community groups' intersectional political consumerism.

Black women's leadership, whether hindered, stifled, or celebrated, played a critical role in the goal-setting and activism in JOIN and TWO. Algorithmic assemblages of race, class, and gender (specifically in the formal leadership structures) shaped organizational strategies and influenced the types of intersectional political consumerism each organization engaged. For

TWO, it was patriarchal and capitalist ideologies that made up the source code that led the organization to engage commercially centered intersectional political consumerism. For JOIN, it was female-led and anticapitalist and benefited from a primary membership that was racially privileged, which gave space for a community-centered strategy of intersectional political consumerism. Democratic socialism served as a guiding ideology underpinning JOIN's priorities, such as guaranteed annual income, food co-ops, and credit unions. There was also a centering of middle-class whiteness, which would nag both organizations in different ways.

Each organization took its own approach to combating the disciplining technologies of the state's welfare policies. TWO positioned itself as a friend in the mutual fight against communism, while JOIN positioned itself as a foe, insisting that the poor be included in the creation of welfare policies and that capitalist profit yield to the needs of the people. Leaders like Dovie Coleman were experts in the state's disciplining technologies and used that expertise in service of poor people.

Rent strikes deployed by both organizations positioned renters as consumers. For TWO, the rank-and-file membership, who were overwhelmingly Black women, were the ones on the picket lines. JOIN, which studied the movement strategies of TWO and other Black organizations, would soon follow suit. While the algorithmic assemblages of race, class, and gender enabled TWO to be strategically effective and relevant vis-à-vis a male capitalist-centered approach to combating the communities' experiences with racism, JOIN tapped into a well of assemblages that united around class and gender lines. Yet, it did not have to contend with race-based questioning around legitimacy in consumer spaces, because JOIN's membership base was made up primarily of poor whites.

Again, the strategies deployed by both these organizations relied heavily on the raced, classed, and gendered assemblages of their leadership and membership bases. The configuration and multitude of identities came together to shape the strategies as well as determine the magnitude of those strategies.

3

MAGNITUDE

Consumer spaces are a gendered magnitude of legitimacy.
Through this struggle, we are magnified.

Roughly seven years after TWO's first fashion show, on April 7, 1969, the women of the Chicago Welfare Rights Organization[1] attended a Sears Annual Fashion Show. The 1969 display was of a different magnitude. Though CWRO did not sponsor the show, it did plan a demonstration in an effort to disrupt the event and draw attention to the disparities that existed between those on welfare and the middle-class patrons of the Sears Corporation. The women wanted to raise awareness about the credit practices of Sears that discriminated against welfare recipients and hoped to make its case by modeling the "current welfare fashions" during the show.

The national boycott of Sears began a month earlier, in March. Coordinated demonstrations took place across the country. In Chicago on March 27, approximately sixty people from CWRO, mostly Black women, marched and picketed the downtown Sears store and met with management. Among CWRO's demands were that Sears enter into a formal agreement with the national organization to offer credit to all its members, credit of at least $150 be extended to NWRO members, and there be no extra credit charges to welfare recipients. The CWRO fashion show demonstrators wore outfits dated five to six years prior, stating that the clothes they were wearing were not sold in stores like Sears and that if Sears granted them credit accounts, they would be able to afford the current fashions that Sears was modeling in the April 7 show. In a press release explaining their motivations for the demonstration, the CWRO stated, "We are not seeking accounts for the purpose of seeking accounts. These accounts will give us the opportunity to 'buy better' clothing for our loved ones and children. It is a known fact that if children feel part of their environment, they participate more in school activities and are more hesitant about dropping out of school. If we were able to clothe them better, we might be able to help stop them from dropping out."[2]

The idea that wearing newer, more expensive clothing would lead to improved school outcomes for the children of welfare recipients, though flawed, illustrates that the women of CWRO were connecting consumerism with structural outcomes such as educational attainment.[3] The invoking of maternal concerns related to children also focused on the same demographic that Sears targeted for attending the fashion show: women and mothers. Whereas in 1961, efforts were made in the press to display TWO as a nonpolitical organization that put on a fashion show organized by women members, CWRO took an event that was initially positioned as apolitical and deliberately politicized and magnified it by bringing issues of disparities to the forefront and putting them on display rather than using fashion to mask such inequities.

This chapter explores how Black women's struggle for legitimacy via consumer credit access was an expression of the magnitude of their advocacy as they highlighted disparities suffered by Black people in consumer spaces. Though Black consumer aspirations that are tied to white middle-class values leave space for neoliberal ideas to creep into Black consumer imaginings and mask structural inequities, I argue that during the welfare rights movement, something else occurred, something that had a level of sophistication and audacity that is often missed and dismissed in tangential and incomplete accounts of Black women's histories. While the construction of middle-class neoliberal identities through consumerism aided the welfare apparatus in deconstructing the poor, Black women began organizing around consumer credit to repurpose these financial tools to benefit poor people. I view these Black women's movement work as both a sophisticated understanding of consumer credit's connections with citizenry rights and a Black feminist technology deployed in service of poor people. Perhaps the women of the movement would not have defined themselves as Black feminists. However, considering that Black feminists argue that our experiences and voices as Black women are valid and that we should be treated fairly and with respect, it's difficult for me not to describe the women of the movement in this way. It's equally difficult to dismiss how they used consumer credit for the purpose of advocating for fair and equal treatment of the poor. This is why I frame their understanding of the link between consumerism and citizenry rights, and the invoking and deployment of consumer credit, as a Black feminist technology.

As chair of the NWRO Way and Means Committee, Etta Horn was responsible for negotiating credit agreements for its members. She provided very pointed commentary related to society's use of credit and its views of the poor. Horn believed that the extension of credit would lead to increased buying power and economic stability for poor people. She viewed corporations' refusal of credit to welfare recipients as an indicator that "there was something wrong with America."[4] Here, Horn is speaking directly to issues of fair play and credit in America for poor people. She is making a statement on how capitalism, big business, and class interact with regard to allocation of resources (e.g., credit). Commenting specifically about the Sears Corporation and its president's refusal of credit for the poor, she said,

> We feel that President Wood is part of the sick society that is prejudiced against the poor. This whole society is run on credit, especially for the rich man. So why can't we have it. The poor need it more than the rich. We're going to disrupt every damn Sears store there is until we get our demand of $150 in revolving credit for every WRO member who has a letter of reference from the organization. We're going to sit-in, march-in, rally-in, sleep-in until the economic oppression of recipients by Sears is ended.[5]

Horn recognized that consumer credit was a solidified technology of the rich and demanded that this technology be made available to the poor. Arthur Wood, president of Sears, served as a straw man for multimillion-dollar capitalist corporations that, according to Horn, represent a sickness in U.S. society that discriminates against and condemns the poor by imposing a different set of rules on them, preventing them from accessing a technology that rich white men have used without restriction to gain profit. Horn is pointing out the power dynamics that exist between political actors representing the rich (namely, company presidents) and the poor (represented by NWRO) and how the consumer market persists in being a space of tension, negotiation, and resistance. When she says there is something wrong with America, she is connecting nationalism, consumerism, and credit and fashioning credit as a Black feminist technology.

Horn was demanding that poor Black women, and the poor generally, be given access to quality merchandise and reasonable interest rates rather than low-quality goods at exploitive rates offered by predatory local merchants. Horn was demanding that the poor be fully integrated into U.S. consumerist society without an additional poverty tax as punishment for their systematic disenfranchisement.

When we think of technology, we typically turn to examples of sophisticated digital devices and platforms with the latest state-of-the-art digital materials and features. We don't often think of the simplicity of the analog world, such as a pencil and paper, as technology. When I think about the broad definition of "technology" as "the application of knowledge for practical purposes," I consider the institution of consumer credit for retail purposes as a technology. And I use this reframing to consider how Black women's demands for and use of this technology facilitated acknowledgment of the poor as consumers with rights and protections. The archival record contains discussion around how, during the 1960s and 1970s, the government desired to prepare high school students to be future consumers to ensure a healthy economy. The public school system was used to educate students about how to be informed consumers and which financial tools they would have at their disposal to engage the consumer market. One of these financial tools was consumer credit. This technology was regulated and deployed for explicitly capitalist purposes.

TRANSFORMATION FROM CUSTOMER TO CONSUMER

During the mid-1960s, we saw much discussion among marketers in the business industry around the distinction between

MAGNITUDE • 93

customers and consumers. Customers were characterized as localized in their interests, loyal to businesses, and having limited influence over how those businesses operated. In contrast, consumers held political positions with larger agendas that extended beyond the local, sought protection of rights, and exerted power and influence as they fought to access those rights. A key distinction in these discussions of customer versus consumer rested in the consumer identity's access to rights and protections. These rights and protections were defined by the state. While customers were viewed as apolitical and docile, consumers were seen as potentially dangerous for businesses. The consumer identity demanded that businesses inform shoppers about the products being sold and protect shoppers from unethical practices.[6]

But the distinction also served another purpose in expressing how differently power was shared and exerted. Whereas customers had some power in terms of offering their loyalty to businesses that served them well, much of the power rested in the hands of merchants, who were allowed to make claims about products and services (through marketing) that served to mislead and/or confuse customers. Because there was little regulation of businesses and what was lawful versus what was ethical (fair) were two distinct spheres, customers—particularly those with few merchant options due to economic and/or geographical restrictions—were largely at the mercy of merchants. This is particularly relevant to African American customers, who were more vulnerable to exploitation by businesses that price gouged and sold inferior products.[7] Consumers, on the other hand, had an intermediary in the form of the government, which would demand that merchants adhere to fair business practices and attempt to educate consumers so they could make more discerning and informed decisions.

The U.S. government has over a century's history of legitimizing white citizens as consumers. In 1906, Congress passed the Pure Food and Drug Act as a way of protecting white citizens from inaccurate and/or misleading food labeling (Stein 1980). This regulation is important to note because it marked the government's first intercession as a protector of white customers. I emphasize that protection was explicitly for white citizens because, during the time of the legislation's passing, African Americans still were not allowed to vote, and they were denied access to much of the labor market and restricted from much of consumer life. The right to vote and gainfully work were (and are) cornerstones of U.S. citizenship, as is access to the consumer market—as consumers.[8]

In 1914, the Federal Trade Commission was created to protect consumers and promote competition among businesses. The (white) consumer movement, which is defined as "the totality of organizations, institutions, regulations, activities, and viewpoints directed at improving consumer welfare," was a response to the mass production and consumption explosion during the late nineteenth and early twentieth centuries and set in motion political action in the form of lobbying and the creation of organizations to address fair market labor issues (Tiemstra 1992, 2). Workers wanted fair wages, but they also wanted more leisure time. As highlighted in *Consumer Society in American History*, "to the extent that they produced the nation's foods, they deserved to enjoy their fair share of the fruits of their labor. For most white American workers the work week steadily declined: from sixty-four hours in 1850, to sixty by 1890, to fifty-five by 1914, to forty by 1930s" (Glickman 1999, 3).

The first iteration of this consumer movement, which was prolabor and predominantly white and female, was quickly labeled "communist." We get a glimpse of how the algorithmic assemblages of race, class, and gender negotiate and navigate within the realm of power, dictating government protections. In

MAGNITUDE • 95

this case, sexism and classism provided the source code for how to delegitimize the first iteration of the consumer movement. Whiteness alone was not enough.

President Franklin Delano Roosevelt's New Deal helped bolster consumer activity following the Depression. To address unemployment, Roosevelt formed the Civilian Conservation Corps (CCC) to employ eighteen- to twenty-five-year-olds. The government wanted people to work so they could earn a wage, which would enable them to participate in the economy as consumers. After World War II, consumerism was once again lifted as the torch of capitalism, shining light on the evils of communism. In an effort to bolster the economy and revitalize consumption, advertisers targeted the baby boomer generation with new "needs" (Glickman 1999). White Americans were eager to spend, and white businesses were eager to sell, but not without some backlash from the second iteration of the consumer movement.

During this time, the relationship between consumers and industry changed with the intercession of more government regulations, thus further limiting industry power and placing it in the hands of customers. So that capitalism could be beneficial for everyday white American as well as the wealthy white industrialist, the government had to heavily regulate industry activities. Such regulations not only protected customers but also set expectations that government would intercede if they were not treated fairly by businesses. The regulating role of the government also set the stage for the legitimizing of citizens as consumers who were entitled to certain rights. However, the government's new role as protector of consumers did not include African Americans. Much of the South still had segregated consumer spaces, which proved to be contested areas ripe with protest; "taking a seat at a lunch counter as a paying customer was one of the most powerful forms of political action taken by Civil Rights activists in the 1950s" (Ritzer 2007, 706).[9]

While this distinction between consumer and customer provides some liberatory power, through education of the consumer, this power is filtered through the government and therefore is far from complete By educating customers, the government was turning them into consumers and thus legitimizing the consumer identity. Those who control the transitioning process ultimately control the end result, so the opportunities for resistance become limited. But the message that is perpetuated is that the power, however incomplete, is in the hands of the informed consumer. Organizations such as the Better Business Bureau (BBB) helped manage consumers' frustrations and keep them focused on merchants, which resulted in the (perhaps unintentional) hindering of critique around larger economic issues, such as increases in food prices and cost of living, or the lack of jobs due to discriminatory hiring practices in certain targeted communities that had many patrons. It was somewhat predictable that the program of constructing the consumer included a built-in deflector of resistance against the state. The government's source code always includes firewalls.

City and state governments would continue to build structures, such as education, that would support the consumer movement as an apparatus with which to promote capitalist ideology. In this context, discussions around the transition of citizens from customers to consumers, and the government's efforts in facilitating that process, become much clearer. Earl Lind, president of the BBB of Metropolitan Chicago, was appointed to the Consumer Education Curriculum Development Committee, and Mayor Daley set up a budget in support of the Consumer Education Plan to establish multiple counseling centers throughout the city to educate people about issues of buying and

MAGNITUDE • 97

credit. Illinois was the first state to require that consumer education be included in high school curricula. In a 1968 speech to the Illinois Retail Merchants Association, State Senator Cecil Partee, who pushed for the consumer education legislation, stated,

> The young who will be adult buyers of tomorrow must be given the knowledge that consumer credit is a vital part of their future lives—either a great opportunity or a frightful menace to their economic and social lives. They must see consumer credit for what it is—an economic device through which they may acquire what they want and pay for it out of future earnings. They must be impressed with the understanding that consumer credit serves to maintain the important balance between America's production, distribution and consumption. They must be taught that properly regulated and properly used consumer credit is absolutely essential to acquire the sales volume needed for more and more jobs, more and more spendable income and more and more taxes to pay for the solvent operation of an enlightened Nation.[10]

Without explicitly saying as much, Partee clearly drew consumer education—and consumerism generally—into the realm of the political. This statement about education perpetuates capitalist logic as superior; it was never questioned whether or not the promotion of artificial growth, which would be further perpetuated by consumer credit tools, was necessary or desirable. Consumer credit as technology was deployed to advance this capitalist logic of expanded spending as necessary and desirable. The senator asserted that the only way for an "enlightened nation" to generate jobs was through increased sales volume, and without explicitly saying so, he acknowledged that U.S. citizens could not support such volume through their own current earnings. So, the proposed solution was to sacrifice expected future earnings to keep up with the consumption required by the capitalist system to maintain itself. Not only is the relinquishing of future earnings a privileged position of those who are confident in their job security (which would exclude those in poverty as well as those vulnerable to racist work environments), it also leaves no room for critique related to why this type of economic growth is the only option offered.

By controlling the curriculum, the state essentially obscured the general public's understanding of the economy and consumerism's role to the perpetual benefit of capitalism. And consumer credit was the technology used to make these concessions palatable to the public. The Black women of the welfare rights movement used this capitalist technology of the state and turned it against itself through their insistence that poor Black women should have access to this "enwhitened" consumer nation via credit. That the consumer-citizen's historical foundation was built on a legal system of exclusion of nonwhite people, and that the state connected citizens' ability to carry out their civic duties through one means—a capitalist consumer society—meant that Black people were doubly minimized. That Black women would take this exclusionary technology and refract back on to this capitalist society its citizenry demands, and then deploy the consumer-citizen logic in service to magnifying the needs of the very group it was designed to subjugate, demonstrate a sophisticated level of Black technophilia.[11]

CONSUMER EDUCATION AND RIGHTS LEGISLATION

Though certainly not prominently displayed in discussions, there is evidence that the educational apparatuses and consumer organizations made some (albeit limited) outreach to African Americans as potential consumers. Nationally, BBBs were reaching out to African American consumers, including offering buying advice and encouragement for new Black homeowners.[12] Locally, consumer education efforts included those at African American Chicago high schools such as DuSable. In 1968, the Better Business Bureau of Metropolitan Chicago began an organized effort to educate consumers, including focusing some resources toward Black consumer education.[13]

But prior to the federal government's curriculum interventions and the BBBs' educational efforts, white Chicago Woodlawn-area business owners' interest in the African American consumer market. In May 1961, the Industrial Areas Foundation contacted the National Opinion Research Center (NORC) on behalf of the Woodlawn Business Men's Association requesting research on the Woodlawn consumer market. Specifically, WBMA was interested in conducting a survey to determine the existing and potential consumer market in the predominantly Black Woodlawn area. It wanted to know whether or not higher-income Black people in Woodlawn shopped outside the community, patronizing Woodlawn businesses' primary retail competition, and it sought information about efforts that could be made to "win neighborhood consumers to the street." NORC declined the invitation, stating that its research related to projects of broad public interest and referring WBMA to "existing commercial research organizations."[14] For NORC, "broad" meant white. Still, WBMA's request to NORC to understand the consumer market in Woodlawn demonstrates an acknowledgment of and interest in (middle-class) African Americans as desirable consumers.

In contrast, African American business owners, professionals, and consultants across the country had long understood the existence and value of the Black consumer market. The National Association of Market Developers (NAMD), formally organized in Nashville at Tennessee A & I State University in 1953, was created specifically to collect and share information about the "Negro market," develop standards of professional conduct for businesses, and protect the image of "Negro marketeers.'"[16] Organizations such as NAMD not only served to acknowledge and legitimize the Black consumer market, it also helped expose the market's political power and potential.

Spending power has often been invoked as a proxy for value and respect for communities. There was great hype leading up to the moment in 2013 when the Black consumer market reached the $1 trillion mark. That was also around the time of massive calls for boycotts of businesses and encouragement to patronize Black-owned businesses. In response to the state-sanctioned violence carried out by local police against Black people, hashtags such as #BlackOutBlackFriday and #NotOneDime encouraged African Americans to mobilize and withhold their dollars until reforms were made. These activities serve as examples of how African American communities still deploy strategies of politicized consumerism.

In the 1950s, industry boycotts also encouraged Black customers to use their purchasing choices and speak with their dollars. By the 1960s, consumer advocacy and the promotion of fair treatment and protections in the marketplace had long been on the minds of Black people. In 1960, the Chicago Urban League initiated a project on consumer credit education that was concerned with what the league viewed as an increase in exploitation of Black customers. The historical role and treatment of African Americans in the consumer market included being ignored, disrespected, and exploited by white businesses (Weems 2009). While gains had been achieved in home and business ownership, increased wealth and education, and urbanization—all of which contributed to opening opportunities for Black people through the creation of a so-called negro market—these gains also opened opportunities for further exploitation. This exploitation was exacerbated by the in-migration of Blacks from rural and southern communities along with dishonest credit practices of predatory businesses. These were the same practices that Black women activists of the welfare rights movement would later attempt to shield themselves from through acquiring consumer credit from reputable national department stores such as Sears.

Along with the migration of Black people from the South came an increase in wage garnishments, so the Chicago Urban League launched a credit education initiative focused on teaching better buying practices. The league's primary focus was related to credit, communicating to community members the current Illinois statutes related to credit buying. While organizations like the Chicago Urban League focused on protecting Black customers, the government was concerned about creating informed white consumers. And so, in 1962, it passed the Consumer Bill of Rights, which included protections such as the right of consumers to be informed about products and services and to be offered competitive prices.[17] Additional legislation would soon follow, with the goal of adding more consumer protections (see table 3.1).

While the state was securing protections for white consumers via legislation, Black communities were engaging in grassroots efforts to stave off unfair consumer practices. For example, a 1961 flier targeting Black customers, simply titled "Beware," contains a page-long warning to customers about unscrupulous merchants, stores, contracts, and solicitors. The informational material highlights business practices such as by dealers who did

TABLE 3.1 CONSUMER EDUCATION AND RIGHTS LEGISLATION, 1960–1980

Year	Legislation	Description
1962	Consumer Bill of Rights	States that consumers have the right to (a) safe products, (b) be informed about products and services so they can make informed choices, (c) choose from a variety of products and services at competitive prices, and (d) be heard as their comments relate to consumer government policy.
1967	IL Senate Bill 977—Consumer Education Bill	Requires that students in public schools study courses that include instruction in the area of consumer education, including but not limited to installment purchasing, budgeting, comparison of prices, and an understanding of the roles of consumers interacting with agriculture, business, labor unions, and government in formulating and achieving the goals of the mixed free enterprise system.
1968	Truth in Lending Act	Part of the Consumer Credit Protection Act that requires lenders and creditors to disclose the annual percentage rate (APR), term of the loan, and total costs to the consumer before any agreement is signed.
1970	Fair Credit Reporting Act	Part of the Consumer Credit Protection Act that regulates how consumer reporting agencies use consumer credit information and ensures that consumers have access to their credit information as well as the right to have any inaccurate information corrected in a timely manner.
1976	Equal Credit Opportunity Act	Part of the Consumer Credit Protection Act that ensures that consumers seeking credit will not be discriminated against based on religion, sex, race, color, marital status, national origin, or age or because they receive public assistance.

This legislation is public law. Relevant congressional records can be found on the Congressional Record website, https://www.congress.gov/.

not explain finance charges and/or did not list retail prices on merchandise. Among a list of unscrupulous businesses, the flier names State Jewelers and Clothiers, State Furniture, Ellis Jewelers and Clothiers, Chicago Jewelers and Clothier, and all Furniture Dealers. In particular, State Jewelers and Clothiers was the target of a legal case for its enforcement of an inaccurate wage assignment for the brother of a patron. Henry Honore's lawsuit stated that wage assignments were served for Michael Reese Hospital, where he was employed as an oxygen technician, despite the fact that the firm had prior notification that his signature was a forgery. Though Honore's case was one of mistaken identity, those willingly entering into such agreements had little legal recourse regarding enforcement. If customers fell behind on their payments (often as a result of having to pay excessive interest fees), merchants could obtain a court order to garnish all but $45 of their weekly wages every week until the debt was paid. In these cases, the state was working in favor of the merchants.

Despite this collaboration whereby local merchants weaponized the state, African Americans viewed themselves as a political force in consumerism's realm of power and validated themselves as legitimate consumers. The "Beware" flier was one example of how they were organizing and educating their communities so their legitimacy would be acknowledged by white power structures like the state and merchants alike. They were "tinkering" with the state's capitalist technology even before credit's mainstream deployment via Illinois public schools.

The state government and the local BBB were several years behind the Chicago Urban League in considering the need for more extensive consumer education—specifically credit education—for the citizenry.[18] In 1967, Illinois Governor Otto Kerner approved Senate Bill 977, which amended the School Code of Illinois (section 27–12:1) and stated, "Pupils in the public schools in grades 8 through 12 shall be taught and be required to study courses which include instruction in consumer education, including but not necessarily limited to installment purchases, budgeting, and comparison of prices."[19]

A December 1967 memo to Illinois school administrators from the superintendent of public instruction, Ray Page, addresses two bills: 19H, dealing with the teaching of U.S. history and requiring lessons about more ethnic groups throughout the year, and 977, which dealt with consumer education. The irony in the memo rests in its discussion of seemingly unrelated bills with directly related issues. One of the major failings of scholars of mainstream consumption in providing postmodern theories has been their lack of historicizing consumerism in the context of identity when attempting to uncover structural relationships between the material and the ideological. How history is taught and whose history is taught (and from what perspective) greatly influences our ability to understand and be critical of various relationships and their implications.

Just as bill 19H called for ethnic diversification of the curriculum, understanding the consumer movement and its impact on society requires a more inclusive investigation of how variously gendered and racialized consumers have shaped, innovated within, and been impacted by this capitalist technology. As we uncover the various histories of consumer activism as told and lived by African American women, we are able to offer different theories around how consumerism exposes relationships of power and resistance and the degrees to which positionality influences meaning making.

Bill 977 passed as the result of the collaborative efforts of the BBB of Metropolitan Chicago and the state government during the 1960s-1970s to incorporate consumer education into the public school curriculum.[20] The formal guidelines that developed through this collaboration stated that the objectives of consumer education included helping students "to understand the role of the consumer in our economy, . . . to develop the ability to make rational choices among alternatives, . . . to show the relevance of economic principles to personal economic competence and develop basic economic understanding requisite for responsible citizenship, . . . [and] to become aware of dependence on society for consumption, and of reciprocal responsibilities."[21] This focus on consumer education signaled the connecting of consumerism with national economic health and responsible citizenship. The nation's dependence on consumption was not questioned but encouraged. The use of the public school system as an apparatus to push for the education of students as future consumers had perhaps an unintended consequence of extending access to consumerism to African Americans.

Consumer education topics in public schools included types of consumer credit, the use and cost of credit, consumer credit laws, and information about borrowing money, buying goods and services, and renting or owning a home. The curricular materials also provided information and references for teachers and students, including listings of available films and slides. One filmstrip, titled "Price of Credit," featured the main character Frank, who was a white male recently laid off and defaulting on his car payments, and focused on educating him about consumer credit and his responsibilities in becoming an informed consumer. That the white male character was laid off and unemployed is noteworthy, given the narratives around Black female WRO members and their so-called deservingness of credit tied to their employment status.

The necessity for educating citizens about their rights and obligations served to bring an emerging national movement to the forefront. The state used the public education system to promote its newest capitalist technology. And by using the Illinois school system as a conduit for promoting consumer credit, the federal government also conceded to an acknowledgment of Black people as consumers as well as citizens.

NWRO AND THE SEARS CAMPAIGN

When NWRO began targeting national chain stores such as Sears and Montgomery Ward on March 27, 1969, in a campaign to secure credit-buying rights for welfare recipients, the organization provided the following rationale: "This became a pilot program, with purposes of ensuring welfare recipients' nondiscriminatory treatment by narrow-minded local credit personnel; remove poor people from the exploitation of unscrupulous ghetto merchants, and give poor people the security of knowing that, when large or special items, such as beds, stoves, winter clothing, etc., are needed by their families they will have credit available at reputable stores to permit them to secure good merchandise at reasonable prices."[22] The idea that major white retail stores would have the best merchandise and services and that access to those services would somehow lead to less exploitation of the poor is taken as fact without much critique. This stance is peculiar given the historical context of Black and poor people's experiences with white consumer spaces. In some cases, time served as an organizing structure for which campaigns, as well as which targets, were chosen.

The Sears campaign began just before Easter, as NWRO promoted narratives around seasonal consumerism such as the following: "Welfare Recipients need credit arrangements with Sears and other stores. At certain times of the year, in the fall, at Christmas time, in the early summer, and <u>Now</u> [<u>sic</u>] with

Easter and the beginning of warm weather, it is necessary to make larger purchases for the family than at other times. Welfare recipients should be able to buy on credit the special needs of the season."[23] The needs that were the subject of these campaigns were in large part directed by family seasonal desires. Though new Easter clothes would not be considered a necessity for life and health, NWRO members saw them as necessary for dignity and a demand that mothers were willing to fight for on behalf of their children.

As the campaign continued into October, NWRO fliers and communications for local welfare rights organizations emphasized its "Credit for Christmas" push to secure an agreement with Sears and other stores. According to Hulbert James, the NWRO director of field operations,

> Opposition to the credit campaign comes from two sources: a) real conservatives, who judge our tactics to be threatening; b) fiscal conservatives, who feel that poor people will not pay their credit accounts. The credit campaign became a national issue only after a year of experimentation in Philadelphia where several large stores extended credit to welfare recipients, and it turned out that their rate of repayment was higher than in the general population. One must realize that a welfare check is guaranteed income! At present, the basic factor in extending credit is income; but it should be ability to repay. I would like to suggest that the only way welfare families can live in the city on $3,000 a year is to be more economical than the average person. Welfare families will know how to make credit repayments.[24]

James had good reason to address concerns about the poor's ability to responsibly manage their government benefits. From the time of Roosevelt, Black poor people had been stigmatized and viewed as incapable of making good consumer choices with their relief payments. Roosevelt's policies were susceptible to the same paternalism we later saw during the welfare rights movement. As Kimberley Phillips notes in *AlabamaNorth*, "By 1934, 80 percent of the Black population received either direct or indirect relief. Superadded to the disproportionate burden of unemployment, those African Americans on relief did not receive cash like white recipients; instead, Blacks had to buy from stores authorized to fill orders. In justification, the Cuyahoga County relief administration claimed that African Americans 'would prove unable to properly manage their affairs' if they gave direct payments to the poor" (Phillips 1999, 197).

The democratic socialist policies of the Roosevelt administration, which would assist in slowing the underdevelopment reestablished after Reconstruction, were fiercely attacked during the Cold War, when the national anticommunist sentiment weakened the effectiveness of the Black civil rights struggle. It is important to note that though the women of the welfare rights movement viewed access to credit as a right to which they were entitled, the use of such credit was frequently positioned as extending only to special one-time purchases of items, such as appliances, or special seasonal items. Credit, as a technology, was not positioned as an instrument that would allow the women to sustain a lifestyle beyond their means. Credit was presented as a budgetary rather than a lifestyle tool. Yet, there is an inconsistency in the message that credit was simply a way for the poor to obtain needed items they otherwise couldn't afford because they lacked capital or savings and the Sears protest calling for access to the latest fashions as well as the seasonal pushes for Easter clothes and Christmas items. NWRO members attempted to appeal to middle-class white women's sense of empathy by highlighting the disparities in the quality and newness of garments or ability to buy holiday gifts, which were heavily encouraged by marketers and by a shifting consumerist society that insisted these items were necessities.

Inequity was embedded in a system that required certain groups to pay higher prices for goods and services. Consumerism as a democratizing tool was a myth of capitalism, which masked this embedded inequity (and allowed the exploitation of African American consumers to go unchecked) while disingenuously purporting equity as achieved through consumer choice. The notion that consumers have power through their choice of where they spend their money provides agency for those who are disenfranchised but lacks acknowledgment of the entrenched inequalities that are reinforced through neoliberalism. Unsurprisingly, this strategy of acquiring retail credit for the poor backfired and served to further cast welfare recipients in the broader movement as unwilling to work and perpetually seeking handouts for which they were undeserving.

In February 1967, the Welfare Council of Metropolitan Chicago, understanding the implications of viewing the poor as consumers, took formal positions on several consumer issues. The Welfare Council, an advocacy organization composed of a conglomerate of social service agency representatives that later became the United Way of Chicago, issued position statements on the need to abolish the "wage process."The statements included the need to prohibit withholding the wages of consumer borrowers who defaulted, to change default remedies such as deficiency judgments that exceed the original cost of the item, and to more clearly and fully disclose credit charges. In June 1968, the Welfare Council also issued a statement of support for a guaranteed annual income. It interpreted poverty within a context of the marketplace and understood the poor as a type of consumer several years before the consumer rights movement began to gain momentum. During the 46th Annual Meeting of the Welfare Council of Metropolitan Chicago, on February 23, 1961, G. Edward McClure, executive director of the Evanston United Fund, delivered a speech in which he compared the shopping center with welfare services and, by extension, retail customers with welfare clients:

> Convenience, accessibility—whatever you choose to call it—has been an important consideration in the retail field. It is good business sense to have stores grouped together—a drug store, a department store, a supermarket, an apparel shop, and so on— so that the customer can save time and effort. This principle was recognized long ago when our neighborhood business districts developed, and it has been pursued even more consciously in our modern shopping centers. The key to the effectiveness of such a center, whether it is a shopping center or a welfare center, is the extent to which the various services needed by the customer, or client, are available to him.[25]

Though McClure was attempting to make a point about the need for increased efficiencies of the welfare system and the importance of proper planning to best serve welfare recipients' needs, the choice to compare welfare services to a shopping center and to invoke marketplace language speaks to the insidious ways in which neoliberal thinking began infiltrating the welfare discourse. That supporters of welfare would offer up consumer spaces as a model for welfare systems served to reify notions of individual choice or freedom, market-based approaches to achieving democratic outcomes and (economic) growth, as well as the achievement of health through consumption.

In 1970, NWRO Executive Director George Wiley and Etta Horn coauthored a statement titled "Consumer Credit and the

Poor," which was presented to the Senate Banking and Currency Committee. Among other issues, the statement highlighted the need for poor families to have access to credit at fair interest rates so they could make large purchases for which they are unable to save.[26] Horn also compared Sears and Montgomery Ward, in which Wards was viewed as reasonable and ideal (as a corporation) because of its willingness to extend credit to welfare recipients. Still, there were conflicting views within NWRO about whether credit was viewed as a citizen's right. Though Wiley and Horn stated in "Consumer Credit and the Poor" that credit was a right of all citizens, when asked this question during a February 6, 1970, interview, NWRO Director of Field Operations James said, "We do not say that credit is a 'right.' The issue is one of exploitation. Poor people have obtained credit for quite a while—from ghetto merchants, but at higher rates, and for shoddy goods. One of the ways we can get more money into poor homes is to get them cheap credit, well-made products, guarantees on quality, in respectable stores. We are trying to tell merchants that they must change their practices."[27]

Remember that during the 1960s, retail credit was considered a new and novel financial tool for consumers. Public schools were beginning to educate high school children on the function of credit in society, and for many consumers—particularly poor consumers—credit was viewed as part of a liberatory financial management strategy ushering in flexibility and choice. While NWRO had a multitude of goals in service to the nation's poor, the credit campaign was revolutionary in that it fought for the poor to access what was, at the time, a relatively new offering of major retailers as opposed to unscrupulous merchants who exploited vulnerable Black communities.

Not only were NWRO credit campaigns directly related to the larger consumer movement taking place during the same period, but NWRO national headquarters personnel also connected their personal consumer experiences to skills they felt were transferable to the labor market. Jonquil Lanier, in her application for employment as an administrative assistant, included the following among her qualifications for the position: "Consumer buying and comparative shopping—We took many shopping trips, had parent meetings, developed, compared and tested recipes designed for low income families."[28] Another applicant, Constance Sadlow, wrote in her cover letter, "I am constantly waging my own private battles in this field against false interest charges, poor public services, rude and deceitful sales people, defective appliances, etc."[29] It is unknown whether these applicants were successful in securing positions with the organization. But it is clear how aware the public was of NWRO's campaigns and association with consumer-related issues. Those wishing to work for the national headquarters recognized the NWRO's interest in the consumer space and used that knowledge to communicate their personal alignment with the organizational goals. And NWRO was not alone in this interest.

The Consumer Action Bedford-Stuyvesant (CABS), a community organization in New York, seeing a need for the poor to access credit, formed the Consumer Action Credit Union. Gladys Aponte, executive director of CABS, stated, "We have proved to the League of Credit Unions and the regional office of the Federal Credit Union Bureau that poor people are capable of utilizing middle-class institutions by adjusting them to their own needs."[30] In Waterbury, Connecticut, the low-income area of Berklee also sought a credit union as a solution to the community's credit needs and its desire for economic control. The New Opportunities for Waterbury (NOW), a consumer action group that serviced a low-income area of Berklee, envisioned cooperative economic institutions working together to generate wealth in the community. Gaudencio Obligacion, assistant director of NOW, stated,

> When NOW opens a branch office of a credit union in Berk-lee . . . it will be a step closer to complete community control. . . . A person will be able to cash his check at the credit union and buy food stamps. Afterwards he will be able to go downstairs to the buying club. This keeps the money right where it belongs. . . . This money can be put in the credit union for people to borrow. As the club continues to grow it eventually can open a neighborhood grocery store and even a supermarket.[31]

Accessibility to credit through credit unions for several low-income communities offered inroads to broader opportunities to engage as consumers without perpetuating overtly capitalist values. This type of community credit-seeking, in contrast to the corporate credit-seeking employed for NWRO's Sears campaign, had the direct goals of strengthening the entire community using middle-class institutions rather than strengthening the status of individuals through the acquisition of middle-class aspirations.

CREDIT AND CLASS ASPIRATIONS

During the time when the state was using the education apparatus to push consumer credit technologies on the next generation of potential consumers and consumer protection legislation was being passed, there was significant public debate around whether or not poor people had the right to be consumers if they were not engaged in the formal workplace.

An analytical deconstruction of a document created by NWRO, "Being Poor Is Expensive,"[32] exposes the distinctions between the middle-class consumer and the poor consumer and how these distinctions served to reify class inequities and left poor consumers worse off in the consumer market. The document is found in a collection of files that includes materials related specifically to NWRO's guaranteed annual income (GAI) campaign. GAI documents in the same folder utilize arguments similar to those outlined in "Being Poor Is Expensive," suggesting that the arguments were commonly used when articulating the specific challenges facing the poor.

"Being Poor Is Expensive" is clearly in conversation with the debates occurring during the welfare rights movement. In contrast to the numeric facts and figures given in institutional reports, the NWRO document takes an ethnographic approach to communicating the lived experiences of the poor, similar to other narratives that the organization produced. The document's methods are notable because they speak to the rejection of a conventionally quantified, perceivably "objective" presentation in favor of a subjective and qualitative rendering of the experiences of the poor. The document is also important because it clearly positions the poor as consumers and offers a critique of access to consumer spaces rather than a critique of the poor as flawed. The document mentions the specific challenges faced by the poor to gain access to credit, and it concludes with a statement related to the elusiveness of credit for the poor. It makes the case that (low-interest) credit offered to middle-class consumers is a tool with the potential to assist the poor in managing their finances and obtaining access to consumer spaces.

The document suggests that middle-class consumers have the benefit of time on their side, in that they can afford to use the fluctuation in pricing of goods and services to their advantage. Section one of "Being Poor Is Expensive," "Time of Purchase," poses the question, "Of what use is a sale on children's summer clothing in October, when a poor family can't even afford to purchase a winter coat?"[33] The argument is that because they are not perpetually deprived, middle-class consumers have the privilege of waiting for certain foods to go on sale, buying in bulk when those items are reduced, and that, generally, they have the privilege of shopping out of convenience rather than necessity.

The temporal component was key to WRO members' demands for access to consumer goods, spaces, and tools. Speaking to access, Rose Thomas, a leader of the New York–based NWRO group, Concerned Parents for Adequate Welfare, stated, "Well, I would like to stay here in Queens, have my own home and a station wagon. Mostly to get around, especially when I see sales on a lot of things I like, and I try to travel on the bus. When I get there, I see so much and I can't travel back with it. Food especially, groceries, meats. Sometimes clothing."[34]

This was much more than an issue of consumer convenience. The issue of available consumer options and choice was viewed as one of social justice. The Chicago Archdiocesan Committee on Poverty (ACP) advocated for nearby shopping for residents of Lawndale, Cabrini-Green, Englewood, and Altgeld Gardens (African American areas with high concentrations of poverty). The committee drew attention to rising food prices and a dearth of major grocery store chains in these areas, and it offered several solutions to address these issues.

ACP became involved with the Self-Help Action Center (SHAC) in 1973. SHAC, a nonprofit program that began in 1968, sold and distributed food in impoverished areas. Paul Horvat and Dorothy Shavers created the program. Horvat's personal biography seemed to greatly influence his political consumerist perspectives:

116 • MAGNITUDE

As a youth in Yugoslavia during the early part of this century, Horvat identified with the land, with what it produced, and very early developed a concern for broader distribution of food. Having lived through both World Wars and under various political regimes, his concern for food distribution and self-determination has not wavered. He carried his concerns with him to the United States in 1952 and, after becoming financially self-sufficient here, he began to organize food buying clubs, sponsor demonstration sales and tried to sell the concept of consumers purchasing food directly from producers.[35]

Horvat was able to make connections between politics and food distribution and sought to offer people alternatives to the sale and distribution of food that were more independent of large corporations and promoted socialist rather than capitalist ideas. Dorothy Shavers, a Black Southside Chicago resident and teacher who grew up in Arkansas on a cotton farm, contacted Horvat after reading an article about his ideas around food distribution. Having seen both rural and urban poverty, and curious about the impact of malnutrition on children, Shaver believed that food cooperatives and buying club concepts could greatly benefit the poor. She engaged in and promoted community-based intersectional political consumerism via the food-buying club and joined Hornet around values that placed the needs of poor people over profit.

The "Being Poor Is Expensive" document also speaks to the choices that are available to middle-class consumers around geographical options and store choice (e.g., shopping around for the best prices and merchandise), the higher quality of products available to middle-class consumers, and the flexibility of payment options available to middle-class consumers, including access to credit. "The poor have no flexibility in the method by which they must make purchases. It is almost impossible for a poor family to obtain credit without collateral. Even if they manage to obtain credit, the poor become trapped by exhorbitant [sic] carrying charges, high interest rates, and unreliable merchants. Conversely for most Americans credit is an outlet to cost effectiveness and financial convenience."[36]

It was under this premise that the NWRO organized a major campaign to secure credit for its members. Similar to TWO's direct-action efforts during the Square Deal Campaign, local welfare rights organizations marched on local businesses to apply pressure to secure credit for the poor. This site of struggle was set in the consumer market and centered on choice—choice as freedom. NWRO pursued companies such as General Mills, Procter & Gamble, and The Sterling Drug Company, requesting that these companies give coupons redeemable for General Motors products as a way to "distribute a share of your great wealth to those poorest of the poor."[37]

Though NWRO was unsuccessful in gaining support from these companies, the request signals the politicizing of consumerism (Kornbluh 2003). Women of the NWRO felt they had a right to choose what their needs were and to consumer choice in meeting those needs. The Home Economics Unit of the Cook County Department of Public Aid offered "homemaking education," which included sewing classes. As one NWRO member indicated, welfare mothers of the NWRO wanted to buy clothes off the rack like middle-class white women did and not spend their time and energy making clothes. That member was resisting the notion that the poor had endless disposable time to be used in such ways.

During the 1960s, focus was not only on consumerism as part of civil rights but also on intersectional aspects of identity and oppression and the impact of assemblages on consumer experiences. The pursuit of consumer credit from a major retailer like Sears exemplifies how Black women were transforming the government's financial technology of credit into a Black feminist technology that considered NWRO members' racialized, classed, and gendered position in the consumer market to meet their specific needs and exercise their citizenry rights, while detaching those rights from the employment driver in the government's capitalist machine. That was a complex maneuver in a climate that was growing increasingly hostile toward the poor generally and poor Black women specifically. Still, Black women spoke loudly and boldly about the conditions they experienced in the consumer marketplace.

In a July 31, 1966, speech to the National Urban League (NUL) during its annual conference, NUL Assistant Secretary of Labor Esther Peterson emphasized the need to focus specifically on the conditions and issues of "Negro women." "Equality in the marketplace belongs right beside equality in education, in housing, in job opportunity and in the polling booth. . . . Not having enough income is only part of the predicament. In many cases, for a variety of reasons, the price paid by the poor for products and services is higher than the price paid by those with higher incomes. There seems to be an extra penalty for being poor. The people with the least money are often the ones who pay the highest prices."[38] Peterson brought attention to the realities of those who occupied the social locations of Black, poor, and female. Her emphasis on the marketplace demonstrated her belief that consumer spaces were a site of struggle, similar to educational and housing spaces, and required critical analysis to uncover systemic inequities that were embedded within a capitalist society.

While Peterson's comments do not overtly link capitalism and consumerism with the oppression of poor Black women, they do signal a desire to center women—specifically African American women—in discussions of social problems affecting the race. Again, we see Black women's magnitude in a sophisticated and deliberate practice of connecting the realm of consumerism with systemic inequities. The comments also serve to link women with consumer concerns, in some ways reifying consumerism as a gendered realm accessed by women. Still, these consumer concerns cast Black women as deserving of protections against the punishments of poverty systems. The Advisory Council on Public Welfare recognized this as well in its recommendations to the secretary of Health, Education and Welfare when it stated, "Public welfare is the only governmental program operating in the United States today which has as its assigned task the provision of an ultimate guarantee against poverty and social deprivation."[39] There were separate standards of "social deprivation" for poor African American women as opposed to middle-class white women.

For example, when the *Washington Post* ran a story on Johnnie Tillmon and NWRO in 1968, the response was swift and unsympathetic. Responders to the article, mostly white women, characterized welfare recipients as irresponsible, unwilling to work, inadequate parents, and eager to take advantage of taxpayers who were struggling to make ends meet themselves. The NWRO members' efforts to gain freedom through choice (of consumer goods) used consumer credit as technology to navigate and resist the tensions that existed between their deprived consumer conditions and their middle-class aspirations. The social deprivation experienced by NWRO members also served to illuminate the gap that existed between poor Black women and middle-class white women as related to the treatment, material realities, and proximity to choices and, by extension, available acts of citizenship. This gap is precisely what the women of the movement were attempting to illustrate by creating the deliberate spectacle of "Welfare Fashions" during the Sears fashion show in 1969. The garments modeled were the manifestation and presentation of the social deprivation and social affluence that existed between the space of these two groups and a demonstration of the material failures of the welfare system, which Black women's advocacy for consumer credit as a Black feminist technology served to further illuminate and challenge.[40]

Still, there were inconsistencies with NWRO's approach of engaging capitalist businesses with hopes of obtaining equitable outcomes. That a capitalist marketplace would be expected to serve as a site for promoting equity across classes demonstrates the failings of a strategy deeply disconnected from ideology. The Blackening and feminization of poverty served to shift the larger narrative around what minimal conditions for the poor were acceptable in a capitalist society. That led to the narrative that the typical person on family assistance was a Black female head of household, though according to the Departments of Labor and Health, Education, and Welfare, in 1971, those family heads of household receiving child care assistance were 60 percent male and 62 percent white, and those receiving family assistance benefits were 54 percent male and 55 percent white. Despite these realities, public opinion related to the welfare rights movement and its activists and organizers was extremely hostile and racialized (as Black).

NWRO also sponsored "Live on a Welfare Budget" weeks in which members encouraged concerned middle-class citizens, including the wives of public officials, to try living on a welfare food budget for a week and contribute the difference between the welfare budget and what they would usually spend to their local welfare rights organization.[41] The welfare budget challenge illuminated the ways in which the state commodified the social

MAGNITUDE • 121

lives of the poor and highlighted how this type of drastic commodification was intolerable for those accustomed to a middle-class lifestyle. Just as the case of the welfare fashions, NWRO's welfare budget weeks were successful in demonstrating the social deprivation of the poor by highlighting the differences in consumer patterns, options, and expectations between the poor and the middle class.

But in thinking about Black women of the CWRO's sophisticated framing of consumer credit and its potential to serve the needs of poor people, I return to the notion of technology. The women's practical application of knowledge about consumer credit and its use for acquiring goods they may not otherwise be able to afford, while playing to white middle-class expectations associated with U.S. citizenship, was deliberate and strategic. These women recognized the additional poverty premium they were paying to engage in consumer spaces and demanded relief (from businesses that exploited their marginalized position) and acknowledgment as consumers. The goal wasn't to dismantle capitalism; instead, the goal was to improve the material conditions of poor Black women and their families to obtain some degree of capitalism's promise to white middle-class consumers. The main issue with this strategy was that capitalism's promise was not intersectional—and therefore not applicable to poor Black women. However, that did not stop their demands.

Clearly, there were contradictory roles of consumer credit as both a liberatory (middle-class) technology utilized by the poor and a neoliberal mechanism serving to mask growing gaps in income and social deprivation. The NWRO Sears campaign was a commercially based form of intersectional political consumerism, entrenched in freedom from poverty through liberalism in the form of consumer choice, the perpetuation of capitalism in the form of consumer credit, and proximity to white middle-class materiality through its imitation. Despite the radical approach to consumer advocacy, which lasted several years, NWRO's Sears Credit Campaign failed to engage capitalist mechanisms such as retail credit to sustain equitable outcomes. In contrast, the cooperative economic consumer options, such as food-buying clubs (like JOIN's Leland Food Buying Club) and credit unions, were forms of community-based intersectional political consumerism that promoted socialist ideals.

The difference in approaches also illuminates how local organizations engaged actors on a local level while NWRO, as a national organization, attempted to tackle national retailers to obtain credit for their affiliated chapters. NWRO's top-down approach to organizing around consumer credit was not only logistically driven but also influenced by the national leadership's proximity to middle-class whiteness. This proximity influenced the national organization's stated aspirations for what the poor deserved from consumer spaces. Though NWRO's entrenchment in freedom from poverty through liberalism (choice), capitalism (retail credit), and proximity to white middle-class materiality did not lead to success with the Sears campaign, the pursuit of consumer credit as a Black feminist technology of access pushed the boundaries and imaginaries of what Black women demanded and deserved.

The welfare apparatus deconstructed the poor via middle-class neoliberal consumer identities, yet Black women had a sophisticated way of exploiting neoliberalism's artificial connections between consumer credit and citizens' rights. Black women magnified the disparities between poor and middle-class people, using consumer spaces (such as fashion shows) to expose what they viewed as deprivation, tying their demands to consumer spaces to their rights as citizens. They demanded that Black women be treated fairly, and part of that fairness was fair access to the same credit offered to the middle class.

Consumer credit served as both a neoliberal mechanism to mask structural inequities and a liberatory middle-class tool utilized by the poor. This apparatus was perpetuated by the public school curriculum in the government's efforts to shape the narrative around the consumer's role in the economy to explicitly promote capitalism. It wasn't that the women of the movement were unaware of that; they understood that if capitalism was to rule the day, they had a place there as well—despite not being in the workforce. Women of the welfare rights movement tapped into this capitalist consumer technology and demanded access to consumer credit as citizens, disconnecting this right from workforce membership. They short-circuited the neoliberal consumer-citizen logic to make the case that poor people had a place in the society as citizens and that the government had a responsibility to ensure they had means and access to exercise their citizenry rights. That is how they transformed consumer credit into a Black feminist technology.

The Black women of the movement used consumer credit to push the boundaries of individual choice, capitalism, and middle-class materiality. Freedom of choice in the consumer market was viewed as a way of alleviating other structural inequities caused by poverty, whether freedom to buy fashionable clothes off the rack, stock up on groceries when they are on sale, or purchase big-ticket items such as appliances with assurance that the products are of good quality.

4

BOND

When the National Welfare Rights Organization began operation, the infinity link, which was emblematic of the organization, was initially open-ended. According to NWRO, as the years stretched on and poor people continued to organize and exercise their rights, the link gradually began to close.[1] As the organization would later learn, the link remained perpetually open-ended, as the work of organizing the poor proved to be complex and thorny. Many of the groups that the Chicago Welfare Rights Organization represented had deep and complicated local histories that existed prior to the creation of NWRO. CWRO began with four preexisting welfare rights groups in Chicago. NWRO later opened a CWRO office and recruited staff, including Dovie Coleman and Nezzie Willis.[2] These organizers and their staff worked to build up CWRO and recruit more local groups to the organization.[3] These preexisting welfare rights organizations remained autonomous in their decision-making and operations.[4]

This chapter begins with a description of the welfare policies created by the Nixon administration (what I call "analog algorithms of poverty") and NWRO's efforts to organize against those algorithms[5] as it advocated instead for a guaranteed annual income. Analog algorithms have a finite set of terms and procedures, and therefore they produce a finite set of outcomes. The model of an analog algorithm does not account for dynamic, changing circumstances. I frame poverty policies of the time as analog algorithms of poverty because of their rigidity and unwillingness to consider the dynamic, changing needs of those in poverty.

Nixon's welfare policies during the late 1960s and early 1970s were punitive and based on rigid, static definitions. These analog algorithms of poverty were biased, in that they reified constructions of deserving and undeserving poor, demonized poor Black women specifically, and ultimately reproduced inequities through the promotion of capitalism, patriarchy, and racism. I argue that the collapse of NWRO began with the aggressive assault by the Nixon administration's analog algorithms of poverty and that this rigidity and perpetuation of inequities against those in poverty persists today. In this chapter I also explore how these analog algorithms, based on various poverty metrics and punitive ideologies, led to the commodification of the social lives of the poor. The attempts by the Nixon administration to standardize the budgets of the poor impacted not only their consumer choices but also their vulnerability to exploitation by the state and private businesses.

ANALOG ALGORITHMS OF POVERTY AND NWRO'S RESPONSE

During President Lyndon Johnson's term, a major aim of his Great Society was the eradication of inequalities through government policies targeting poverty and deprivation.[6] In August 1966, public assistance in Illinois was paid to 402,742 people in the amount of $25.4 million.[7] Five major public assistance programs operated in Illinois during the 1960s targeting five groups: dependent children, elderly people, people who were blind, people with other disabilities, and those needing general assistance.[8] A total of 37,565 Chicago-area families received assistance through the Aid to Dependent Children (ADC) program, and 250,362 people from 95,155 families received some form of aid from Cook County programs.[9] Politicians in Illinois and across the nation viewed these expenditures as excessive and began to move away from reducing income inequalities and toward reducing government program expenses. October 1966 expenditures for these Cook County programs alone were estimated at $14.7 million.[10] As soon as Nixon took office in 1969, he began pushing forward analog algorithms of poverty to address increased expenditures.

A special study of the Illinois Aid to Dependent Children program from April to June 1969, which focused on providing information that identified those capable of obtaining employment, including a focus on locating absent parents, found that there were 67,900 mothers in the home[11] and 114,100 absent fathers. Those absent fathers contributed $847,500 per month toward the support of dependent children.[12] The twenty-four-page report also determined that of the 67,900 mothers living in the home, 78 percent were unemployed.[13] The report focused on identifying those unemployed and determining their reasons for being unemployed. If the reasons were deemed by the Department of Public Aid to be "illegitimate" (meaning these women were able-bodied, in good health, and had skills that could be used toward employment), the government's goal was to transition them into employment and off the assistance rolls.

For those African Americans most affected by such policy changes, finding enough jobs to employ everyone proved challenging, as high concentrations of unemployment generally centered in poor Black neighborhoods in the city. Also, the "employ everyone" approach was somewhat at odds with NWRO's and CWRO's stance that welfare recipients—specifically mothers—should have the right to choose whether they wish to participate in the capitalist workplace or remain at home to care for their children while being provided with a livable income.

According to data from the Bureau of Labor Statistics (July 1968–June 1969), unemployment rates in Chicago's predominantly Black West Side neighborhoods were two and a half times greater than the unemployment rates for the entire city.[14] In addition, the bureau found the following for those West Side neighborhoods: teenagers in the area made up 12.3 percent of the labor force versus 7.6 percent for the city; adults were more likely to be in the labor force, with 49 percent of adult women working compared with 45 percent for the city and 85 percent of adult men compared with 82 percent for the city;[15] and one in four West Side residents who were not working indicated that they wanted to work, compared with one in ten nationally.[16] BLS data also showed that teenage workers on the West Side were more likely to have white-collar jobs and adult workers more likely to have blue-collar jobs, though all jobs were concentrated in low-skill positions;[17] four in ten women in the area age twenty-five years and over had completed four years of high school, versus three in ten men;[18] one in eight full-time workers on the West Side made less than federal minimum wage, and women were four times more likely than men to earn less than minimum wage (which was $65 per week in 1969[19]); and 20 percent of four-person families were low income.[20] It is worth reiterating that people in these communities wanted to work and were working at higher rates (while earning less) than reported for the city, but their choices were limited. There were not enough jobs for people in poor communities who wanted to work, and those who were able to find jobs found them in low-skilled positions paying less than they needed to keep them out of poverty.

In November 1969, the Chicago Urban League (CUL) issued a subcommittee report regarding President Nixon's welfare proposals. It referenced a $27 million monthly expenditure by the Cook County Department of Public Aid (CCDPA). The report stated that CCDPA was responsible for the welfare of 330,000 people from 119,000 families.[21] The needs and expenses of the poor were growing steadily. Still, by the late 1960s, a strong and ferocious backlash against welfare programs had begun. Nixon proposed massive reforms in the form of the Family Assistance Program (FAP), whose authors included Daniel Patrick Moynihan.[22] NWRO strongly resisted Nixon's welfare reform, though in theory, any type of guaranteed income plan was considerably progressive.[23]

NWRO's specific objections were that Nixon's proposed guaranteed annual income of $1,600 was too low and that the work incentive program constituted "slave labor" that sought to benefit corporate industrialists at the expense of the poor. NWRO's position on Nixon's FAP stated,

> NWRO's response must be to escalate the "welfare crisis" which forced Nixon to make his token proposals; continue to press demands for school clothing through more militant action; launch campaigns and lawsuits for free school lunches for all school children; step up the boycott and action against Sears Roebuck to get credit from all major department stores; plan for campaigns against Proctor [sic] & Gamble and other corporate giants in the consumer products industry, and make them share their

profits with poor people by giving $5,000 family allowance grants to NWRO members; plan now for winter action for clothing, furniture, and full utility checks, plan now to get middle income supporters to live on the Nixon "illfare" food budget for a week in November; plan new campaigns to recruit low-paid workers and other poor people into the movement and onto the welfare rolls.[24]

NWRO's strategy was to overwhelm the welfare system by adding eligible poor people to the welfare rolls and forcing the government to implement the organization's proposed changes to fix the system once and for all. NWRO had hoped to break the algorithm in an effort to capitalize on its inability to scale and illustrate its limitations. Clearly, NWRO viewed the consumer market as a key strategic component of this plan, with its insistence on targeting large corporations and demanding that they not only extend services to the poor but also be accountable to these citizens by contributing a share of profits to them—demands that were inconsistent with neoliberal capitalism. NWRO was attempting to connect welfare benefits with consumer needs. Its insistence that the relationship between corporations and consumers should be similar to that between the government and its citizens not only spoke to a desire for mutual benefit and reciprocity but also attempted to explicitly integrate a socialist agenda as it simultaneously strove to legitimize the poor as consumers.

NWRO also issued a formal statement related to its position on Title I and the proposed changes to the Elementary and Secondary Education Act (ESEA), which exposed the organization's views on power and how it was negotiated between the poor and the local, state, and federal governing bodies. The organization opposed the revenue-sharing proposal, which sought to redirect education money to local and state governments. NWRO's main objection was that without the federal government regulating these funds and ensuring that the poor and disabled were considered, local and state politicians would fight among themselves over the money. Specifically on this issue, NWRO stated, "Because there is no provision for Federal regulations, the money would go where the power is. Federal regulations are necessary to protect the needs of the powerless."[25] The organization did not believe that the local and state governments were concerned with the needs of the poor. The poor were described as "powerless" and, interestingly, the federal government was viewed as a protector and potential advocate for the poor.

NWRO's concern was that the state would corrupt local school boards if given latitude with funding, and this would result in money being redirected to schools that served areas with higher incomes. The efforts of NWRO to organize parents and demand that Title I be retained so that, among other things, parents would receive supportive services that allowed for money for "clothing, transportation, medical and dental care, books, supplies and food programs,"[26] spoke to the organization's focus on mobilizing local community members who were its core membership base (primarily poor African American women). Its attempts to subvert the local and state systems of government spoke to the brokenness of these systems and their lack of promotion of democratic ideals.

Illinois Governor Richard Ogilvie became the state government target of major demonstrations by various Chicago welfare organizations as a result of the massive cuts to welfare that occurred in the state in 1971.[27] The new state rules went into effect on November 1, with cuts to welfare general assistance as well as medical allowances.[28] George Dunne, president of the Cook County Board of Commissioners, filed suit to block Ogilvie's plan to cut welfare programs. Cook County Circuit Court Judge Daniel Covelli approved a temporary restraining order to stall Ogilvie's plan to withhold $6.4 million per month in welfare funds to Cook County. The Illinois Supreme Court upheld the restraining order.[29]

One solution to addressing the $6.4 million gap in funds was to have the county screen some 54,000 general assistance recipients to determine their eligibility to receive benefits (because the general assistance funds came from the state, whereas funds for dependent children and the aged, blind, and disabled were partly funded by the federal government).[30] Also during this time, the House passed a bill requiring mothers and children sixteen and older receiving assistance under the Aid to Dependent Children program to register for public work or have their welfare benefits revoked.[31] Though welfare caseworkers seemed to be invested in getting much-needed funds to their clients, they were at least equally if not more concerned with their own job security, as the cuts were not only to welfare benefits but also to public aid staff.

As Ogilvie struggled to reduce Illinois's welfare expenses, asking that the federal government take over public aid, California Governor Ronald Reagan was making major cuts to his own state's welfare caseloads.[32] Reagan would later roll out a nationwide assault on welfare with his ascension to the U.S. presidency. The analog algorithms of poverty continued to hold the line.

CWRO, led by Chair Ruby Mabry, had a strong presence during the demonstrations against the welfare cuts.[33] Interestingly, the daily discourse during November 1971 in newspapers such as the *Chicago Tribune* and *Chicago Sun-Times*, contained much discussion about the politicians, judges, budgets, and spending and very little about the welfare recipients themselves or the leaders who organized them—leaders like Ruby Mabry. Mainstream media outlets contributed to the erasure of Black female leadership, either through the occasional highlighting of white priests' marches or Jesse Jackson's involvement in demonstrations through Operation Breadbasket or through a focus on rich white men who made up the state legislature and public aid leadership.[34] The diminishing and erasure of Black women leadership served to reify the message in discussions of how the welfare system should operate that welfare recipients were objects of need rather than subjects of resistance worthy of respect and inclusion.

POVERTY METRICS PROVIDE ALGORITHMIC STRUCTURE

In Virginia Eubanks's *Automating Inequality*, she discusses the use of technology as a "rational" response to volume and how it served to perpetuate bureaucracy, reinforce barriers to human services, and reify inequalities of systems used to manage the poor. Poverty is intentionally constructed, often by governmental algorithms. The way poverty is constructed and who falls within these definitions serve a societal purpose that typically benefits the orchestrators of poverty. Just as there is power in poverty's orchestration, there is also power in its measurement (in this case, the underlying structure of the analog algorithms of poverty). Policy approaches that rely on methods that equate quantification with universality carry a false sense of objectivity that is then used to produce false generalities (Mohanty 1984). Assertions based on the presence of large numbers—particularly related to poverty metrics—reinforce misogynoir in state welfare policies. And much of the tension that existed between NWRO and the Nixon administration over poverty policy focused on how poverty was measured.

There are two general measurement categories of poverty— or, rather, two primary ways of organizing poverty policies:

absolute (employed by the government at the time of the welfare rights movement) and relative (advocated for by NWRO). These various metrics have been used to delineate between the so-called deserving and undeserving poor. But these metrics also help us understand where power resides (and where it resided at the beginning of the movement). How those who are labeled as poor feel about their situation is irrelevant to government policy makers, and typically, the poor are not in a position to reject this labeling anyway. As Lewis Coser stated in his 1965 "Sociology of Poverty" article, "Historically, the poor emerge when society elects to recognize poverty as a special status and assigns specific persons to that category. The fact that some people may privately consider themselves poor is sociologically irrelevant. What is sociologically relevant is poverty as a socially recognized condition, as a social status. We are concerned with poverty as a property of the social structure" (1965, 141).

These poverty definitions either reinforce or challenge dominant ideologies. For example, consumption as a base absolute poverty metric reinforces capitalism. Absolute income metrics used by the government were embedded in patriarchy, as they were based on a family of four (specifically, a man, a woman, and two children). Nixon's and Ogilvie's policies, with their breakdowns for need and thresholds for determining who was in poverty, were absolute measures. Embedded within the valuation and commodification of life was a dehumanizing element that exposed ideologies (or source code) around what the government felt the poor deserved. Further, the extreme focus on rigidly quantifying poverty hid the racist roots of these poverty categories (Gillborn, Warmington, and Demack 2018). Since numbers and corresponding categories are neither neutral nor natural, these constructions are embedded with dominant system bias and political decisions that are made around which data are selected and how data are categorized (Castillo and Gillborn 2022). For example, during the late 1960s, the government felt that a poor family of four should be able to get by on $1,600 per month.

NWRO's version of the guaranteed annual income (GAI) was a shift to a relative poverty measure. Relative poverty metrics go against the grain of the liberalism that was prominent during the time of the welfare rights movement. The construction of liberalism began to shift between World War I and II from classic liberalism, with the insistence on limited government control and interference, to a form of New Deal liberalism, which attempted to temper capitalism in an effort to save it (Gerstle 1994). Still, what remained consistent with liberalism in its various forms throughout history was its unwillingness to significantly disrupt other dominant systems, such as capitalism, patriarchy, and racism. That sheds light on our understanding of the environment in which social scientists would come to produce influential research related to poverty in the United States during the 1960s and 1970s and the narratives that NWRO and CWRO had to contend with. The ideologies of racism, capitalism, and patriarchy provided a deeply flawed foundational source code with which to construct a deserving/undeserving dichotomy.[35]

Absolute poverty measures have thresholds that remain constant over time, have a minimum measurable subsistence level, do not fluctuate with changes in standard of living, and are conceptually easy to understand and gain consensus around (Iceland 2006). Absolute poverty measures are also convenient inputs for analog algorithms. Simply thinking of the poor as merely numbers allows policy makers to make supposedly logical and objective policy decisions that do not engage the very people these policies are meant to impact. It also does nothing to inform our understanding of how the poor manage their available resources to make ends meet (or not).

Another consideration is that poverty is not a static condition, just as poor people do not experience finite sets of conditions. Yet absolute poverty measures do not consider increases in standards of living. NWRO's charge to public officials to try living on a welfare budget was an attempt to demonstrate the practical challenges of managing such limited resources, a particularly difficult task during a time of rising food prices and high inflation.

Relative poverty measures focus on how close or far the society is from total egalitarianism. Poverty is determined to be relative to the income of the overall population. Relative poverty measures include, for example, average income of people at the lowest income percentile of the population, or the number of people whose income is less than the mean income of the population (Blackwood and Lynch 1994). Relative measures are also sensitive to periods of economic growth and recession and are more responsive to income inequity.

The egalitarian approach of relative poverty measures was counter to the neoliberal shift that was emerging during the time of the welfare rights movement. Advocacy for absolute or relative measures was becoming more polarized between the very wealthy and the rest of the population. High unemployment rates, coupled with stifled wages, reduced returns on financial investments (such as housing and stock markets), and a general perception that people's children will be less well off compared with a generation ago, speak directly to one's perception of income adequacy.

Simply put, these measures greatly influence how we construct the poor. If we want the poor to include those with higher levels of education, those who are male or male-headed households, or those who do not receive welfare assistance, there are appropriate measures that will include them. Likewise, there are also appropriate measures to exclude them. To have a poor population that the majority of people can directly identify with would jeopardize the position of the very wealthy and, in all likelihood, provoke revolution. That NWRO encouraged more people to identify as poor in an attempt to overrun the system and force reforms had the potential to reduce the stigma of living in poverty. However, there was also a risk of formally stigmatizing larger groups of people who were eligible for benefits but had not previously asked for them.

When looking at the poor in these terms, it is apparent that, far from being an objective measure of subsistence, how "the poor" is defined and classified is ripe with political implications. And the implications of a poor population perceived as being overwhelmingly Black and female were severely felt by the welfare reform movement and NWRO. If we consider the poor as being defined by their acceptance of assistance and declassified from any previous status once their "private trouble" become a public burden (Simmel and Jacobson 1965, 138), the Blackening and feminization of poverty proved a convenient scapegoating strategy for the very wealthy who, in a decade's time, would come to widen their income gap to obscene levels by arguing that poor Black women were willingly burdening everyone else. And those in power used analog algorithms of poverty to loosen themselves of that burden.

In the 1960s and 1970s, the gross national product (GNP) was a commonly used measure of absolute income. The GNP measures national income and national expenditures in a particular country plus net property income from abroad (e.g., dividends, interest, and profit). During the welfare rights era, the GNP was between $691.03 and $1,549.20 (in billions).[36] See table 4.1

BOND • 137

TABLE 4.1 GROSS NATIONAL PRODUCT DURING THE WELFARE RIGHTS ERA, 1965-1975

Year	GNP (1972 dollars—in billions)	Gini coefficient
1965	691.03	–
1966	756.00	–
1967	799.58	.399
1968	873.40	.388
1969	943.98	.391
1970	992.73	.394
1971	1077.65	.396
1972	1185.93	.401
1973	1326.38	.397
1974	1434.23	.395
1975	1549.20	.397

for details. Though U.S. economic income was rising, that growth was not a valid metric of citizen welfare. Growth is just that—growth. Relative income measures look for the degree of inequity in income distribution. The Gini coefficient is the most widely known example of a relative income measure. It measures how equally distributed are an individual's or household's income or consumption levels within an economy. The measure ranges from 0, indicating perfect distribution equality, to 1, which indicates perfect distribution inequality.

Between 1947 and 1968, the Gini coefficient decreased,[37] with a decrease in income inequality for families of 7.5 percent. America's Gini coefficient in 1969, during the start of the Nixon administration, was .391. It increased slightly but remained relatively stable through the end of the welfare rights movement and has since trended upward. That indicates that the nation continues to expand income and consumption disparities as the gap grows between those who are very wealthy and those who are poor.[38]

These metrics[39] have significant implications, in that the government's use of absolute metrics influenced how it determined what poor people needed (in the racialized and gendered context of a Blackening and feminization of poverty). The goal was not egalitarianism but, rather, meeting a minimum level of subsistence. These metrics provided the blueprint for how the government would impersonally commodify the lives of the poor.

In contrast, NWRO pushed for relative metrics, which considered quality of living and the changing standard of living. The organization used its own GAI as the mechanism by which it commodified the social lives of the poor. Though different from the government's absolute measures, NWRO's GAI still relied on a standardized budget that required a commodification and, at times, reification of attitudes about the lives of the poor.

The NWRO's insistence on a GAI to better manage poverty called for a level of respect for the poor that acknowledged their ability to make sound budgetary decisions for themselves and their families without further government intervention and/or surveillance. All measures of poverty are not equal, and therefore they cannot be used interchangeably. But just as important as what the measures evaluate is how they shape the discourse and change the face of poverty. Metrics that create the female-headed family as the face of poverty must contend with patriarchy.[40] Measures that create the welfare recipient as the face of poverty must contend with liberalism. As Alice O'Connor (2002) notes in her criticisms of poverty research,

That this tension [between understanding poverty rooted in individuals or structures] has more often been resolved in favor of the individualist interpretation can be seen in several oft-noted features in poverty research. One is the virtual absence of class as an analytic category, at least as compared with more individualized measures of status such as family background and human capital. A similar individualizing tendency can be seen in the reduction of race and gender to little more than demographic, rather than structurally constituted, categories. Poverty research treats the market and the two-parent, male-headed family in much the same way, as inevitable, naturally occurring ways of ordering human relations rather than as institutions that are socially created and maintained. (9)

As more nonwhite people began using welfare, and as gender roles began to shift, the welfare professional agenda shifted from developing a new, more comprehensive system to improving the unpopular ADC.[41] Welfare recipients were presented as single mothers with individual issues, and welfare workers began to conflate welfare as an income support program with "rehabilitation" efforts. By focusing on individual behaviors rather than larger assemblages of race, class, and gender (issues of racism, poverty, and sexism), policy makers and their opponents avoided acknowledging that Black mothers were not able to find employment, much less employment with a living wage. As Rhonda Williams states in *From Welfare to Workfare*, "Liberal welfare experts helped to undergird white privilege and arguably contributed to a weightier anti-black backlash against public assistance. The negative public response was intensified by the vitriolic Louisiana and New Jersey campaigns targeting primarily black recipients as 'loafers' in 1960 and 1961, and by the rise of welfare-rights protests predominately led by black women in the mid 1960s and 1970s" (Williams 2006, 345).

Analog algorithms of poverty, including its measures and strategies, served to reify existing racist and sexist source code, which further perpetuated poverty rather than alleviating it. So, just as the poet Audre Lorde asserted that you cannot dismantle the master's house with his tools, it seems outrageous to think we could address structural issues of poverty using measures that reinforce those structures. The major disconnect in the poverty discourse when using cultural analysis is that this analysis is interested in determining and identifying a poor subculture, not in measuring poverty (Williamson and Hyer 1975). And the major disconnect between the state and NWRO in its fight for a guaranteed income was a difference in beliefs around whether poverty was to be individually exorcized or structurally overcome.

Dispelling myths about who was on welfare went hand in hand with defining who was considered poor and thus eligible for benefits. Despite the realities that more whites than Blacks were on welfare and that fraudulent welfare cases made up less than 1 percent of the rolls,[42] the fact that the movement's leadership was overwhelmingly Black and female served to further encourage the demonizing of welfare recipients as well as Black women generally. NWRO, in its efforts to fight for a guaranteed annual income that would relieve poor families of having to pinch every penny and still end up short was as much an attempt to reclaim poor Black women's personhood and freedom of choice as it was an attempt to manage poverty.

POOR PEOPLE, CONSUMER CHOICE, AND THE WORK-PAY BOND

Under Wiley's direction, NWRO set GAI as a national campaign. The organization, which partnered with the National Tenants Organization (NTO) and the Southern Christian Leadership Conference (SCLC) to develop the Poor People's Platform, also called for the federal government to protect the rights of tenants to organize and negotiate collective bargaining agreements with private landlords.[43] These demands were in the context of a more aggressive presence of government regulations protecting the rights of consumers.

Also during this time, Chicago's West Side Organization (WSO), which would later become a CWRO-affiliated welfare union with a membership of more than fifteen hundred, mobilized its members to fight for a federal guaranteed income program.[44] Given the excessive unemployment and large number of mothers with young children in the area, WSO recognized that strategies other than demanding more jobs were required.[45] Kenwood-Oakland Community Organization (KOCO), modeled after WSO, also protested in favor of guaranteed income.[46] Its Black female leadership, which included Ruth Walker, organized poor residents on Chicago's Near South Side around welfare grievance issues as well as overall improvements to welfare programs, such as a guaranteed income.

There were a variety of arguments for a guaranteed income. They included the need for an income guarantee system because of concern over technological developments that would lead to automation.[47] The view was that such rapid automation would result in loss of jobs and a break in the work-pay bond whereby people would work without pay (because technology would alter the type of work humans would be inclined to do). The argument concluded that a guaranteed minimum income would protect from this technological unemployment.[48] This perspective spoke to both the concerns of organized manufacturing laborers that their jobs would become obsolete and they would not have adequate income to replace what would be lost and to concerns of the poor who were unemployed or unable to find employment that paid a livable wage.

There was also an argument that an economy that relied solely on wage earnings to ensure sustained growth would ultimately slow and fail, whereas a system that allowed for a guaranteed income would maintain high levels of demand for goods and services (particularly during times of technological job displacement).[49]

Arguments around job displacement resulting from technological advances were not considered nearly as seriously as those related to consumer demand. The concern about ensuring sufficient consumer demand to maintain GNP growth was frequently offered by economists.[50] There was a direct connection between consumerism as a mechanism for growing the economy and guaranteed adequate income as a mechanism for managing poverty. While economists were able to get the attention of some legislators, more concerning than the worry that such a plan would result in increased inflation was the feminization and Blackening of poverty, which severely distorted the narrative toward an evaluation of deserving and undeserving poor and the measures needed to incentivize them to work.

NWRO, understanding the impact of race in determining appropriate resources for the poor, publicly opposed making people identify their names or races in the 1970 Census. The organization cited the "extermination of the Black Panthers and the under-representation of Blacks in Congress" as examples of

BOND • 143

how identifying the poor as Black would disadvantage the movement to allocate government funds toward assisting the poor.[51] NWRO was attempting to disrupt the inputs for the analog algorithms of poverty. However, the narrative around the Blackening and feminization of poverty would prevent the severing of the work-pay bond that NWRO was seeking. According to the *Guaranteed Annual Income Newsletter* (*GAIN*), "The nation has long accepted, its adherents state, that no one in the society should starve—why, in the midst of unheard-of affluence, do we permit people to live in and suffer from poverty. Opposition to this idea comes from those who still maintain that no man, able to work, should be paid for not working."[52]

For a nation that found Black people to be undisciplined, lacking a work ethic, and pathologically flawed because of single-mothered households, the Blackening and feminization of poverty helped explain how the country could be satisfied with the fact that Black people (even women and children) suffering from poverty. The view of Black women as the "mules of the world" would not allow the (white) U.S. collective conscience to divorce income from work. For white women, patriarchal gender roles allowed for the privilege of an option, without ridicule, to remain at home with children. However, Black women were expected to work. Though more whites than Blacks still lived in poverty during that time, the extreme focus on urban Blacks as a result of the narrative around the Blackening and feminization of poverty laid a path that would not only halt consideration of a guaranteed income for all citizens but would, within the next decade, lead to a government-orchestrated full-on assault on the poor.

Collaboration between the University of Chicago's School of Social Service Administration and its Ad Hoc Committee for a Guaranteed Income resulted in the publication of the

Guaranteed Annual Income Newsletter (GAIN).[53] The Ad Hoc Committee's goal was to promote the adoption of a government-guaranteed adequate income,[54] and it began publishing *GAIN* in June 1966 to educate those interested in poverty and welfare issues about both sides of the GAI debate.[55] One of NWRO's strategies for obtaining political power to win a guaranteed adequate income was through coalition building and developing a wider base. NWRO stated, "by broadening our organizational base with inclusion of the organized blind, aged, disabled, we, in essence, will be developing the power needed to acquire an adequate income program."[56]

Extending the focus to include those groups not only made more visible the population of poor people of color with disabilities whose adequate income needs were higher than the average per-person cost of someone on public assistance but also resisted the Blackening and feminization of poverty by bringing into the organizational fold poor white male individuals.[57] Though the organization had been concerned since its inception with the needs of all poor people, this strategic reassertion (of solidarity with all assistance recipients) in response to Nixon's welfare reform suggested that NWRO understood some of the ways the algorithmic assemblages of race, gender, and class of its base impacted how power was negotiated and legitimized. Though the organization's formal campaign related to securing a guaranteed income for the poor, in January 1970, Chicago organizations including CWRO, TWO, KOCO, CUL, the Lawndale People's Planning and Action Committee, and CCDPA and other local organizations also began working collaboratively on the issue of guaranteed income. Under the direction of CWRO's Ginger Mack, these groups took part in a conference to discuss the best ways to inform the working poor about the wage supplement program.[58]

BOND • 145

Initially, NWRO had determined that an adequate annual income for a family of four living in an urban area in 1969 would be \$5,500,[59] but in 1971, it determined that number should be \$6,500.[60] For Chicago, NWRO determined that the GAI should be \$6,760. In addition to calling for adequate income, NWRO pushed for grants for clothing and furniture to ensure that recipients adhered to a minimum standard of "health and decency." As NWRO's guaranteed income promotional materials stated,

> In calculating its budget NWRO specifically rejected the official Poverty Level as a measure of what a family needs to live at a minimum adequate level. The Poverty Level was devised by the Social Security Administration on the basis of the Agriculture Department's economy food plan. But the Agriculture Department has said that the economy food plan "is not a reasonable measure of basic money needs for a good diet. The public assistance agency that recognizes the limitations of its clientele and is interested in their nutritional well-being, will recommend a money allowance for food considerably higher than the cost level of the economy plan."
>
> The Social Security Administration ignored the USDA warning. They took the cost level of the economy plan and simply multiplied it by three to determine the total "poverty level" budget for a family of four. This procedure is made totally inappropriate because, in addition to the Agriculture Department's own statement, the Bureau of Labor Statistics has pointed out that a family of four has a total budget closer to four or five times the cost of it's [sic] food component.[61]

Embedded in the discussion of how the cost and poverty levels are devised by the Social Security Administration (SSA) is a general assertion that the sum of one's social life can be commodified. Within these discussions are negotiations of power over who has the legitimate right to determine the commodified needs of citizens. Though there are other spaces of struggle and resistance, such as NWRO's proposed adjustments around the cost of housing and clothing, this specific example illustrates how the organization used other government institutions, such as the Department of Agriculture and Bureau of Labor Statistics, to attempt to invalidate another—namely, SSA. In essence, NWRO is finding legitimacy in one part of the government to refute the legitimacy of another part, thus turning the analog algorithms of poverty on themselves. But this explanation of reasoning on the part of NWRO also serves as an example of how the organization resisted what it felt were oppressive systems that limited the choices that could be made within the realm of consumerism. These absolute poverty measures, which focus solely on the poor, look at how many people are poor, how much money would be required to raise them above the poverty threshold, how income is distributed among the poor, or some combination of these.

Absolute poverty measures minimum subsistence based on a family budget (Williamson and Hyer 1975). Within this frame, there are many opportunities to institutionalize views and biases around what the poor deserve. Something perceived as an objective measure can, in reality, be highly subjective, in that the rules that apply to the poor (in terms of what is determined that they need and how much is allotted for each of those determined items) do not apply to anyone else. As noted in Williamson and Hyer's article, "The Measurement and Meaning of Poverty," "The SSA poverty index is well suited to what has been referred to as a 'head count' measure of poverty. Such a measure tells us how many fall below the specified poverty line, but tells us nothing about the difference in degree of poverty between families below the line. It also leads to a rather arbitrary difference in classification between families with incomes a few dollars above the poverty line and those with incomes a few dollars below the poverty line" (1975, 653).

Though food is necessary for survival, NWRO rejected the idea that SSA could legitimately determine what amount constituted "above poverty level" as well as the means by which one would rise above that level. In this way, as in the case of clothing and furniture grants, consumerism is a site of struggle over the legitimacy of needs and choice. But even as NWRO is resisting the mechanism used to commodify the social lives of the poor, it is also reifying a commodification of the poor in attaching its own proposed weekly, monthly, and yearly values to food, housing, furnishings, clothing, personal care, and recreation.[62] A power struggle or negotiation occurs when a group or organization such as SSA is determining adequate levels or thresholds for life, particularly the lives of the poor. And within that commodification, beliefs about a certain group's worth (in this case, the poor) are uncovered, which are based on the presumptions about what that group would need and what those needs would cost. This commodification is the by-product of the state's analog algorithms of poverty.

CONSUMER PAWNS OF BUSINESSES AND THE STATE

Consumerism is key to understanding the relationships among the state, private business, and the poor. *Kiplinger Washington Letter*, a Washington, D.C., publication circulated to business owners, stated a positive outlook on customer issues following Nixon's election, including expected increases in consumer spending.[63] That optimism would prove to be short-lived, as unemployment remained high, wages remained stagnant,[64] and food prices increased. Businesses were left holding their breath to see whether Nixon's economic program would stimulate spending and result in growth. NUL became cautiously optimistic regarding Nixon's plan, specifically the wage and price freezing that "could enable Black people to purchase more with their limited dollars."[65]

Just prior to Nixon's election, during the 1968 uprisings and protests following King's assassination, businesses and governments became very concerned with managing the discontent of area Blacks. In Chicago, a "riot study committee" was established to determine the causes of the April 1968 uprising in Chicago's West Side neighborhoods and the resulting $10 million in damage to property. The report determined that "the pent-up resentment of Negroes against the economic system was apparent in the selectivity of targets for looting and burning."[66] Most businesses in the Black communities that experienced these uprisings were white-owned,[67] and only white-owned businesses were deliberately targeted and burned.[68] A number of these businesses were known to "sell low-quality products at high prices" and engage in sharp, often ruthless, credit practices. It is important to note, though, that more local merchants than major chain stores were likely to extend credit to welfare recipients because they were often inclined to sell inventory due to lack of adequate storage space.[69] "They often refuse to permit the return of defective merchandise. Many local white merchants admit to higher prices but justify them on such grounds as higher insurance costs, higher credit losses and a high incidence of shoplifting. The relationship between this large group of merchants and their customers is not a constructive one of mutual respect."[70]

BOND • 149

Though this information was reported to the local government—specifically Mayor Daley—little was done to address the issues of customer exploitation at the hands of merchants.[71] The exploitive relationship between the poor and merchants also extended to the reaches of, and was facilitated by, the local, state, and federal governments. During a time of consumer rights legislation, in which the government served as the defender of middle-class white customers, the poor were being identified as a bloc to be manipulated.

During the first NWRO convention, held on August 27, 1967, James Farmer and Dick Gregory gave addresses. During his comments to the NWRO delegates, Farmer made a clear connection between consumers and the poor as well as consumers and political activism. "Workers have organized . . . tenants are organizing tenants . . . consumers are organizing as consumers . . . the poor have a great strength, when you organize you must organize politically—because the answers will be found in politics."[72] NWRO viewed its members as citizens who are entitled to engage in political activism—viewed in this book through the analytical lens of intersectional political consumerism—for the purposes of organizing poor people around marketplace issues. And NWRO viewed itself as an appropriate vehicle through which to carry out that work.

While Farmer's comments focused on the political possibilities of organizing the poor, Gregory's comments illuminated the collusion between government and private businesses to exploit and disempower the political potential of the poor as consumers. During his speech at the inaugural NWRO meeting, he stated, "five minutes after a nigger get his check, you right wing bastards got it. . . . So if they cut off relief checks in the morning, just in the state of Illinois, that $17M, 5 minutes after those checks come through, that white folks don't have—then he'll come up with $17M and in 10 months tops that $170M knocked out of the state of Illinois economy, the damn state would collapse."[73] Here, Gregory is speaking about the amount of welfare aid distributed in the state of Illinois during the 1960s and how the government relies on its subsidized income to keep the state economy healthy. In 1967, Illinois spent $488 million statewide and locally for public welfare assistance.[74] In 1968, 43.7 percent of total government expenditures was spent on social welfare.[75] That included health, education, veteran, and insurance programs in addition to public aid. Gregory made the point that the state and national economies continued to rely on the poor as both a subsidized income stream and a scapegoat. He provided the following reasoning for why the government relies on the institutionalization of poverty via subsidized income programs:

> That's why they'll give you the money, and they won't give you nothing else with it, 'cause they know in giving you the money in this hand, they gone get it in this hand over here. That's why they never tried to do anything but give you money. They not doing you a favor. . . . How many of you have ever kept $5 out of a [welfare] check? . . . That goes back into this country's economy. So you got to understand this. White folks done got mad at niggers over the economy. Why you think they haven't fired us?[76]

Gregory is explicit in his assertion that the government is not benevolent and remains unconcerned with the needs of the poor. When he says "why you think they haven't fired us?," he is speaking to the government's obsession with the health of the economy for the benefit of the wealthy and that the government remains intentional in its efforts to maintain poverty because it serves capitalism to do so. He is pointing out how poverty and capitalism are bound together. Consider that during the time,

Cook County was the largest user of food stamps in the country and that recipients in September 1966 paid $1,017,797 for $1,398,770 worth of food stamps (for 82,466 people or 26,063 households).[77] This meant that over $1 million was funneled into the Cook County economy through food stamps alone, at a discount to poor people of only 27 percent. In other words, for just $380,973, the government was able to get over $1 million from the poor and funnel $1,398,770 in food stamps into the economy.

The food stamp program, like other welfare benefits, essentially used the poor as a vehicle by which the government could subsidize its own economic system—either through subsidizing private businesses or, via the Department of Agriculture, subsidizing farms. Indeed, the government was not doing any favors for the poor. Of those families eligible for food stamps, only 53 percent participated in 1969, stating that lack of participation was because the program was too costly, too limiting, and inconvenient.[78] There were other voices in addition to Gregory's who pointed out how the connection between the government and the poor was a way of subsidizing the economy. An opportunistic view offered in *Outlook* magazine[79] stated that by extending credit to welfare recipients, businesses had an opportunity to exploit the deteriorating economic conditions, because there would likely be an increase in unemployment and therefore an increase in the number of people going on welfare. The logic was that retailers could access a market that had once been ignored, sell off their lower-end merchandise that middle-class patrons are less likely to buy, and maintain a steady revenue stream from retail sales that are essentially subsidized by the government. As Irene Gibbs, a welfare recipient from Jamaica Queens, New York, stated, "They don't do nothing for poor people. Welfare clients are catching particular hell. People say how much money the welfare client gets. Most of the welfare check goes to the slum landlord, Con Edison and the Brooklyn Union Gas Company. And they're the same folks who are saying welfare people should work."[80]

Gregory's view was that the poor were needed so the capitalist economy could maintain itself, "'cause the capitalist system in this country functions on 85 percent credit. And black folks, not to mention poor white folks, but black folks cash value in America is $17B, its $27B if you want to get our credit, multiply $27B by 85 and that's what we owe. And we owe all of that to white folks. . . . Don't let nobody tell you they doing you some favors because they giving you some money. Look beyond that check and ask why. Because they have to."[81]

In addition to critiquing the capitalist system that perpetuates sustaining poverty, Gregory speaks to the importance of credit in a capitalist society as well as the importance of the poor as credit holders. Recall that during this time, NWRO had launched its campaign against Sears and other major department stores in an effort to secure credit and eradicate discriminatory credit practices that would exclude the poor. Here, Gregory is saying that businesses (though they may appear to not want the poor as consumers) rely heavily on the poor. When he says "And we owe all of that to white folks," he is commenting about how debt leaves Blacks in servitude to the white capitalist system and how this system is dependent on that exploitation.

Whether it is consumer credit as technology or welfare policy as algorithm, what is evident is that at the intersection of the welfare and consumer rights movements of the 1960s through the 1970s, a battle for power of legitimacy and choice sat at the feet of a capitalist system driven by consumer desire and demand. The strategic roles of Black women leaders in demanding that poor people be included as consumers and that their choices be considered when determining income thresholds for poverty speak to the defiance they exhibited against the state and a complicated relationship with capitalism.

Though measures are sought that are objective and apolitical, like algorithms, they often expose underlying biases and serve to replicate existing ideologies. These ideologies demonized, devalued, and discredited poor Black women of the welfare rights movement. And yet, when these technologies continued to hold the line for misogynoir, Black women and the local organizations they led drew their own lines and formed their own bonds—bonds that connected dignity with freedom of choice, resisted the standardizing and disciplining of the state, and rejected technologies such as the analog algorithms of poverty. These technologies constructed a particular generalized Black woman who Black women did not recognize as themselves. This rejection of such state constructions is part of what freed women of the welfare rights movement to erect opposing constructions of themselves—constructions that demanded the resources of the state while refusing the exploitation of the state and marketplace that were encoded in the labor market.

I define the welfare policies of the Nixon administration as analog algorithms of poverty because of their static rigidity and standardizing of poverty terms and outcomes. Their perpetuation and refusal to acknowledge the dynamic needs of those under the institution of poverty served to discipline and commodify the lives of the poor. Absolute and relative poverty metrics were at odds as the state battled to construct the poor based on a quantified minimal level of sustenance, while NWRO fought to cast the widest net possible of who could be categorized as poor in an effort to push the government to take up quality of life issues in a society that lived and died by consumer choice.

NWRO used calculus different from that of the state to commodify the social lives of the poor. This commodification was manifested in the form of a demand for a guaranteed annual income. CWRO leaders demanded agency to make budgetary decisions for their families, freedom to raise their children without the coercion of a capitalist labor market, and acknowledgment that it was not Black women who were flawed but, rather, a capitalist technology that demanded participation via consumerism without providing equal opportunities for such participation.

In considering realms of power—specifically the Blackening and feminization of poverty—we see the shaping of narratives around poverty measurement and policy that stifled the efforts of the welfare rights organizations toward a universal income. While state technologies distorted Black women of the movement beyond their recognition of themselves, those technologies were also used by these same women to expose the exploitive relationships among industry (businesses and corporations), the state, and the poor. Consumerism has and will likely always be a site of struggle for the legitimacy of needs and choice.

CONCLUSION

This book is my attempt to reimagine the activities, circumstances, occurrences, and outcomes of the welfare rights movement through the lens of Black feminist technologies. I explored realms of power as instruments of a specific capitalist technology that served to isolate and contain the poor during the 1960s and 1970s. The public and private consumer industries; local, state, and federal governments; economic policies; and the Blackening and feminization of poverty all came together during this time to perpetuate capitalism and a consumerist society.

I began my journey simply trying to understand what happened during those years. I wanted to hear from the Black women of the movement in their own words about their challenges, triumphs, and priorities. As a secondary curiosity, I sought to understand how the academic discourse broadly and the archives specifically talked about and viewed the Black women of the movement. When I identified over one million results from the JSTOR database, I was excited. I had gotten caught up in the same worship of quantification and big data that I often caution against. I was eager to play with my shiny new tools to computationally make sense of the realms of power I'd identified related to consumerism within the movement and the treatment given in academic discourse of Black women involved in it.

That excitement turned to frustration as I found erasures, misreadings, distortions, and, in some cases, complete misfires. The experience using computational tools paralleled what I encountered in the physical archives, only instead of a specific database search for Black women in the context of business and industry and poverty coming up suspiciously empty, I'd find meeting minutes from various male-led welfare organizations (that I could speculate were likely typed by women) with no mention of women's perspectives in the documents. Or, worse, I discovered in official records of powerful organizations such as IAF derogatory language used to describe Black women in what was supposed to be professional correspondence . That led me to wonder how technology was not only mimicking the devaluation of Black women in the archives but also continuing the perpetuation of that devaluation in the academic discourse. It's partly the reason I found an intersectional analysis of consumerism to be so critical to defend against the epistemic violence of both the digital and physical archives, as well as better and differently understand the experiences of Black women who led the Chicago welfare rights movement. I kept returning to the reframing of technology as a way to reread and reinscribe the contributions of Black women's activism in the movement.

Intersectional political consumerism is any activity motivated by one's intersecting social locations that uses and/or targets sites of consumerism to influence how resources are allocated to benefit the political condition of that group. Consumer spaces and industries were a battle site of legitimacy for the Black women of the movement. Welfare organizations across Chicago and the nation benefited from Black women's formal and informal leadership. Whether it was TWO, whose formal leadership was male

CONCLUSION • 157

and procapitalist, or JOIN, whose leadership was female and anticapitalist, welfare organizations were deploying intersectional political consumerism with purpose and accuracy. CWRO leaders like Dovie Coleman had expert knowledge of state technologies. And by using their experiences with and knowledge of the state's discipling technologies, Black women of the Chicago welfare rights movement propelled themselves into the future by adopting and adapting new technologies for their own purposes. I'm inspired by their focus and clear vision related to the lives they wanted for themselves and their communities and the boldness with which they demanded their dignity.

Understanding and connecting the historical legacies of the parallel movements of consumer rights, women's rights, and civil rights helped to contextualize the tremendous barriers as well as the sophisticated work these Black women committed themselves to as they strove for the rights of poor people—they were each other's harvest. The ineffectiveness of these movements in computing in parallel reiterates the destructive nature of anti-Blackness. If your movement has a goal of liberation but does not include Black women, it is shortsighted.

Black women of the welfare rights movement faced tremendous challenges against algorithmic assemblage of race, class, and gender that would impact and shape not just their movement strategies but also the outcomes. These assemblages would lead JOIN down a path of community-based intersectional political consumerism, and TWO would follow a path of commercially based intersectional political consumerism. While JOIN wanted buying clubs and food co-ops in their neighborhoods, TWO demanded access to large chain supermarkets in their community. The rent strikes conducted by both organizations positioned poor and working-poor apartment dwellers of slum housing as legitimate consumers with legitimate expectations and demands. The differing intersectional political consumerisms of JOIN and TWO served multiple purposes. Though the two organizations were very different ideologically, they shared the belief that the poor could achieve political and economic power by invoking their rights as consumers.

Though commercially based forms of consumerism have been the most prevalent, today we see a resurgence of some previously deployed community-based strategies to address current structural issues that continue to haunt us. We have "mom co-ops" where single mothers are pooling resources to share in housing and childcare costs and responsibilities, in addition to tenant organizing in the form of rent strikes and unions in the wake of the COVID-19 pandemic. We are seeing examples of people's growing desire to change their relationship with the consumer marketplace and refocus collective attention on prioritizing the needs of people over profit. It makes me wonder about the relationship between this type of intersectional political consumerism and ruling economic policies and whether a shift away from commercially based and toward community-based intersectional political consumerism might change how we construct our economic policies. If consumers began to demand, for example, tenant unions with collective ownership of properties, might that lay a path for policy that would encourage profit sharing within a highly stratified and exploitive rental housing market? We've also seen, in the last decade, in response to the state-sanctioned violence carried out against Black people, calls for African Americans to mobilize and withhold consumer dollars until reforms are made. Hashtags such as #BlackOutBlackFriday and #NotOneDime serve as examples of how egregious injustices against African American communities have been met with strategies that include political consumerism.

CONCLUSION • 159

Black women of the welfare rights movement recognized that the relationship between the citizenry and consumerism was filled with complexity and tensions. And in the case of consumer credit, they used these circumstances to make the case for not just access to credit but also to disconnect the relationship of the citizen-consumer from work. There were social, political, and cultural implications of neoliberalism to contend with in these efforts to divorce workforce participation from beliefs around who was a so-called deserving consumer. In the same way that, a decade earlier, TWO took up the heavy load of attempting to emulate middle-class values through consumption, NWRO and CWRO took up the mantle in the form of a national consumer credit campaign. Though the CWRO leaders attempted to draw attention to the expensiveness of poverty and the ways in which the poor were taxed for their condition, seeking retribution from a private capitalist entity such as Sears served instead to further inflame hostilities toward the poor. Unmoved, the Black women of the movement demanded access to the same consumer technology that was available to middle-class women and cemented that demand in an argument that consumerism was essential to social life in a neoliberal capitalist society.

This neoliberal capitalist society was perpetuated by many institutions, including the educational system. The Chicago public school curriculum disseminated a narrative that through this new consumer credit technology, future earnings could be forfeited in exchange for gratification in the present. It was presented as sound economic policy that would allow for continued growth of the economy. But what of those who could not rely on a promise of future earnings because of their unemployment status? Simply put, the Black women of the welfare rights movement would not be left behind.

Not only did Black women of the movement refuse to accept the idea that poor people should be omitted from the conversation around credit, they also refused to be excluded from conversations around how poverty was determined. As rigid analog algorithms of poverty attempted to standardize poverty terms and outcomes—and poor people's social lives along with it—Black movement leaders rebutted the engagement of quantitative absolute metrics of poverty. We can learn a lot from the skepticism around quantitative metrics and the erroneous view that they are objective and superior to other forms of inquiry. We can also resist external attempts to define and dictate our social lives, as well as efforts to quantifiably arrest our human experiences.

In reflecting on how the measurement of poverty has changed over the last fifty to sixty years (from the time of the welfare rights movement to today), I'm struck by how little has changed regarding the formulas and approach that are used. Though economists at the Census Bureau and Bureau of Labor Statistics have created new supplemental poverty metrics, I imagine these economists are part of the same scholarly community that authored the hundreds of thousands of academic articles related to the economy and consumer market that I searched in the JSTOR database—the same scholarly community that engaged little discussion around race, class, and gender and erased poor Black women entirely. We need to reconsider the ways in which we measure poverty and move toward more relative poverty metrics to elucidate the growing stratification in the nation and how that stratification is shaped by algorithmic assemblages of race, class, and gender.

The Black women of the movement were fighting on multiple fronts. They were fighting not only for their experiences to be reflected in how poverty was measured, but also to shape the narrative around which resources were needed and their right to

CONCLUSION • 161

make their own consumer and financial choices to meet those needs. The analog algorithms of poverty were not only rigid, they were also paternalistic in determining a minimal level of sustenance, and they narrowed the choices available to poor people using a complex apparatus that included calculations, surveillance, and demands to work.

A major priority of both the national and Chicago-based welfare rights organizations was to secure a guaranteed annual income. From a consumerism standpoint, that allowed for the removal of a major barrier to the citizen-consumer connection: employment. It also provided the poor with stability and a means with which to more effectively engage consumer credit and the flexibility it offered. Again, CWRO leaders wanted respect for their ability to make budgetary decisions for themselves and their families. The guaranteed annual income became a site from which source code (ideologies) around what the poor deserved could be dissected. It also provided another mechanism by which the state could subsidize itself through filtering funds to businesses via the poor. Both the state and welfare rights leaders used cash benefits as a way to commodify the social lives of the poor. Whereas the state's focus was constriction, Black women of the movement focused on expansion—expansion of resources, expansion of opportunities, and expansion of choice, and freedom of choice that also had the potential to disrupt the consumer market itself.

I can imagine a society in which people, having their basic needs met and being free of the stress associated with getting by, are able to refocus their energy and creativity in ways that are more aligned with their talents and interests rather than being directed by massive corporations. What might be created if everyone had the flexibility and freedom to pursue their interests in the same way that more heavily resourced people do? What might Black

162 • CONCLUSION

women create, and what products might we flood the consumer market with, if we were not contending with disproportionately negative health outcomes, excessive student loan debt, medical debt, exorbitant childcare expenses, and job segregation?

Following the economic, political, and social consequences of COVID-19, we see renewed conversations and experiments around GAI or universal basic income with no strings attached gaining the attention of policy makers and government officials. To date, twenty-nine states are testing universal basic income programs. Preliminary findings from these experiments show measurable improvements in health, employment, and financial stability among program participants. The programs suggest that, contrary to the narratives about the poor, people have the ability to govern themselves and make sound choices for themselves and their families. This is not dissimilar to Hulbert James, NWRO's director of field operations, noting that Philadelphia's welfare recipients who received credit from several large stores (in 1970) repaid at higher levels than the general public. We have yet another opportunity to reimagine our relationship to consumer choice and poverty policy.

The Black women of the welfare rights movement also exposed the hidden ideologies of anti-Blackness that were embedded in the state's poverty metrics and policies. Reading the local, state, and federal government's "source code," I found that the Black women of the movement combatted hostile algorithmic assemblages and analog algorithms of poverty by writing new procedures, new (self-) definitions, and new code. Even as organizations such as IAF were openly antagonistic toward Black female leaders, made efforts to undermine Black women's authority, and remove them from positions of power, Black women remained in the business of advocating and battling for legitimacy via access to consumer spaces. As the state apparatuses of education and commerce magnified consumer credit as technology, we see a strategic

CONCLUSION • 163

magnification by Black women of credit technology as a way of retooling the consumer-citizen narrative.

To audaciously demand rights—specifically rights to middle-class consumer tools such as credit—and insist that these rights be unbound from employment status demonstrated these women's level of commitment to obtaining a standard of living that kept poor people's dignity intact. Simply, Black women rejected the analog algorithms of poverty that used metrics to commodify their lives and forever bind them to the state. Guaranteed income and guaranteed credit were their response to the work-pay bond.

The lesson and the challenge of Black women's experiences during the welfare rights movement remains the government's symbiotic and exploitive relationship with the poor. The in[ter]jection of poor people into discussions of credit and consumer access cleared a path for future industries to target poor consumers and create entire markets around subprime lending. Though Black women of the welfare rights movement engaged financial tools as Black feminist technologies to improve the immediate material conditions of a population demonized and ignored by the state, the financial tools and technologies of today perpetuate an exploitation akin to the unscrupulous local merchants that welfare rights activists fought against nearly fifty years ago.

And though the archives, in their violence, tried their best to erase the contributions of these women via the politics of preservation and accessibility, those contributions still found ways to spring forth. I cannot capture what has been lost to lack of consideration (i.e., conservation, documentation, equitable distribution, respect), but I can invoke their names so that others will know and remember that they existed.[1] Marion Stamps. Dovie Coleman. Dovie Thurman. Catherine Dandridge. Rosa Pitts. Ada Moore. Dorothy Shavers. Nezzie Willis. Ruby Mabry. Ginger Mack. Few among us have such clarity of purpose as the women of the Chicago welfare rights movement.

Often movements are discussed and evaluated based on some measure of success or failure; success if they achieved the goals of the movement and failure if they did not. I do not want to reify the conventional measures of social movements or capitalist standards of success. Black women have rarely had the luxury of defining success for themselves and having that definition acknowledged and left alone. What I have learned from the study of these women and the welfare organizations they led and served is that they made it a practice to resist oppressive structures and enact their agency. They created and recreated their own standards again and again in service to themselves, their families, and their communities. These daily moments of resistance are inspiring. In my view, their success is demonstrated in the many moments when they individually and collectively insisted that their needs and desires were valid. These Black women were successful in that they saw themselves as deserving of a standard and quality of care, a bit of "that middle-class season of fun," that was denied to them (but freely pushed on the middle class). The women were successful in creating space to divorce one's dignity from one's relationship to the workforce.

The women of the movement were able to organize collectively to demand the attention of major retailers. The issuing of such benefits as retail credit through NWRO membership brought about a group consciousness that exploited the contradictions of freedom and white middle-class materiality. Their refusal to be ignored and dismissed was a victory in itself. They claimed victory with every Black woman who led a neighborhood welfare rights organization. Victory with every direct action. Victory with every arrest. Victory with every campaign. Victory with every demand. Victory with every reimagined technology. Their legacy rests in our ability to know and remember their resistance and resolve.

APPENDIX A

ARCHIVAL COLLECTIONS

ACORN Records, 1965–2008

Annetta Dieckmann Papers Records, 1944–1976

Better Business Bureau of Metropolitan Chicago records, 1940–1980

Charles Chiakulas Collection

Chicago Council on Urban Affairs

CORE (Congress of Racial Equality), Chicago Chapter Archives

Industrial Areas Foundation/Saul Alinsky Papers

Chicago Urban League (CUL)

Hull House Association Papers

Institute of the Church in an Urban Industrial Society

Movement for Economic Justice Records

Brenda Eichelberger/National Alliance of Black Feminists Papers

National Welfare Rights Organization Papers—Unprocessed

Peggy Terry Papers, 1937–2004

Social Action Vertical File, 1960–1980

Scholarship, Education and Defense Fund for Racial Equality

Wisconsin, Division of Community Services: Bureau of Planning
and Implementation Files, 1950–1984

George Wiley Papers, Early Civil Rights and Poverty Activities
1949–1975

166 • APPENDIX A

ARCHIVAL SITES

Chicago History Museum Research Center, Chicago, IL

Daley Library, University of Illinois Chicago, Chicago, IL

Moorland-Springarn Research Center, Howard University, Washington, DC

Walter P. Reuther Library, Detroit, MI

Wisconsin Historical Society, Madison, WI

APPENDIX B

isted below are the six queries created in JSTOR on January 19, 2015. On reviewing several articles from the search query results to ensure the search terms were accurate, I requested the metadata through JSTOR's Data for Research website (http://dfr.jstor.org), which enables researchers to make large data set requests.

JSTOR SEARCH CRITERIA

All texts in the collection should accord with the following parameters in a full-text search query of the DFR database: Language—English; Year of Publication—1965–2014.

- Search query for "Condition—Race/Class/Gender"—All of these words: "(black OR "African American" OR "afro American" OR negro OR colored AND poor OR poverty OR "welfare recipient" OR underclass OR disadvantaged AND girl* OR wom?n OR female* OR lady OR ladies)" DFR beta search with parameters—1965–2014, English only. Search terms yielded 892 results.

168 • APPENDIX B

- Search query for "Economic Policy/Neoliberalism"—All of these words: "(neoliberal* OR liberalism OR "economic liberalism" OR "classical liberal")" in Full-Text + All Fields DFR beta search with parameters—1965–2014, English only. Search terms yielded 110,375 results.

- Search query for "Business/Consumerism"—All of these words: "(Consumerism OR consumer* OR customer* OR patron* OR patronage)" in Full-Text + All Fields DFR beta search with parameters—1965–2014, English only. Search terms yielded 668,386 results.

- Search query for "Governance/Welfare"—All of these words: "("great society" OR "welfare rights" OR "Welfare Rights Movement" OR "NWRO" OR "government assistance" OR "AFDC" OR "aid to families with dependent children" OR "ADC" OR "aid to dependent children" OR "TANF" OR "temporary assistance for needy families" OR "guaranteed adequate income")" in Full-Text + All Fields DFR beta search with parameters—1965–2014, English only. Search terms yielded 31,096 results.

- Search query for "Governance/Law"—All of these words: "(legislation OR law* OR legal OR right* OR "civil right" OR government OR judge OR plaintiff OR defendant OR court* AND "NWRO")" DFR beta search with parameters—1965–2014, English only. Search terms yielded 89 results.

- Search query for "Governance/Citizenship"—All of these words: "(citizenship OR citizen* OR "tax payer")" DFR beta search with parameters—1965–2014, English only. Search terms yielded 731,559 results.

NOTES

INTRODUCTION

1. Throughout the text, I use the terms "Black women" and "African-American women" interchangeably when referring to diasporic Black women residing in the United States.

2. Algorithmic assemblages are defined as the combined effects of race, class, and gender interactions with institutional apparatuses. Inspired by Jasbir Puar's work (2020), I am using "assemblages" as a way to activate intersectional analysis, specifically as related to exposing algorithms of the state. While many read Puar's work as a response to and critique of Crenshaw's intersectionality, I understand her reading of intersectionality as existing within or as assemblage. Therefore, I use Puar's concept of assemblage to signal intersectionality and the ways in which social locations can reverberate across various realms of power.

3. Whiteness or other social frameworks of privilege are not masked. Instead, intersectional political consumerism is used to show how privileged social positions operate differently within the consumer space.

4. See Jenkins (2002, 84). See also Bourdieu (1993).

5. I define "ideology" as a systematic way of understanding and making meaning of the social world that grounds thinking and action. See also Patricia Hill Collins, *Black Feminist Thought* (New York: Routledge, 2000) and *Black Sexual Politics: African Americans, Gender, and the New Racism* (New York: Routledge, 2005).

170 • INTRODUCTION

6. The focus on quality products derived from African Americans paying inflated prices for inferior products. As a result, they were sensitive to product quality.

7. Wiley had been an associate director for the Congress of Racial Equality (CORE) and later formed the Poverty/Rights Action Center (along with Ed Day and Tim Sampson). See also *Guaranteed Annual Income (GAIN) Newsletter*, vol. 1, no. 2, July 1966, 4, series IV; box IV, 104; folder 1174. Columbia University Library.

8. Richard Rogin, "Now It's Welfare Lib," *New York Times* magazine, September 27, 1970, distributed by the National Welfare Rights Organization [hereafter cited as NWRO]. Social Action vertical file ca. 1960–2002, box 56, folder Welfare Rights Org, p. 6

9. See "As Convention Opens: Rift Erupts at Welfare Rights," *Afro-American*, August 19, 1969, box 7, folder 8, National Convention, 1969, (Detroit) Washington, George Wiley Papers, NWRO.

10. *Guaranteed Annual Income (GAIN) Newsletter*, vol. 1, no. 4, September 1966, series IV; box IV, 104; folder 1174, p. 3, Chicago Urban League.

11. John Lewis, "Black Voices," *Afro-American*, August 30, 1969, box 7, folder 8, National Convention, 1969, (Detroit) Washington, Wiley Papers, NWRO; "Report to the Interreligious Foundation for Community Organization," George Wiley, Correspondense [*sic*], Reports, and Notes, 1968–1973, period covered May 1–December 31, 1968, Wiley Papers, NWRO. For a copy of the constitution drafted after the convention, see also Wiley Papers, box 7, folder 4, Constitutions and Bylaws, 1967–1971 National Welfare Rights Organization Constitution, August 27, 1967. For a statement of organizational structure and the organization chart and operating structure, see Wiley Papers, box 7, folder 5, Organizational Descriptions and Proposals, 1968–1972 and undated document titled "National Welfare Rights Organization Organizational Structure," 1972.

1. HARVEST

1. Dictionary.com broadly defines "Technology" as the practical application of knowledge or "the sum of ways in which social groups provide themselves with the material objects of their civilization." Algorithms

I. HARVEST • 171

are simply sets of rules, procedures, and processes that are used to solve a recurrent problem (which can be analog or digital).

2. Despite these violences, some scholars have recognized the impact of archival violence and developed strategies to combat it. See Kimberly Springer (2005) and Bettye Collier-Thomas (2001) for discussions on the use of oral histories, as well as Ashley Farmer's discussions of "archiving while Black" (2018).

3. I searched the JSTOR digital library using the search terms listed in appendix B. I created six queries to create six subcorpora, each related to at least one realm of power identified in the study.

4. Using the topic modeling software Mallet, I constructed an analysis with an output of fifty topics for each of the six queries. Mallett allows the researcher to set the output for the number of topics based on the distribution of topics in the data. Fifty was chosen as a manageable number for analysis, which provided coherent topics.

5. These results come from a subcorpus of the 1.5 million documents that focused specifically on "consumerism" search term results.

6. Intermediate reading of text is a process that falls between the close readings associated with traditional research and the distant readings associated with topic modeling output. To evaluate the relationship between the word lists and the texts used to generate them, researchers developed a simple tool that scans the word-to-topic assignments for each document and returns a list of titles that have a given percentage of words assigned to topics of interest.

7. The document titles found in this intermediate reading were representative for topic 17. Each document had a specific distribution of topics. The threshold (for analysis of topic 17) of at least 70 percent was used to identify representative document titles, meaning that at least 70 percent of the listed documents were composed of words associated with topic 17.

8. The term "misogynoir" was coined by Moya Bailey. See *Misogynoir Transformed: Black Women's Digital Resistance* (2021) for Bailey's arguments related to anti-Black misogyny.

9. See Catherine Knight-Steele's *Digital Black Feminism* (2021) and Legacy Russell's *Glitch Feminism* (2020).

10. See Lizabeth Cohen's work about the citizen consumer in *A Consumer's Republic: The Politics of Mass Consumption in Postwar America* (2003)

11. Foucault, Michel. 1988. *Power Knowledge*. New York, NY: Random House.

172 • I. HARVEST

12. See also Lisa Duggan's *Twilight of Inequality: Neoliberalism, Cultural Politics, and the Attack on Democracy* (2003) and Jody Melamed's "The Spirit of Neoliberalism: From Racial Liberalism to Neoliberal Multiculturalism" (2006) for discussions of how neoliberalism masks inequities while claiming to resolve them and efforts to cast neoliberalism as a democratic capitalist modernity, which in reality only serves to perpetuate white supremacy under the guise of race-neutral policy.

13. United States. 1988. The Kerner Report: The 1968 Report of the National Advisory Commission on Civil Disorders First pantheon ed, New York: Pantheon Books.

14. Hall et al. (1996) saw consumerism as a way of dismantling class and reshaping how workers saw themselves; not as producers but as consumers. Though items were encoded with meaning during their production, this meaning making was not complete until the actual product was consumed. Therefore, consumers have agency to determine the meaning of these items despite what the producers or marketers may have intended.

15. Moynihan, Daniel. 1965. The Negro family: The case for national action. Washington, DC: Office of Policy Planning and Research, US Department of Labor.

16. Some of the items identified included high-dollar items such as refrigerators and other appliances, beds, and winter clothing.

17. ACORN was a national nonprofit umbrella organization formed in 1970 to lobby for and mobilize low- and moderate-income families. Areas of focus included affordable housing, wages, and voter registration.

18. Wilson (1987) attributes this to the Moynihan report's chilling effect on liberals and social scientists, who, in response, refused to discuss culture, thus allowing conservatives to dominate the conversation and cast the urban poor in the worst light—as undeserving poor.

19. See Mead's *Beyond Entitlement* (1986) for the argument that welfare undermines citizenry obligations that the poor should work.

2. BUSINESS

1. The organization was later renamed "The Woodlawn Organization" (also abbreviated TWO) in 1961.

2. Saul Alinsky Papers (IAF Records) Box 27 Folder 456 Woodlawn-The Woodlawn Organization-Fashion Show-newspaper clippings Dec, 1961-Dec, 1962 Article Titled 'Cavalcade of Fashions'.

2. BUSINESS • 173

3. The National Welfare Rights Organization was plugged in to consumer issues, as demonstrated by the organization's presence at various conferences that focused on consumer rights. The Urban Coalition's conference held an "Urban Consumer Clinic" in June 1973. NWRO chairperson Johnnie Tillmon attended to represent the organization. One topic discussed at the clinic on consumerism was how "Blacks, Browns, Native Americans, Ethnic Whites and other minorities" might collaborate to obtain economic and political power. See Movement for Economic Justice Records [hereafter cited as MEJ Records], box 11, folder 7, National Urban Coalition (NUC). The Southern Regional Council's Food Stamp Meetings, held in 1974, were attended by NWRO; see MEJ Records, NUL. Several consumer groups also were represented, such as the Consumer Federation of America and the National Consumer League; see Consumer Concerns—Food Stamps, MEJ Records, box 23, folder 2. MEJ, which worked closely with welfare organizations to provide administrative support and resources, also participated in consumer information conferences; see National Consumer Information Center Convention, January 11–16, 1976, MEJ Records, box 12, folder 17.

4. *NOW (News of Welfare)*, vol. V, no. 23, September 30, 1971, Hull House Association Papers, series VIII, box 42, folder 480.

5. NWRO Boycott discussions, similar to the case with discussions of boycotting Standard Oil in Mexico (see Workshop report, Social Action Vertical File ca. 1960–2002, box 36, folder National Welfare Rights Organization), frequently mentioned imperialism, the company's perpetuation of it, and the group's need to divest from such endeavors.

6. Consumer Credit (Harlem Consumer Education), Scholarship, Education and Defense Fund for Racial Equality Records, 1944–1976, box 51, folder 19.

7. Public Interest Economic Center and Foundation, 1973–March 1974, Movement for Economic Justice, box 3, folder 3

8. "Tenants Find a New Source of Power: At Issue, Rights of Residents— and Consumers," *National Observer*, August, 8, 1966, Industrial Area Foundations Records [hereafter cited as IAF Records], box 64, folder 798, IAF Records-TWO-Chicago, 1965–66.

9. Flyer titled "Lawndale and East Garfield Pk on a Rent Strike," Charles Chiakulas Collection, box 32, folder Lawndale Tenants Union (Lawndale Union to End Slums).

174 • 2. BUSINESS

10. Though these organizations were clearly affiliated with NWRO, they did not hold themselves accountable to NWRO in any way with regard to their decision-making and activities. These organizations were loosely affiliated with and detached from the national organization. JOIN was an active participant in early NWRO meetings; see attendance list for the National Welfare Rights Meeting, Chicago, Illinois, August 6–7, 1966, Social Action Vertical File ca. 1960–2002, box 36, folder National Welfare Rights Organization (Poverty Rights Action Center). Local organizations did participate in some national organization's activities; see also memo from Sam Clark, September 1966, 3, Social Action Vertical File ca. 1960–2002, box 36, folder National Welfare Rights Organization (Poverty Rights Action Center). However, NWRO had no oversight of these organizations, so their level of connection to anything the national campaigns were calling them to do—such as rent strikes, boycotts, or demonstrations—was likely not directed, organized, or coordinated with NWRO but were parallel activities. These organizations were tapping into the larger needs of poor people that existed nationally rather than taking their cue from NWRO.

11. For more information on West Woodlawn, see memorandum from Nicholas von Hoffmann to Saul Alinsky regarding West Woodlawn, May 22, 1959, IAF Records, box 27, folder 459, Woodlawn-TWO-general & miscellaneous-correspondence and memoranda February–September 1959; and seven-page memo to Fred Ross from Nicholas von Hoffman regarding TWO, November 27, 1962, 27, IAF Records, box 64, folder 798, Industrial Areas Foundation Records—TWO-Chicago, 1965–66. For more history of Woodlawn, see documents titled "Woodlawn Fact Sheet," n.d., and "Woodlawn Project," n.d., IAF Records, box 64, folder 800, Industrial Area Foundation TWO-Chicago 1958–1961.

12. "A Movement of the People," *Awareness*, vol. 1, no. 1, May 1961, 1, IAF Records, box 28, folder 465, Woodlawn-TWO-general & miscellaneous May–September 1961; letter to Right Reverend Monsignor Vincent Cooke, Catholic Charities of Chicago, from Alinsky, Industrial Area Foundations, June 9, 1959, IAF Records, box 64, folder 800, Industrial Area Foundations TWO-Chicago 1958–1961.

13. Proposal titled "The Woodlawn Cooperative Project," n.d., 2, IAF Records, box 27, folder 459, Woodlawn-TWO-general & miscellaneous-correspondence and memoranda February-September 1959;

2. BUSINESS • 175

memorandum regarding West Woodlawn to Alinsky from von Hoffman, May 22, 1959, IAF Records, box 27, folder 459, Woodlawn-TWO-general & miscellaneous-correspondence and memoranda February–September 1959.

14. For more information on rapid white flight in the area, see memorandum regarding the state of Woodlawn at this time to Alinsky from von Hoffman, November 23, 1960, IAF Records, box 64, folder 800, Industrial Area Foundations TWO-Chicago 1958–1961.

15. "A Movement of the People," 3.

16. "A Movement of the People"; "Woodlawn: An Urban Battlefield," *Chicago Sun-Times*, vol. 14, no. 28, April 9, 1961, IAF Records, box 29, folder 475, Woodlawn-TWO-clippings-miscellaneous March-April 1961.

17. Letter to Alinsky from Juan Sosa, corresponding secretary of the Temporary Woodlawn Organization, January 6, 1961, IAF Records, box 28, folder 462, Woodlawn-TWO-general & miscellaneous-correspondence and minutes of meetings January 1961.

18. More background and history about Alinsky and TWO can be found in *Awareness* newsletter. See "A Movement of the People" and 1962 "Chicago's Woodlawn—Renewal By Whom?," *Forum*, May 1962, reprinted and published by TIME, Inc., IAF Records, box 27, folder 446, Woodlawn-The Woodlawn Organization-articles May-November 1962. For more information on why the Industrial Area Foundations Back of the Yards model was viewed by some as problematic, see "Woodlawn: The Head-On Clash of Urban Forces," *Chicago Sun-Times*, April 9, 1961, 36, IAF Records, box 29, folder 475, Woodlawn-TWO-clippings-miscellaneous March-April 1961.

19. "Rift in Woodlawn Alliance Widens," *The Bulletin*, vol. 3, no. 28, April 20, 1961, IAF Records, box 29, folder 475, Woodlawn-TWO-clippings-miscellaneous March-April 1961.

20. "The Woodlawn Cooperative Project," n.d., 3.

21. Regarding the relationship among Alinsky, the Industrial Area Foundations, and the Roman Catholic Archdiocese, see also Saul Alinsky, "The IAF—Why Is It 'Controversial'?," *Church in Metropolis*, Summer 1965, "The Archdiocese Responds," 16, IAF Records, box 30, folder 502.

22. "The Woodlawn Cooperative Project," n.d., 4.

23. Letter to Right Reverend Monsignor Vincent Cooke, Catholic Charities of Chicago, from Saul Alinsky, Industrial Area Foundations, June

176 • 2. BUSINESS

    9, 1959, 3, IAF Records, box 64, folder 800, Industrial Area Foundations TWO-Chicago 1958–1961.

24. Memorandum regarding the state of Woodlawn at this time to Alinsky from von Hoffman, November 23, 1960, IAF Records, box 64, folder 800, Industrial Area Foundations TWO-Chicago 1958–1961.

25. Letter to Reverend Robert McGee, president, Temporary Woodlawn Organization, from Alinsky, August 15, 1961, IAF Records, box 28, folder 465, Woodlawn-TWO-general & miscellaneous May–September 1961.

26. For more information on race demographics and the church's role in the creation of TWO, also see "A Movement of the People," 3.

27. "The Great Debate in Chicago," *Presbyterian Life*, June 15, 1961, IAF Records, box 28, folder 465, Woodlawn-TWO-general & miscellaneous May–September.

28. "Woodlawn: An Urban Battlefield."

29. According to the U.S. Census, in 1960, the area of Woodlawn (community area/census tract 42) was 89 percent Black, while the area of Uptown (community area/census tract 3) was 60 percent Appalachian white. See LeGates and Stout (2011) and Pacyga (2009) for information on Woodlawn and Obermiller et al. (2000), Guy (2007), and Frost (2001) regarding Uptown.

30. "What's the Toughest Neighborhood in America? Wrong," True October 1971, Peggy Terry Papers, series JOIN, box 3, folder 8, JOIN Community Union, 1966.

31. "Who Pays For Black Lung Disease? A Working Man's Wages?," *Chicago's Free Weekly Reader*, vol. 6, no. 8, November 19, 1976, Peggy Terry Papers, series JOIN, box 3, folder 8, JOIN Community Union, 1966.

32. Document titled "Purpose of JOIN," March 1966, 1, Social Action Vertical File ca. 1960–2002, box 23, folder JOIN Uptown Community Union Chicago.

33. Booklet printed by the SDS titled "Get Ready for the Firing Line," March 1968, 1, Terry Papers, series JOIN, box 3, folder 16, The Firing Line, 1967.

34. Flyer titled "JOIN," n.d., Social Action Vertical File ca. 1960–2002, box 23, folder JOIN Uptown Community Union Chicago

35. Statement and list of demands presented to Mayor Daley and Superintendent O. W. Wilson from JOIN Community Union, September 10, 1966, and flyer titled "A Message to the Unemployed Workers," n.d.,

2. BUSINESS • 177

Social Action Vertical File ca. 1960–2002, box 23, folder JOIN Uptown Community Union Chicago.

36. "In Poverty, They Help the Poor," *Chicago Daily News*, July 3, 1965, Terry Papers, series Uptown Chicago, box 6, folder 4, Living and Working Conditions in Uptown, 1963–1968; "JOIN Progress Report," December 16, 1965, Social Action Vertical File ca. 1960–2002, box 23, folder JOIN Uptown Community Union Chicago.

37. The northern cities were chosen because the North was viewed as less tumultuous and would allow northern students to do tangible things, such as organizing, fundraising, and conducting research. See "Get Ready for the Firing Line," 3.

38. Document prepared by Peggy Terry titled "Organizing Poor Whites in Uptown, Chicago: A History and Prospectus of JOIN Community Union," Terry Papers, series JOIN, box 3, folder 19, Org. History etc. 1966–68.

39. "The Apparatchik," *New Republic*, July 24, 1965, Terry Papers, series Uptown Chicago, box 6, folder 4, Living and Working Conditions in Uptown, 1963–1968; "Get Ready for the Firing Line," 3.

40. "Get Ready for the Firing Line," 3.

41. Flyer titled "Poor People's Campaign for Poor People's Power," n.d., Terry Papers, series Poor People's Campaign, box 6, folder 2, Poor People's Campaign, 1968; "Purpose of JOIN," 2.

42. "White Woman's Drive to Aid Poor People," *Jet* magazine, June 13, 1968, 17, Terry Papers, series JOIN, box 2, folder 8, Civil Rights Movement 1961–1969.

43. "White Panthers Hand Out Free Food, Talk Survival," The Lerner Press, October 9, 1972, Terry Papers, series Uptown Chicago, box 6, folder 6, Intercommunal Survival Committee, 1972.

44. In 1967, the newsletter had a circulation of six thousand. See letter Lowell Kirby from Peggy Terry regarding *The Firing Line* newsletter, September 22, 1967, Terry Papers, series JOIN, box 3, folder 5, Correspondence, 1963–1997.

45. Peggy Terry, "Let's Get It On," *The Movement*, January 1968, Terry Papers, series JOIN, box 3, folder 9, Organizing Committee, 1966–68.

46. Terry, "Let's Get It On."

47. Huey Newton cofounded the Black Panther Party in 1966.

48. "Get Ready for the Firing Line," 3.

49. "Get Ready for the Firing Line," 6.

178 • 2. BUSINESS

50. "Get Ready for the Firing Line," 6.

51. Terry, "Let's Get It On."

52. "Purpose of JOIN," 3.

53. Organized by Martin Luther King, Bayard Rustin (national coordinator of the Solidarity Day march), and Ralph Abernathy, the Poor People's Campaign of 1968 encouraged people all over the country to come to Washington, D.C., in May 1968 to address the issues of decent wages, job training, removal of poor people due to urban renewal, police harassment, and adequate welfare. See "Poor People's Campaign for Poor People's Power," n.d.

54. Program title "Solidarity Day in Support of the Poor People's Campaign," June 19, 1968, Terry Papers, series Poor People'seoples Campaign, box 6, folder 2, Poor People's Campaign, 1968.

55. Transcription of Peggy Terry's speech at Solidarity Day, "'Solidarity Day' Speech at Lincoln Memorial, June 19, 1968," Terry Papers, series Poor People's Campaign, box 6, folder 2, Poor People's Campaign, 1968.

56. Dovie Coleman was a key Chicago leader of JOIN and WRDA in Uptown. WRDA, KOCO, and JOIN also participated in the June 30 demonstrations that would mark the formal beginning of the NWRO. See document produced by the Poverty/Rights Action Center, "Round-Up of June 30th Welfare Demonstrations," June 28, 1966, 4, George Wiley Papers, National Welfare Rights Organization, box 14, folder 9 (NWRO) Birthday Demonstrations, 1966–1970. See also "Cities Participating in June 30th Nationwide Welfare Demonstrations," 1967, which names Dovie Coleman and the Welfare Recipients Demand Action (WRDA), in Wiley Papers, box 14, folder 9 (NWRO), Birthday Demonstrations, 1966–1970. Also see NWRO Papers—Unprocessed collection, box 2150, a collection of documents from NWRO papers, for meeting minutes, informational materials, and advocacy and recruitment letters from the Chicago Friends to their middle-class contacts asking for support. The documents also describe Coleman's background before she joined the NWRO and became the first staff member and organizer for the CWRO office. Eleven months prior to her appointment to the CWRO office, Coleman started WRDA. In 1964, she began working with JOIN. In 1966, Coleman was chosen as the Illinois state representative for NWRO and also served as its financial secretary and a member of the NCC. See also *Feminist Coalitions: Historical*

2. BUSINESS • 179

Perspectives on Second-Wave Feminism in the United States by Stephanie Gilmore (2008) for more information regarding Black female leadership in welfare rights organizations, including the efforts of Dovie Coleman and Dovie Thurman (WRDA).

57. JOIN Community Union press release, May 23, 1966, regarding protests at the Cook County Welfare office, Social Action Vertical File ca. 1960–2002, box 23, folder JOIN Uptown Community Union Chicago.

58. Document titled "Steering Committee Poor People's Campaign," Terry Papers, series Poor People's Campaign, box 5, folder, 9 Poor People's Campaign, 1968.

59. See the introduction of Dovie Coleman (as the organizer for the CWRO office) in the meeting minutes of Chicago Friends Welfare Rights Organization, document titled "Chicago Friend Welfare Rights Organizations," n.d., 1–3, NWRO Papers—Unprocessed collection, box 2150.

60. "Poor Marchers: Actors in a Drama," *Washington Post*, May 1, 1968, Terry Papers, series Poor People's Campaign, box 5, folder 9, Poor People's Campaign, 1968.

61. JOIN Community Union press release, May 23, 1966.

62. Dovie Thurman also worked with the Economic Research and Action Project.

63. "Why I Went to Jail," JOIN Community Union newsletter, vol. 2, no. 7, May 27, 1966, Terry Papers, series Uptown Chicago, box 6, folder 4, Living and Working Conditions in Uptown, 1963–1968.

64. JOIN Community Union press release, May 23, 1966, 2.

65. The JOIN members (or "Trespassing Trio," as they were called in the JOIN newsletter) were bonded out of jail and released eighteen hours after arrest. They then returned to the Cook County welfare office with fifty additional members. See JOIN Community Union newsletter, May 27, 1966, Terry Papers, series Uptown Chicago, box 6, folder 4, Living and Working Conditions in Uptown, 1963–1968.

66. JOIN Community Union newsletter, vol. 2, no. 11, July 4, 1966, Terry Papers, series Uptown Chicago, box 6, folder 4, Living and Working Conditions in Uptown, 1963–1968.

67. "JOIN Marches."

68. Four-page booklet, "How Did The National Poor People's Coalition Get Organized?," n.d., 3, Terry Papers, series Poor People's Campaign, box 6, folder 1, Poor People's Campaign, 1968.

180 • 2. BUSINESS

69. JOIN Community Union coordinator's report, May 15, 1967, Social Action Vertical File ca. 1960–2002, box 23, folder JOIN Uptown Community Union Chicago.

70. Peggy Terry, "Welfare Rights," JOIN Community Union newsletter, vol. 3, no. 3, February 16–28, 1967, Terry Papers, series JOIN, box 3, folder 20, Org. History etc. 1966–68.

71. The names of delegates are in IAF Records, series 1, box 27, folder 448, Woodlawn-TWO-convention delegate list February–May, 1962.

72. See also attacks on Johnson, a TWO female staff member, memo to Saul Alinsky from Leon Finney re: Woodlawn Report, dictated on April 16, 1966, received on April 18, 2, IAF Records, box 64, folder 798, Industrial Areas Foundation Records—TWO-Chicago, 1965–66. See also eight-page memo to Alinsky from Dick Harmon, dictated on April 2, 1966, received on April 4, and transcribed on April 5, 5–6, IAF Records, box 64, folder 798, Industrial Areas Foundation Records—TWO-Chicago, 1965–66.

73. Memorandum regarding West Woodlawn to Alinsky from von Hoffman, May 22, 1959, 3, IAF Records, box 27, folder 459, Woodlawn-TWO-general & miscellaneous-correspondence and memoranda February-September 1959.

74. Nine-page memo to Alinsky from Leon Finney regarding TWO, dictated on August 13, 1966, received and transcribed on August 17, 3, IAF Records, box 64, folder 799; IAF Records—TWO, 1965–66.

75. Memo to Alinsky from Finney regarding T.W.O., 3.

76. Seven-page memo to Fred Ross from Nicholas von Hoffman regarding T.W.O., November 27, 1962, 2–3, IAF Records, box 64, folder 798, Industrial Areas Foundation Records—TWO-Chicago, 1965–66.

77. West Woodlawn Women's Community Club newsletter, July 12, 1954, IAF Records, box 30, folder 500, Woodlawn Union-bulletins and constitution February 1954–September 1955.

78. West Woodlawn Women's Community Club newsletter, n.d., 2, IAF Records, box 28, folder 465, Woodlawn-TWO-general & miscellaneous May–September 1961.

79. For others, the checkered history between the Industrial Area Foundations and Woodlawn residents led to general hostility toward TWO. TWO was criticized for its affiliation with the IAF by clergy who defected from the pastor's alliance as well as the Associated Block

2. BUSINESS • 181

Clubs of Woodlawn (a splinter group). These community members withdrew from TWO because they disagreed with the aggressive union-type strategies of IAF against the South East Commission to organize and redevelop Woodlawn. Associated Block Clubs of Woodlawn (and Greenwood block club) president L. Eugene Harrison stated that IAF was "following the same line they did in Woodlawn in 1954 when they tried to set up an organization and failed. Nicholas Von Hoffman is in charge now, as he was seven years ago. IAF organizers preach fear and hatred, stir up discontent, exploit antagonisms, try to pit one group against another. . . . They tried to undermine the existing interracial community group, United Woodlawn Conference, attacking the Conference's program of organizing block clubs." See "Rift in Woodlawn Alliance Widens," *The Bulletin*, vol. 3, no. 28, April 20, 1961, IAF Records, box 29, folder 475, Woodlawn-TWO-clippings-miscellaneous March–April, 1961. For detail on the Welfare Union, see also document titled "The Woodlawn Union," n.d., IAF Records, box 30, folder 500, Woodlawn Union-bulletins and constitution February 1954–September 1955. Von Hoffman attempted to organize in Woodlawn in 1954. Note that the United Woodlawn Conference was part of the SECC that started plans for urban renewal and conservation for the south campus area. See "Woodlawn: The Head-On Clash of Urban Forces," *Chicago Sun-Times*, April 9, 1961, IAF Records, box 29, folder 475, Woodlawn-TWO-clippings-miscellaneous March–April 1961; as well as the bifold pamphlet titled "United Woodlawn Conference," IAF Records, box 30, folder 500, Woodlawn Union-bulletins and constitution February 1954–September 1955, which explains the conference's affiliation with the South East Chicago Commission. The political allegiances were clearly drawn. Many people in Woodlawn had long memories and resented IAF for what was perceived as its outside agitation and tampering or undermining of the community's efforts to organize itself.

80. "Control Your Own Community," *The Crusader*, vol. 20, no. 45, April 15, 1961, IAF Records, box 29, folder 475, Woodlawn-TWO-clippings-miscellaneous March–April 1961.

81. "'Muscle Men' Infiltrate Woodlawn Organization," *New Crusader*, vol. 20, no. 42, March 25, 1961, IAF Records, box 29, folder 475, Woodlawn-TWO-clippings-miscellaneous March–April 1961.

182 • 2. BUSINESS

82. "Woodlawn Operators Move in for Big Kill," *New Crusader*, April 8, 1961, IAF Records, box 29, folder 475, Woodlawn-TWO-clippings-miscellaneous March–April 1961.

83. The Protestants were upset because they felt the Catholics had basically bought the IAF and would therefore push its own agenda of maintaining the racial segregation in the area. See Ken Pierce, "Calls Segregation Charge 'Grossly Irresponsible,'" *Chicago Maroon*, vol. 69, no. 62, March 10, 1961, IAF Records, box 29, folder 475, Woodlawn-TWO-clippings-miscellaneous March–April 1961; "Church Supports 'Hate Group,'" *Chicago Maroon*, vol. 69, no. 61, March 3, 1961, IAF Records, box 29, folder 475, Woodlawn-TWO-clippings-miscellaneous March–April 1961; and letter to Right Reverend Monsignor Vincent Cooke from Reverend Martin Farrell, September 15, 1959, IAF Records, box 64, folder 800, Industrial Area Foundation TWO-Chicago 1958–61. The reality was that the majority of Blacks were not Catholic, and the Catholic churches in the area and surrounding areas were losing parishioners due to white flight. See sixteen-page document outlining a proposed program by the Industrial Area Foundations targeting Woodlawn as a neighborhood to be organized, IAF Records, box 64, folder 800, Industrial Area Foundation TWO-Chicago 1958–61. To maintain the status quo would mean a stabilization of parishioners. Alternatively, the Protestants and Catholics could attempt to build a parishioner base of a darker hue. Though the IAF stated that its intentions were to develop an "integrated pattern" throughout the city (as demonstrated by its Back of the Yards initiative), some felt IAF was more concerned with keeping Woodlawn Blacks where they were. The Lutherans had backed out because of the strategies and financial support given by the Catholics. See also "'Muscle Men' Infiltrate Woodlawn Organization," *New Crusader*, vol. 20, no. 42, March 25, 1961; "Church Supports 'Hate Group,'" *Chicago Maroon*, vol. 69, no. 61, March 3, 1961; and untitled article, *The Bulletin*, March 9, 1961, IAF Records, box 29, folder 486, Woodlawn-TWO-Square Deal Campaign Board of Arbitration-newspaper clippings March 1961.

84. "Woodlawn Operators Move in for Big Kill."

85. Alinsky, 'The IAF—Why Is It 'Controversial'?," 13–14.

86. See "TWO's Two-Fisted War on Chicago Slum," *National Observer*, November 26, 1962, IAF Records, box 64, folder 801, Industrial Area

2. BUSINESS • 183

Foundation Records—TWO OSC, 1959–62. The article highlights Alinsky and names him as founder. Compare this with the *Chicago Defender* article dated November 19, 1962, "Ministers vs. Evils of Urban Renewal," which also provides a history of the organization but does not highlight Alinsky in a significant way. But then the *Defender* does the same thing the next day with an article calling Alinsky "the man behind TWO." See "Found: A General to Lead a Slum Army," *Chicago Defender*, November 20, 1962, IAF Records, box 64, folder 801, Industrial Area Foundation Records—TWO OSC, 1959–62. This white savior idea seemed to permeate for white as well as Black people.

87. An undated memo from the NWRO strategic action conference planning committee references reports on "alternative economy" that recognize communes and co-ops to be superior to capitalism in ending sexism and racism. See Workshop Report, Social Action Vertical File ca. 1960–2002, box 36, folder National Welfare Rights Organization.

88. Document titled "Basis for the Development of a Woodlawn Community Rehabilitation Plan," January 5, 1961, 1, IAF Records, box 28, folder 462, Woodlawn-TWO-general & miscellaneous-correspondence and minutes of meetings January 1961; document titled "Statement and Motion Offered at the South East Commission Board Meeting," February 13, 1961, 2, IAF Records, box 28, folder 463, Woodlawn-TWO-general & miscellaneous correspondence and memoranda February 1961.

89. "Statement and Motion Offered at the South East Commission Board Meeting," 2.

90. It proposed to take 60th to 61st Streets, Stoney Island to Cottage Grove for the south campus; see "A Movement of the People."

91. "A Movement of the People"; "Up from Apathy—The Woodlawn Experiment," *Commentary*, vol. 5, no. 37, May 1964, IAF Records, box 64, folder 801, Industrial Area Foundation Records—TWO OSC, 1959–62.

92. From the beginning, TWO's interest included business and commerce objectives in the community; it did not start as a desire to build a movement (revolutionary) but more as a reactionary measure (reformist) in response to landownership and usage (which are premised by capitalist framing).

93. "Basis For the Development of a Woodlawn Community Rehabilitation Plan," 1–3; "How University of Chicago Was Stopped by a Fighting

184 • 2. BUSINESS

Community," *Chicago Defender*, November 21, 1962, IAF Records, box 64, folder 801, Industrial Area Foundation Records—TWO OSC, 1959–62.

94. By 1976, Uptown residents would be displaced by the building of Harry Truman College. See the interactive project by Professors Gayatri Reddy and Anna Guevarra, "Dis/Placements: A People's History of Uptown, Chicago" (https://dis-placements.com/uptown-timeline-main), which chronicles the displacement in the Uptown area.

95. Response to questionnaire for Lakeview-Uptown Community Council from Luevelle (Peggy) Terry, n.d., Terry Papers, series Uptown Chicago, box 6, folder 6, Intercommunal Survival Committee, 1972.

96. "Tenants Find a New Source of Power: At Issue, Rights of Residents—and Consumers," *National Observer*, August 8, 1966, IAF Records, box 64, folder 798, Industrial Area Foundation Records-TWO-Chicago, 1965–66.

97. "Slum Building Undergoing Repairs as Result of TWO," *Daily Defender*, November 2, 1961, IAF Records, box 29, folder 478, Woodlawn-TWO-clippings-miscellaneous November 1961–March 1962.

98. "Rent Strike in Woodlawn," *Woodlawn Booster*, October 17, 1962, IAF Records, box 29, folder 479, Woodlawn-TWO-clippings-miscellaneous April–October 1962.

99. "'This is Slum'; Renters Strike," *Chicago Daily News*, December 8, 1961, IAF Records, box 29, folder 478, Woodlawn-TWO-clippings-miscellaneous November 1961–March 1962.

100. The following articles are in IAF Records, box 29, folder 478, Woodlawn-TWO-clippings-miscellaneous November 1961–March 1962. "S. Side Tenants Strike Against Landlord," *Chicago Sun-Times* December 9, 1961; "Tenants Stage Big Rent Strike," *New Crusader*, December 16, 1961; "T.W.O. Pickets Home of Landlord as 'Rent Strike' Issue Heads to Court," *Daily Defender*, January 10, 1962; "Woodlawn Tenants March on Home of Area Landlord," *The Bulletin*, January 11, 1962; and "TWO Pickets Slum Landlord's Swank Home on South Shore Dr.," *New Crusader*, January 20, 1962.

101. "Rent-Struck Tenants Get TWO's Help," *Chicago Courier*, December 23, 1961, IAF Records, box 29, folder 478, Woodlawn-TWO-clippings-miscellaneous November 1961–March 1962; "T.W.O. Gives Coal to

2. BUSINESS • 185

Rent Strike Tenants," *Daily Defender*, December 21, 1961, IAF Records, box 29, folder 478, Woodlawn-TWO-clippings-miscellaneous November 1961–March 1962.

102. "Tenants Stage Sit-In," *The Bulletin*, March 1, 1962, IAF Records, box 29, folder 478, Woodlawn-TWO-clippings-miscellaneous November 1961–March 1962; "Lights Shut Off; 25 In Flat Seek Refuge In Church," *Chicago Daily Tribune*, February 27, 1962, IAF Records, box 29, folder 478, Woodlawn-TWO-clippings-miscellaneous November 1961–March 1962; and "Lights, Heat Off, Church Shelters Rent 'Refugees,'" IAF Records box 29 folder 479 Woodlawn-TWO-clippings-miscellaneous April 1962–October 1962.

103. "T.W.O. Unit Huddles with Landlord Over 3 Flats," *Daily Defender*, February 21, 1962, IAF Records, box 29, folder 478, Woodlawn-TWO-clippings-miscellaneous November 1961–March 1962.

104. "Tenants Plan Legal Action After Electricity Is Cut Off," *Chicago Daily News*, February 27, 1962, IAF Records, box 29, folder 478, Woodlawn-TWO-clippings-miscellaneous November 1961–March 1962.

105. "TWO Wins Second Rent Victory in Slum Case," *Chicago Daily Defender*, July 5, 1962, IAF Records, box 29, folder 479, Woodlawn-TWO-clippings-miscellaneous April 1962–October 1962.

106. See the following articles for more TWO-sponsored rent strike details. "TWO Visits Three In Rent Fights," *Woodlawn Booster*, June 27, 1962; "TWO Gets First Rent Agreement," *Woodlawn Booster*, June 13, 1962; "Picket Cyrus as 'Slumlord,'" *Chicago Daily Defender*, April 10, 1962; "TWO, Block Club Fight Landlords," *Woodlawn Booster*, September 18, 1963; "TWO Gives Landlords 'Repair or Else' Order," *Chicago Daily Defender*, October 31, 1963; Ulysses Blakeley and Charles Leber, "Woodlawn Begins to Flex Its Muscles," *Presbyterian Life*, September 15, 196212.

107. A copy of the May 1966 agreement between JOIN and landlord Max Gutman of 4107–15 North Broadway, Chicago, can be found in the Social Action Vertical File ca. 1960–2002. box 23, folder JOIN Uptown Community Union Chicago. In the agreement, the landlord agreed to make improvements to his properties. Rent strikes also took place for the residents of 4240 Kenmore Avenue. See the flyer titled "JOIN Victory," n.d., Social Action Vertical File ca. 1960–2002, box 23, folder

186 • 2. BUSINESS

JOIN Uptown Community Union Chicago. The flyer communicated a successful negotiation between the organization and the Kenmore building landlord

108. "Strike Victory," *JOIN Newsletter*, vol. 2, no. 10, June 27, 1966, Terry Papers, series JOIN, box 3, folder 15, Welfare Rights, 1964–68.

109. Press release, "NWRO Winter Action Campaign Ideas," February 24, 1969, 5, Social Action Vertical File ca. 1960–2002, box 36, folder National Welfare Rights Organization.

110. JOIN Community Union coordinator's report, June 7, 1967, Social Action Vertical File ca. 1960–2002, box 23, folder JOIN, Uptown Community Union Chicago.

111. "Purpose of JOIN," 5.

112. "Purpose of JOIN," 4.

113. Statement and list of demands presented to Mayor Daley and Superintendent O. W. Wilson from JOIN Community Union, September 10, 1966, Social Action Vertical File ca. 1960–2002, box 23, folder JOIN Uptown Community Union Chicago.

114. "JOIN Progress Report," 3.

115. "JOIN Progress Report," 2.

116. All the organizations referenced were affiliated with NWRO at one time. See amphlet from the Poverty/Rights Action Center dated January 15, 1967, listing the welfare rights organizations nationwide identified by PRAC in Social Action Vertical File ca. 1960–2002, box 36, folder National Welfare Rights Organization (Poverty Rights Action Center). See also information regarding WSO and JOIN, letter to welfare leaders and organizers from George Wiley, November 14, 1966, 1, in Social Action Vertical File ca. 1960–2002, box 36, folder National Welfare Rights Organization (Poverty Rights Action Center); and information regarding KOCO and JOIN, memo by Sam Clark, September 1966, in Social Action Vertical File ca. 1960–2002, box 36, folder National Welfare Rights Organization (Poverty Rights Action Center). See also Membership and Chapter Records, 1967–1972, NWRO Membership listing, July 1, 1970, 6; NWRO Membership listing December 3–5, 1971, 3; and NWRO Membership listing February 4, 1972, 6, in George Wiley Papers, National Welfare Rights Organization, box 8, folder 4. Also see "Minutes of Meeting to Form City Wide Welfare Union JOIN, KOCO and

2. BUSINESS • 187

WSO," July 30, 1966, Terry Papers, series JOIN, box 3, folder 15, Welfare Rights, 1964–68.

117. Joint press release from JOIN, KOCO, and WSO, "Recipient Groups Support William Robinson as New Head of Welfare Department," 1966, Terry Papers, series JOIN, box 3, folder 15, Welfare Rights, 1964–68.

118. Document titled "School of Community Organization: Introduction," n.d., Terry Papers, series JOIN, box 3, folder 2, Community School Adult Educ. Materials, 1965–68.

119. "School of Community Organization: Introduction."

120. Flyer titled "What Is TWO?," n.d., IAF Records, box 28, folder 464, Woodlawn-TWO-general & miscellaneous March-April 1961.

121. "Negro Civic Group Assails 'Welfarism,'" *Chicago Daily News*, March 24, 1962, IAF Records, box 27, folder 450, Woodlawn-The Woodlawn Organization-Constitutional Convention clippings; "Woodlawn Organization Created from 'Melting Pot' of Different Groups," *Chicago Defender*, June 2–8, 1962, IAF Records, box 64, folder 800, Industrial Area Foundation TWO-Chicago 1958–61.

122. There was much excitement that this new organization would provide a militant presence that some community members felt was lacking in Chicago's Black organizations. See "The Woodlawn Organization," *Chicago Defender*, April 18, 1962, IAF Records, box 64, folder 800, Industrial Area Foundation TWO-Chicago 1958–61.

123. "Fourth Annual T.W.O. Convention," *The Woodlawn Organization Self-Determination Newsletter*, Convention Issue, vol. 2, no. 4, May 14, 1965, IAF Records, box 27, folder 450, Woodlawn-The Woodlawn Organization-Constitutional Convention clippings; "Third Annual T.W.O. Convention Agenda, " *The Woodlawn Organization Self-Determination Newsletter*, Convention Issue, vol. 1, no. 5, April 17, 1964, IAF Records, box 27, folder 450, Woodlawn-The Woodlawn Organization-Constitutional Convention clippings.

124. "Negro Civic Group Assails 'Welfarism.'"

125. TWO had a meeting with Daley in Dec 1961 where they told him "TWO expected to be in on the planning for the rehabilitation of Woodlawn from the beginning" See "Rent-Struck Tenants Get TWO's Help."

126. "Mayor's Planning Approach Commended," *New World*, March 30, 1962, IAF Records, box 29, folder 478, Woodlawn-TWO-clippings-miscellaneous November 1961–March 1962.

188 • 2. BUSINESS

127. The following articles are in IAF Records, box 30, folder 497, Woodlawn Plan of March 1962—clippings: "Woodlawn Blueprint to Blot Out Negroes," *New Crusader*, March 24, 1962; "Mayor to Tell Plan for Woodlawn," *Hyde Park Herald*, vol. 31, no. 9, March 7, 1962; "Get Out: Daley to Woodlawn Negroes," *New Crusader*, vol 21, no. 43, March 31, 1962; and "Our Opinion: The New Woodlawn 'Plan,'" *New Crusader*, vol 21, no. 43, March 31, 1962.

128. "Woodlawn Blueprint to Blot Out Negroes."

129. "Daley Compromises on TWO Demands," *Chicago Sun-Times*, July 17, 1963, IAF Records, box 29, folder 482, Woodlawn-The Woodlawn Organization-newspaper clippings-miscellaneous July–October 1963.

130. "Third Annual T.W.O. Convention Agenda."

131. Black Paper, "On Poverty, Power and Race in Chicago," December 6, 1965, Social Action Vertical File ca. 1960–2002, box 23, folder JOIN Uptown Community Union Chicago.

132. When discussing aids and grants, TWO was referring to $4 million earmarked by the Chicago Dwelling Association. TWO wanted spot clearances of empty, vacated, and dilapidated land and the resale of that cleared land to nonprofit and limited-profit corporations for housing that would be affordable for Woodlawn residents. The organization also pushed for the building of affordable housing for residents (low-rise public housing on scattered sites throughout the city) before the demolishing and spot clearances of other areas. There was also an issue around Black owners of small residences who were not able to afford repairs demanded of them by the Building Department; with TWO insisting that these owners be provided with assistance so they did not lose their homes. See "Third Annual T.W.O. Convention Agenda.". Also see sixteen-page document outlining a proposed program by the Industrial Area Foundations targeting Woodlawn as a neighborhood to be organized, 4, IAF Records, box 64, folder 800, Industrial Area Foundation TWO-Chicago 1958–61.

133. "Future Outlook League—Squad Leaders," March 2, 1961, IAF Records, box 28, folder 464, Woodlawn-TWO-general & miscellaneous March–April 1961.

134. "Service Staff Integrated," March 24, 1961, IAF Records, box 28, folder 464, Woodlawn-TWO-general & miscellaneous March–April 1961.

2. BUSINESS • 189

135. Report on TWO activities from Robert Squires to IAF, "Report on Woodlawn—Robert Squires," March 2, 1961, IAF Records, box 64, folder 800, Industrial Area Foundation TWO-Chicago 1958–61, Document.

136. "Future Outlook League Withdraws From T.W.O.," *Woodlawn Booster*, October 11, 1961, IAF Records, box 29, folder 477, Woodlawn-TWO-clippings-miscellaneous-September–October 1961.

137. The Square Deal Campaign was TWO's premier organizing campaign. According to a *Chicago Defender* article dated November 29, 1962, the campaign was originally suggested by a group of Puerto Rican Woodlawn residents who found that area merchants where cheating them in the same way that Blacks were being cheated. This group would later be part of the "citizen shoppers" team charged with visiting stores in search of short weights and inaccurate and misleading pricing. The Square Deal included creating a code of business ethics related to credit-buying practices, pricing, and advertising. A Board of Arbitrations was governed by the "Square Deal Articles of Agreement," consisting of four representatives of WBMA, four representatives from consumer groups, and one impartial chairman from outside the community who was to be elected by the board members. As stated in the articles of agreement, the role of the Board of Arbitrations was to hear consumer complaints (such as short-weighting and exploitive credit practices) and establish rules for interest rate limits and procedures for dealing with delinquent customers and dishonest merchants. The campaign kicked off with a parade on March 6, 1961, with estimates ranging from six hundred to a thousand demonstrators (mainly Black and Puerto Rican). The campaign was deemed a success after several merchants suspected of cheating customers adjusted their scales and totalizers. A year and a half after the parade, the campaign was still considered active, but with the majority of businesses becoming Square Deal merchants, the campaign was left struggling for purpose. See also John Hall Fish's *Black Power/White Control* (1973, 49) and *Black Self-Determination* by Arthur Brazier (1969).

138. Carlson was viewed as a great "race man" whose loyalties lay with FOL rather than TWO. FOL's primary concern in the area dealt with promoting African American products and improving African American

190 • 2. BUSINESS

employment conditions. And Carlson pitched this idea/program to many organizations over the years in Chicago. There was recognition that FOL had a small but loyal following, and TWO leaders' primary concern with FOL members had to do with ensuring that the people of FOL "fall in line" with the wishes of TWO and not cause dissent within the organization. See "Report on Woodlawn—Robert Squires."

139. "T.W.O. Demands Jobs," *Woodlawn Booster*, vol. 30, no. 31, July 31, 1963, IAF Records, box 29, folder 482, Woodlawn-The Woodlawn Organization-newspaper clippings-miscellaneous July–October 1963.

140. "Food Chain Agrees 12 Negro Jobs," *Chicago Daily News*, November 7, 1963, IAF Records, box 29, folder 482, Woodlawn-The Woodlawn Organization-newspaper clippings-miscellaneous July–October 1963.

141. For information on financial ventures with Blackstone Rangers, see nine-page memo to Alinsky from Leon Finney regarding TWO, dictated on August 13, 1966, received and transcribed on August 17, 1966, 8, IAF Records, box 64, folder 799, TWO, 1965–66.

142. Letter to Reverend Monsignor John Egan with subject title "T.W.O.'s Progress," February 11, 1965, IAF Records, box 64, folder 798, Industrial Areas Foundation Records-TWO-Chicago, 1965–66.

143. Eight-page memo to Alinsky from Dick Harmon, dictated on April 2, 1966, received on April 4, 1966, transcribed on April 5, 1966, IAF Records, box 64, folder 798, Industrial Areas Foundation Records-TWO-Chicago, 1965–66.

144. Memo to Alinsky from Edwin Day regarding "The Woodlawn Organization (TWO)," n.d., IAF Records, box 46, folder 652, Alinsky Correspondence and memos, 1970–71.

145. Brochure for Observer Printing and Publishing, n.d., IAF Records, box 64, folder 798, Industrial Areas Foundation Records-TWO-Chicago, 1965–66.

146. Observer Printing and Publishing memo listing of weekly, semimonthly, and monthly clients, November 29, 1966, IAF Records, box 64, folder 798, Industrial Areas Foundation Records-TWO-Chicago, 1965–66; ten-page memo to Alinsky from Richard Harmon, dictated on March 7, 1966, received on March 8, 1966, and transcribed on March 9, 1966, IAF Records, box 64, folder 798, Industrial Areas Foundation Records-TWO-Chicago, 1965–66, .

147. Brochure for Observer Printing and Publishing.

2. BUSINESS • 191

148. Peggy Terry, "Welfare Rights," *JOIN Community Union Newsletter*, vol 3, no. 4, March 1–10, 1967, Terry Papers, series JOIN, box 3, folder 20, Org. History etc. 1966–68.

149. Peggy Terry, "Welfare Rights," *JOIN Community Union Newsletter*, vol. 3, no. 7, April 6–25, 1967, Terry Papers, series JOIN, box 3, folder 20, Org. History etc. 1966–68; and hand-drawn/handwritten flier, "Are You Tired of High Food Prices?," n.d., Social Action Vertical File ca. 1960–2002, box 23, folder JOIN Uptown Community Union Chicago.

150. JOIN's position on food stamps was that poor people had the right to a decent food stamp program that they could afford and that food stamps should be allowed for the purchase of any commodity of the recipient's choosing. See Welfare Bill of Rights document, n.d., Social Action Vertical File ca. 1960–2002, box 23, folder JOIN Uptown Community Union Chicago.

151. Letter to Frank Pollatsek, Cause of the Month, from Mike James, JOIN organizer, September 25, 1967, Terry Papers, series JOIN, box 3, folder 7, Correspondence, 1963–97.

152. Peggy Terry, "Welfare Rights," *JOIN Community Union Newsletter*, vol. 3, no. 6, March 21–April 5, 1967, Terry Papers, series JOIN, box 3, folder 15, Welfare Rights, 1964–68.

153. "Political Machine," (Terry Papers, series JOIN, box 3, folder 1) describes how politicians such as Daley spent money on airports, highways, street lights, and parking lots, along with the building of McCormick Place, to appease the interest of businesses, to the detriment of the community.

154. Note Alinsky's resistance to the idea of co-ops in Woodlawn, as mentioned in a memo. He sees them as being for "middle income liberals— who actually don't save much of anything in their co-op operation but they have a feeling—they get an emotional satisfaction out of the fact that they belong to a co-op." See letter to Dick Harmon from Alinsky read to Harmon over the phone as verbal notes, March 29, 1966, 3, IAF Records, box 64, folder 798, Industrial Areas Foundation Records-TWO-Chicago, 1965–66.

155. "High Prices and Inflation," November 1966, 2, Terry Papers, series JOIN, box 3, folder 3, Community School Adult Educ. Materials, 1965–68.

156. "Agenda for Organizing Committee Meeting," April 11, Social Action Vertical File ca. 1960–2002, box 23, folder JOIN Uptown Community

192 • 2. BUSINESS

Union Chicago; flyer titled "Boycott Price-Rite," n.d., Social Action Vertical File ca. 1960–2002, box 23, folder JOIN Uptown Community Union Chicago.

157. "Agenda For Organizing Committee Meeting," April 18, Social Action Vertical File ca. 1960–2002, box 23, folder JOIN Uptown Community Union Chicago.

158. For the names of board members, see the 1961 booklet listing Woodlawn Business Men's Association officers and board of directors in IAF Records, box 64, folder 798, Industrial Areas Foundation Records-TWO-Chicago, 1965–66 .

159. "Resolution on Retail Trade," n.d., IAF Records, box 27, folder 451, Woodlawn-TWO-constitutional convention-notes and resolution February 1962.

160. "'Muscle Men' Infiltrate Woodlawn Organization."

161. Press release, "WBMA President Speaks to Knights of St. John," *Woodlawn Booster*, January 31, 1961, 1, IAF Records, box 28, folder 469, Woodlawn-TWO-news releases January–February 1961.

162. "T.W.O. Received $600 Check From WBMA," *Woodlawn Booster*, March 27, 1963, IAF Records, box 29, folder 481, Woodlawn-The Woodlawn Organization-newspaper clippings-miscellaneous January–April 1963.

163. "Interest convergence" is a term coined by Derrick Bell referring to how Black people are able to achieve social justice only when their interests align with those of whites. See *"Brown v. Board of Education* and Interest-Convergence Dilemma" (1980).

164. "TWO's Two-Fisted War on Chicago Slum."

165. "Third Annual T.W.O. Convention Agenda"; memorandum to WBMA membership from WBMA Promotion Committee, May 27, 1961, 7, IAF Records, box 30, folder 492, Woodlawn Business Men's Association-memoranda May 1960–June 1961.

166. Four page memo to Alinsky from Finney regarding Woodlawn, dictated on April 11–12, 1966, received on April 12, 1966, and transcribed on April 12, 1966, 3, IAF Records, box 64, folder 798, Industrial Areas Foundation Records-TWO-Chicago, 1965–66.

167. During its time with TWO, FOL was also interested in co-ops and credit unions. However, that interest in no way usurped its efforts on

3. MAGNITUDE • 193

the commercial front, which was privileged in those efforts. See IAF Records, box 28, folder 463, 5.

168. Flyer titled "How Long Will Welfare Recipients Have to Wait for Christmas?," n.d., Terry Papers, series JOIN, box 3, folder 15, Welfare Rights, 1964–68.

169. "We Demand . . .," n.d., Social Action Vertical File ca. 1960–2002, box 23, folder JOIN Uptown Community Union Chicago; JOIN press release, December 22, 1965, regarding Cook County Public Aid's "Christmas Policy," 1–2, Social Action Vertical File ca. 1960–2002, box 23, folder JOIN Uptown Community Union Chicago.

170. The credit union provided $5 and $10 loans. See JOIN Organizing Committee meeting agenda, June 10, Social Action Vertical File ca. 1960–2002, box 23, folder JOIN Uptown Community Union Chicago.

171. JOIN Organizing Committee meeting agenda.

172. JOIN Organizing Committee meeting agenda.

173. Lizabeth Cohen's *Consumers' Republic* (2003) explores the production of identity as "citizen consumer" by engaging the long relationships among consumerism, democracy, and citizenship. Cohen promotes a convincing thesis that cements consumerism with citizenship. The "consumer republic," which began during the Cold War era and ended in the 1970s, when the individual interests of neoliberals would come to be incompatible with the public's interests, which had been stressed during the consumer's republic era. Her thesis is that after World War II, the public and private were interconnected through the creation of the "citizen consumer" (as the result of a booming economy, suburbanization, etc.), which helped perpetuate democratic ideals and had a perhaps unintentional effect of providing a consumer space of resistance for marginalized groups within the citizenry (African-Americans and women, to name but two).

174. Terry, "Let's Get It On."

3. MAGNITUDE

1. By that time, TWO had become an affiliated organization of CWRO.

2. See press release "Chicago Welfare Rights Organization/NWRO," April 7, 1969, 1–2, NWRO Papers—Unprocessed collection.

194 • 3. MAGNITUDE

3. See Felicia Kornbluh, "To Fulfill Their 'Rightly Needs': Consumerism and the National Welfare Rights Movement" (1997). See also Allison Pugh, *Longing and Belonging: Parents, Children, and Consumer Culture* (2009), regarding the concept of "shielding consumption," which suggests that low-income parents carry out certain consumption practices on behalf of their children in an effort to shield them from the stigma attached with being poor. For example, parents might spend money on expensive clothing and shoes so their children are not ridiculed by peers.

4. NWRO insisted that credit was a viable financial instrument for the poor to meet needs given their restrictive cash flow and that the only available credit was via unscrupulous neighborhood merchants, who charged exorbitant interest rates and engaged in unethical collection practices, which served to further economically marginalize and exploit the poor. NWRO also references rigid welfare policies that discourage saving their benefits. The strategy was for the poor to gain access to reputable companies with fair interest rates to provide flexibility for emergency expenses and larger purchases. See "Consumer Credit and the Poor," 1970, NWRO Papers—Unprocessed collection, box 2105, Folder NWRO. See also an untitled document by Etta Horn discussing the NCC and NWRO credit campaign, n.d., NWRO Papers—Unprocessed collection, box 2105.

5. See "NWRO Launches Sears Boycott," *WROs in Action* newsletter, April 1969, NWRO Papers—Unprocessed collection.

6. The concept of consumerism is also connected with an increase in multinational businesses and customers' feelings of powerlessness in getting satisfaction from these vast, impersonal institutions.

7. For discussions on how African Americans' brand loyalty connects with previous experiences of exploitation in the consumer marketplace, see Robert Weems, *Desegregating the Dollar: African American Consumerism in the Twentieth Century* (1998), and Jason Chambers, *Madison Avenue and the Color Line: African Americans in the Advertising Industry* (2009).

8. For the connection between labor movements and citizenship, see Josiah Bartlett Lambert's *"If the Workers Took a Notion": The Right to Strike and American Political Development* (2019). For discussions related to the labor unions and immigration, see also Ruth Milkman's

3. MAGNITUDE • 195

Organizing Immigrants: The Challenge for Unions in Contemporary California (2019).

9. See George Ritzer, *The Blackwell Encyclopedia of Sociology*, vol. 2: *Consumption* (2007). See also John Dittmer, *Local People* (1994).

10. See memo to Andy Duffy from Michael Caliandro, January 31, 1968, Better Business Bureau of Metropolitan Chicago Records, Consumer Education.

11. See Anna Everett's "The Revolution Will Be Digitized. Afrocentricity and the Digital Public Sphere" (2002).

12. This is likely also a response to anti-redlining legislation, as the Fair Housing Act was passed in 1968.

13. Discussions between Earl Lind, president of Better Business Bureau of Metro Chicago, and Ray Page, Illinois Superintendent of Public Instruction, began in 1967 with the passing of the Consumer Education Bill 977. Plans would not be formalized for another year. BBB of Metro Chicago records show department store credit education materials explaining the differences between a thirty-day charge account, an installment account, and a revolving charge account.

14. See letter to Dr. Peter Rossi, director National Opinion Research Center, from Nick von Hoffman, Industrial Area Foundation, May 23, 1961, IAF Records, box 30, folder 492, Woodlawn Business Men's Association-memoranda May 1960–June 1961.

15.

16. Interracial collaborations also occurred between the state and private organizations to aid in the creation and development of more Black-owned businesses. For information about the CEDC and its efforts to assist small business owners in obtaining financing, see the Chicago Urban League's 1969 trifold brochure titled "Business-like help for small-businesses," produced by the Chicago Economic Development Corporation. Also, see "Interracial Council for Business Opportunity," n.d., which describes the formation of the ICBO on October 30, 1963, as a collaboration between the Metropolitan Council of American Jewish Congress and the Urban League of Greater New York.

17. The Civil Rights Act legislating equal access to consumer spaces, public services, and facilities passed in 1964.

196 • 3. MAGNITUDE

18. On January 12, 1968, Better Business Bureau of Metro Chicago president Lind was appointed by Ray Page, Illinois Superintendent of Public Instruction, to join the consumer education curriculum development committee. The people invited to serve on committee included members of DePaul, Northern Illinois, Loyola, Western Illinois, and Northwestern Universities; local merchants and small business owners; and representatives from local high schools as well as businesses such as Sears, HFC, Montgomery Ward, and Marshal Fields.

19. See memorandum from the State of Illinois Office of Superintendent of Public Instruction, 1967, Better Business Bureau of Metropolitan Chicago Records, series 1, box 14, folder 2, Consumer Education.

20. Consumer education was defined as "the teaching of students in the rights and responsibilities individuals have in the marketplace as the buyer and user of goods and services. It involves an understanding of the total production and distribution processes. An emphasis on the marketing function is essential if the student is to learn how to maximize the utilization of available income for the greatest satisfaction of wants and needs. Consumer Education informs students of the functions and services of private and governmental agencies that operate in the best interest of the public. Private enterprise, as a principle, underlies the subject so that wholesome sellers of goods and services and intelligent buyers and users can have a mutual confidence in transactions." See letter to Dr. William Johnston from Earl Lind, January 25, 1968, Better Business Bureau Records, series 1, box 14, folder 2, Consumer Education.

21. See report titled "Guidelines for Consumer Education," June 1968, 2–3, Better Business Bureau of Metropolitan Chicago Records, series 1, box 14, folder 2 Consumer Education.

22. See "Report to the Interreligious Foundation for Community Organization," from George Wiley, period covered: January 1, 1969 to December 31, 1969, 8, George Wiley Papers, National Welfare Rights Organization, IFCO NWRO Correspondense [sic], Reports, and Notes, 1968–1973.

23. See "Why Don't Buy Sears," n.d., NWRO Papers—Unprocessed collection, box 2143.

24. See "Interview with Hulbert James, 2/6/70 for Seminar of February 16th," 2–3, Wiley Papers, National Welfare Rights Organization, box

3 . MAGNITUDE • 197

11, folder 18 IFCO NWRO Correspondense [*sic*], Reports, and Notes, 1968–1973.

25. See Welfare Council of Metro Chicago booklet titled "How Can We Help the Whole Man? Text of Speeches Delivered at the 46th Annual Meeting," February 23, 1961, Hull House Association Papers.

26. "Consumer Credit and the Poor."

27. See "Interview with Hulbert James, 2/6/70 for Seminar of February 16th."

28. See résumé materials and narrative of Jonquil Lanier for the position of administrative assistant at NWRO headquarters, Wiley Papers, National Welfare Rights Organization, Job Applications and Resumes L–R.

29. See cover letter to Nancy Barnes from Constance Sadlow, December 12, 1969, describing application materials for a secretarial position at NWRO headquarters, Wiley Papers, National Welfare Rights Organization, Job Applications and Resumes S–Z.

30. See Leslie G. Range, "Low-Income Units Form Credit Aids," Institute of the Church in an Urban Industrial Society Archive, May 23, 1967.

31. Range, "Low-Income Units Form Credit Aids."

32. See "Being Poor Is Expensive," n.d. Social Action Vertical File, National Welfare Rights Organization.

33. "Being Poor Is Expensive."

34. See reproduction of the article distributed by NWRO: Richard Rogin, "Now It's Welfare Lib," *New York Times* Magazine, September 27, 1970, 8, Social Action Vertical File, National Welfare Rights Organization.

35. See James Duignan, "Self-Help Action Center (SHAC)," *Marginal Line Newsletter*, vol. 5, no. 2, Summer 1975, 1, Institute of the Church in an Urban Industrial Society Archives-Illinois, Chicago, Archdiocesan Committee on Poverty Newsletter, Marginal Line, 1975–1976.

36. "Being Poor Is Expensive."

37. Letters dated December 16, 1968, from Johnnie Tillmon, NWRO national chairman, and George Wiley, NWRO executive director, to Mr. J. P. McFarland, president of General Mills; Mr. H. J. Morgens, president of Procter & Gamble Company; and Mr. D. J. Fitzgibbons, president of The Sterling Drug Company. See, Social Action Vertical File, box 56, folder Welfare Rights Organization.

38. See the July 31, 1966, press release from the 1966 National Conference of the Urban League in reference to Assistant Secretary of Labor Esther Peterson's conference comments related to the needs of Negro women

198 • 3. MAGNITUDE

and girls. Social Action Vertical File, box 35, folder National Urban League.

39. See report titled "Having the Power, We have the Duty," summary of recommendations to the Secretary of Health, Education, and Welfare compiled by The Advisory Council on Public Welfare, June 29, 1966, Wisconsin, Division of Community Services Bureau of Planning and Implementation Files, 1950–1979, Welfare Recipients Budget Cuts, Poor, Negro.

40. It is important to note that C. Virgil Martin, president of Carson Pirie Scott & Co., served on the advisory council that produced this report, suggesting a corporate interest in public welfare standards and allocation. The recommendations of the council outlined in this report would have allowed for public welfare recipients to have a more prominent role in the marketplace. The report states, "Social services, like those in education, health and recreation, are not only needed by people in their role as consumers but are also a necessary development in furnishing them with outlets to serve in the role of workers."

41. Booklet produced by NWRO titled "Some Ideas on How to Raise $ for Your WRO," June 1, 1971, 10, Social Action Vertical File, box 56, folder Welfare Rights; and Robin, "Now It's Welfare Lib," 5.

4. BOND

1. In materials from the 1973 NWRO convention: convention program booklet titled "Strategies for Survival July 11–15th," n.d., 1, George Wiley Papers, National Welfare Rights Organization, box 7, folder 10, National Convention, 1973 (Washington). See images of the NWRO logo on a sign in red, white, and blue to mimic an American flag, with the words "I support a guaranteed adequate income for all Americans" in the white stripes of the image and the NWRO and the infinity link symbol in the blue section of the depicted flag; Social Action Vertical File ca. 1960–2002, box 36, folder National Welfare Rights Organization, n.d. See also NWRO "Mother Power" sign, n.d., Social Action Vertical File ca. 1960–2002, box 36 folder National Welfare Rights Organization.

2. "Report to the Interreligious Foundation for Community Organization," George Wiley period covered: May 1, 1968 to December 31, 1968,

4. BOND • 199

8, Wiley Papers, National Welfare Rights Organization, box 11, folder 18, IFCO NWRO Correspondense [*sic*], Reports, and Notes, 1968–73.

3. "Report to the Interreligious Foundation for Community Organization."

4. Richard Rogin, "Now It's Welfare Lib," *New York Times Magazine*, September 27, 1970, 5, Social Action Vertical File ca. 1960–2002, box 56, folder National Welfare Rights Organization.

5. Algorithms are sets of rules, procedures, and processes.

6. Richard Hamilton, "Conviction or Convenience: The Trap of the Great Society," *The Nation*, [November 22, 1965], 384, Wiley Papers, Early Civil Rights and Poverty Activities, box 5, folder 8, Moynihan Report and Reaction 1964–66.

7. State of Illinois Department of Public Aid, "Public Aid in Illinois," December 1966, CUL, series IV, box IV 102, folder 1134.

8. Report dated November 30, 1966, to Seymour Simon, president, and members of the Board of Commissioners from John Ballew, acting director of Cook County Department of Public Aid, CUL, series IV, box IV 102, folder 1134, CCDPA Oct. Monthly Report of Activities.

9. Cook County Department of Public Aid report dated November 30, 1966.

10. Cook County Department of Public Aid report dated November 30, 1966.

11. Memorandum, "State of Illinois Department of Public Aid RE: Special Study of ADC April-June 1969," September 29, 1969, CUL, series IV, box IV 102, folder 1134, Special Study of ADC.

12. "State of Illinois Department of Public Aid RE: Special Study of ADC April-June 1969."

13. "State of Illinois Department of Public Aid RE: Special Study of ADC April-June 1969."

14. "BLS Reports on Economic Problems for West Side Neighborhoods of Chicago," n.d., CUL, series IV, box IV 104, folder 1167, Employment Westside.

15. "BLS Reports on Economic Problems for West Side Neighborhoods of Chicago."

16. "BLS Reports on Economic Problems for West Side Neighborhoods of Chicago."

17. "BLS Reports on Economic Problems for West Side Neighborhoods of Chicago."

200 • 4. BOND

18. "BLS Reports on Economic Problems for West Side Neighborhoods of Chicago."

19. "BLS Reports on Economic Problems for West Side Neighborhoods of Chicago," .4

20. "BLS Reports on Economic Problems for West Side Neighborhoods of Chicago," 5.

21. "Subcommittee Report on President Nixon's Welfare Proposals (S.1986 and H.R.14172)," November 19, 1969, CUL, series IV, box IV 102, folder 1134, Advisory Committee on Nixon Welfare.

22. Rogin "Now It's Welfare Lib," 4.

23. Daniel Moynihan's *The Politics of a Guaranteed Income* (1973) discusses Nixon's FAP as a cloaked guaranteed income proposal that was the most radical and progressive legislation (social program) offered by a president (not to mention a Republican) since the New Deal. The program did not call for recipients to work, even though Nixon referred to it as "workfare"; it did not require one-for-one detracting of income for those who were able to find work; and it allowed states to provide supplemental income to those who could not live on just the $1,600 income proposed. Moynihan claimed that it was liberal opposition to the plan, and liberals' unwillingness to side with a Republican president, that led to its ultimate failure. But it was also opposed by southern Dixiecrats, who saw that the plan would lead to more people being deemed poor and therefore eligible for welfare assistance. See Peter Passell and Leonard Ross, review of Moynihan, *"The Politics of a Guaranteed Income,"* *New York Times Book Review*, 1973, Hull House Association Records, series VIII, box 101, folder 1207, Guaranteed Annual Income. See also Michael Harrington, "Failures of Money, Confusions of Mouth," book review, [DATE], 59–60, Hull House Association Records, series VIII, box 101, folder 1207, Guaranteed Annual Income.

24. "Report to the Interreligious Foundation for Community Organization," 10–11.

25. "National Welfare Rights Organization Position on Title I: March 5, 1973," CUL, series IV, box IV, 102 folder 1135, National Welfare Rights Organization. "

26. "National Welfare Rights Organization Position on Title I: March 5, 1973."

4. BOND • 201

27. "No Solution in the Streets," *Chicago Tribune*, November 2, 1971, Hull House Association Records, series VIII, box 38, folder 447, Chicago newspaper clippings on welfare crisis 1971.

28. From Hull House Association Records, series VIII, box 38, folder 447, Chicago newspaper clippings on welfare crisis 1971: "Jon and Abra," *Chicago Daily*, November 2, 1971; "Scott Bypassed for Opinion on Welfare Slash," *Chicago Today*, November 2, 1971; and "No Tax Boosts for Welfare, Ogilvie Repeats," *Chicago Daily*, November 2, 1971.

29. "No Tax Boosts for Welfare, Ogilvie Repeats"; and "State's High Court to Hear More Debate," *Chicago Tribune*, November 2, 1971, Hull House Association Records, series VIII, box 38, folder 447, Chicago newspaper clippings on welfare crisis 1971.

30. "Check of 54,000 on Welfare May Take 2 Months, Not One," *Chicago Sun-Times*, November 5, 1971, Hull House Association Records, series VIII, box 38, folder 447, Chicago newspaper clippings on welfare crisis 1971.

31. Thomas Seslar, "Welfare Jobs Bill Is Sent to Ogilvie," *Chicago Tribune*, November 13, 1971; and "Straining at Welfare Gnats," *Chicago Sun-Times*, December 16, 1971, Hull House Association Records, series VIII, box 38, folder 447, Chicago newspaper clippings on welfare crisis 1971.

32. George Tagge, "Ogilvie and Reagan Disagree on U.S. Role for Welfare," *Chicago Tribune*, November 19, 1971, Hull House Association Records, series VIII, box 38, folder 447, Chicago newspaper clippings on welfare crisis 1971.

33. "2,000 on Dole March in Capital, Demand Increase in Welfare," *Chicago Tribune*, November 9, 1971, Hull House Association Records, series VIII, box 38, folder 447, Chicago newspaper clippings on welfare crisis 1971.

34. Roy Larson, "Don't Cut Welfare, Priests, Nuns Urge," *Chicago Sun-Times*, December 1, 1971; and "Straining at Welfare Gnats," Hull House Association Records, series VIII, box 38, folder 447, Chicago newspaper clippings on welfare crisis 1971 .

35. See Cellini, McKernan, and Ratcliffe (2008) for a review of the literature specific to poverty measures.

36. Real GNP (1972 dollars) in billions; see Balke and Gordon (1986), "Appendix B: Historical Chapter," 783.

37. See Jones and Weinberg (2000).

202 • 4. BOND

38. World Bank, World Development Indicators table (2015); Jones and Weinberg (2000), 7.

39. For GNP, see Balke and Gordon (2000), 783; for gini coefficient, see Jones and Weinberg (2000).

40. See also Fineman (1991) for a discussion on how mothers are constructed within the poverty discourse to perpetuate patriarchy.

41. The Aid to Dependent Children (ADC) program was renamed in 1962 after several eligibility changes to the Aid to Families with Dependent Children (AFDC). There was continued reference in NWRO documentation to the ADC after the name change, so I used ADC to remain consistent with the archival documentation.

42. "Welfare Myth and Reality," *Chicago Sun-Times*, November 23, 1971; and "Straining at Welfare Gnats," Hull House Association Records, series VIII, box 38, folder 447, Chicago newspaper clippings on welfare crisis 1971.

43. "The Poor People's Platform of National Welfare Rights Organization, National Tenants Organization, Southern Christian Leadership Conference," n.d., 3–4, Wiley Papers, National Welfare Rights Organization, box 7, folder 9, National Convention, 1972 (Miami).

44. *Guaranteed Annual Income Newsletter* (*GAIN*), vol. 1, no. 1, June 1966, 4, CUL, series IV, box IV 104, folder 1174.

45. *GAIN*, June 1966, 4.

46. *Guaranteed Annual Income Newsletter* (*GAIN*), vol. 1, no. 3, August 1966, 4, CUL, series IV, box IV 104, folder 1174.

47. Pamphlet titled "Guaranteed Income Plan," July 1966, CUL, series IV, box IV 104, folder 1174, Guaranteed Annual Income.

48. "Guaranteed Income Plan."

49. "Guaranteed Income Plan."

50. *GAIN*, June 1966.

51. Press release from the National Welfare Rights Organization regarding the 1970 Census, n.d., Wiley Papers, National Welfare Rights Organization, box 7, folder 11, National Coordinating Committee Meetings, 1966–72.

52. *GAIN*, June 1966.

53. Letter to Robert Hatch, managing editor of Nation Associates, from Irv Garfinkel, chairman of Ad Hoc Committee for a Guaranteed Income, February 16, 1967, CUL, series IV, box IV 104, folder 1174, Guaranteed Annual Income.

54. *GAIN*, June 1966, 1

4. BOND • 203

55. Press release to the city desk from the Ad Hoc Committee for a Guaranteed Income, February 21, 1967, CUL, series IV, box IV 104, folder 1174, Guaranteed Annual Income.

56. "National Welfare Rights—The Effects of PL 92–603 (HR-I) on the Aged, Blind, Disabled, and AFDC," n.d., 5, CUL, series IV, box IV 102, folder 1135, National Welfare Rights Organization.

57. Cook County Department of Public Aid report, November 30, 1966.

58. Memorandum to Bill Berry from Marion Henley regarding "Wage Supplement," February 3, 1970; and memorandum from Marion Henley from Rosie Simpson regarding "Wage Supplement Program," January 26, 1970, CUL, series IV, box IV 102, folder 1143, CUL WRO Collab. Wage Supplement.

59. Booklet titled "$5500 OR FIGHT," April 1970; and trifold booklet titled "Up the Nixon Plan," n.d., Social Action Vertical File ca. 1960–2002, box 36, folder National Welfare Rights Organization.

60. Booklet titled "The NWRO Adequate Income Plan $6500 Now!," n.d., Social Action Vertical File ca. 1960–2002, box 36, folder National Welfare Rights Organization

61. "The NWRO Adequate Income Plan $6500 Now!," 10.

62. "The NWRO Adequate Income Plan $6500 Now!," 10.

63. "The Kiplinger Washington Letter," February 5, 1971, CUL, series IV, box IV 111, folder 1272, Nixon Econ. Plan Impact.

64. "The Kiplinger Washington Letter," August 20, 1971, CUL, series IV, box IV 111, folder 1272, Nixon Econ. Plan Impact.

65. National Urban League press release, "Statement by Harold R. Sims, Acting Executive Director, National Urban League on President Nixon's New Economic Policy," August 17, 1971, received August 23, 1971, 2, CUL, series IV, box IV 111, folder 1272, Nixon Econ. Plan Impact.

66. "Report of the Chicago Riot Study Committee to The Hon. Richard J. Daley," August 1, 1968, 99, CUL, series IV, box IV 116, folder 1314, Chicago Riot Study.

67. "Report of the Chicago Riot Study Committee to The Hon. Richard J. Daley," 102.

68. "Report of the Chicago Riot Study Committee to The Hon. Richard J. Daley," 99.

69. See Leslie G. Range, "Low-Income Units Form Credit Aids," May 23, 1967, 2, ICUIS, box 29, folder 448, Archive. The article offers a

204 • 4. BOND

perspective on the merchant-consumer relationship that speaks to race and class intersectionality and views the merchant and consumer as working together to mutually support minority-owned local businesses and community members with the hope of controlling the economy of their own community.

70. "Report of the Chicago Riot Study Committee to The Hon. Richard J. Daley," 103.

71. "Report of the Chicago Riot Study Committee to The Hon. Richard J. Daley," 106.

72. From Dick Gregory's audio-recorded speech during the August 27, 1967, NWRO inaugural meeting. The recording is ninety minutes long and can be found at the Wisconsin Historical Society Library Archives in the George Wiley Papers using call number 544A/23.

73. Wisconsin Historical Society Audio recordings UC 544A/23.

74. U.S. Government Spending, State Welfare Spending Rank, http://www .usgovernmentspending.com/compare_state_spending_1967m40a.

75. Ida C. Merriam, Alfred M. Skolnik, and Sophie R. Dales, "Social Welfare Expenditures, 1967–68," *Social Security Bulletin*, December 1968, http://www.ssa.gov/policy/docs/ssb/v31n12/v31n12p14.pdf.

76. Wisconsin Historical Society audio recordings UC 544A/23.

77. Cook County Department of Public Aid report, November 30, 1966.

78. Memorandum, "State of Illinois Department of Public Aid RE: Special Study of ADC April–June 1969," September 29, 1969, CUL, series IV, box IV 102, folder 1134, Special Study of ADC.

79. Eliot Janeway, "Credit Cards for Welfare Clients," *Outlook* magazine, November 1969.

80. Rogin, "Now It's Welfare Lib," 2.

81. Wisconsin Historical Society audio recordings UC 544A/23.

CONCLUSION

1. I was introduced to the practice of know and remember by the group Saving Our Lives Hear Our Truths (SOLHOT). See Ruth Nicole Brown *Hear Our Truths: The Creative Potential of Black Girlhood* (2014) for an articulation of the genius of Black girls and women.

REFERENCES

Balke, Nathan, and Robert Gordon. 1986. "Appendix B: Historical Data Chapter." In *The American Business Cycle: Continuity and Change*, ed. Robert Gordon, 781–850. Chicago: University of Chicago Press.

Bailey, Moya. 2021. *Misogynoir Transformed: Black Women's Digital Resistance*. New York: NYU Press.

Baudrillard, Jean. 1998. *The Consumer Society: Myth and Structures*. Trans. Chris Turner. Thousand Oaks, CA: SAGE.

Bauman, Zygmunt. 1998. *Work, Consumerism, and the New Poor*. Maidenhead, UK: Open University Press.

——. 2002. "Violent in the Age of Uncertainty." In *Crime and Insecurity The governance of safety in Europe*, ed. Adam Crawford, 52–73. Devon, UK: Willan.

——. 2007. "Collateral Casualties of Consumerism," *Journal of Consumer Culture* 7, no. 1: 25–56.

Bayat, Asef. 2009. *Life as Politics: How Ordinary People Change the Middle East*. Stanford, CA: Stanford University Press.

Bell, Derrick A. 1980. "*Brown v. Board of Education* and the Interest-Convergence Dilemma." *Harvard Law Review* 93, no. 3: 518–33. https://doi.org/10.2307/1340546.

Benjamin, Ruha. 2019. *Race After Technology: Abolitionist Tools for the New Jim Code*. Cambridge: Polity.

Blackwood, D. L., and Robert G. Lynch. 1994. "The Measurement of Inequality and Poverty: A Policy Maker's Guide to the Literature." *World Development* 22: 567–78.

206 • REFERENCES

Blei, David M. 2012. Probabilistic Topic Models. *Communications of the ACM* 55, no. 4: 77–84. https://doi.org/10.1145/2133806.2133826.

Bolukbasi, T., K.-W. Chang, J. Zou, V. Saligrama, and A. Kalai. 2016. Man Is to Computer Programmer as Woman Is to Homemaker? Debiasing Word Embeddings." *arXiv* 1607.06520v1 [cs.CL]. http://arxiv.org/abs /1607.06520.

Bonilla-Silva, Eduardo. 2003. *Racism Without Racists: Color-Blind Racism and the Persistence of Racial Inequality in the United States.* Lanham, MD: Rowman & Littlefield.

Bonilla-Silva, Eduardo, and David Dietrich. 2011. "The Sweet Enchantment of Color-Blind Racism in Obamerica." *Annals of The American Academy of Political and Social Science* 634, no. 1:191–206. https://doi.org /10.1177/0002716210389702.

Boris, Eileen. 2002. "On Grassroots Organizing, Poor Women's Movements, and the Intellectual as Activist." *Journal of Women's History* 14, no. 2: 140–43.

Bourdieu, Pierre. 1984. *Distinction: A Social Critique of the Judgment of Taste.* Trans. Richard Nice. Cambridge, MA: Harvard University Press.

——. 1993. *The Field of Cultural Production.* Cambridge: Polity.

——. 2005. *The Social Structure of Economy.* : Polity.

Brazier, Arthur. 1969. *Black Self-Determination: The Story of The Woodlawn Organization.* Grand Rapids, MI: Eerdmans.

Brooks, Gwendolyn. 1994. *Blacks.* Chicago: Third World Press.

Brown, Nicole, Ruby Mendenhall, Michael Black, Mark van Moer, Assata Zerai, and Karen Flynn. 2016. "Mechanized Margin to Digitized Center: Black Feminism's Contributions to Combatting Erasure Within the Digital Humanities." *International Journal of Humanities and Arts Computing* 10, no. 1: 110–25. https://doi.org/10.3366/ijhac.2016.0163.

Brown, Ruth Nicole. 2014. *Hear Our Truths: The Creative Potential of Black Girlhood.* Urbana: University of Illinois Press.

Butler, Octavia. 1995. *Parable of the Sower.* London: Women's Press.

Caraley, Demetrios. 1996. "Dismantling the Federal Safety Net: Fictions Versus Realities." *Political Science Quarterly* 111, no. 2: 225–57.

Castillo, Wendy, and David Gillborn. 2022. "How to 'QuantCrit': Practices and Questions for Education Data Researchers and Users." EdWorkingPaper 22–546. Annenberg Institute, Brown University. https://doi.org /10.26300/v5kh-dd65.

REFERENCES • 207

Cellini, Stephanie Riegg, Signe-Mary McKernan, and Caroline Ratcliffe. 2008. "The Dynamics of Poverty in the United States: A Review of Data, Methods, and Findings." *Journal of Policy Analysis and Management* 27, no. 3.: 577–605.

Chambers, Jason. 2009. *Madison Avenue and the Color Line: African Americans in the Advertising Industry.* Philadelphia: University of Pennsylvania Press.

Claytor, Cassi Pittman. 2020. *Black Privilege: Modern Middle-Class Blacks with Credentials and Cash to Spend.* Stanford, CA: Stanford University Press.

Cohen, Lizabeth. 2003. *Consumers' Republic: The Politics of Mass Consumption in Postwar America.* New York: Vintage.

Collier-Thomas, B., ed.. 2001. *Sisters in the Struggle: African American Women in the Civil Rights-Black Power Movement.* New York: NYU Press.

Collins, Patricia Hill. 1999. "What's Going On? Black Feminist Thought and the Politics of Postmodernism." In *Working the Ruins: Feminist Poststructural Theory and Methods in Education,* ed. Elizabeth St. Pierre and Wanda Pillow. New York: Routledge.

——. 2000. *Black Feminist Thought.* New York: Routledge.

——. 2005. *Black Sexual Politics: African Americans, Gender, and the New Racism.* New York: Routledge.

Coser, Lewis. 1965. "The Sociology of Poverty: To the Memory of Georg Simmel." *Social Problems* 13, no. 2: 140–48. https://doi.org/10.2307/798899.

Countryman, Matthew. 2007. *Up South: Civil Rights and Black Power in Philadelphia.* Philadelphia: University of Pennsylvania Press.

David, M. D. 2016. *Mama's Gun: Black Maternal Figures and the Politics of Transgression.* Columbus: Ohio State University Press.

Dickerson, Amina. 2005. "Dusable Museum." *Encyclopedia of Chicago.* Chicago Historical Society. https://encyclopedia.chicagohistory.org/pages/398.html.

Dittmer, John. 1994. *Local People: The Struggle for Civil Rights in Missouri.* Urbana: University of Illinois Press.

Drake, St. Clair, and Horace R. Cayton. 1993. *Black Metropolis: A Study of Negro Life in a Northern City.* Chicago: University of Chicago Press.

Duggan, Lisa. 2003. *The Twilight of Equality?: Neoliberalism, Cultural Politics, and the Attack on Democracy.* Boston: Beacon.

Eubanks, Virginia. 2019. *Automating Inequality: How High-Tech Tools Profile, Police, and Punish.* New York: St Martin's.

208 • REFERENCES

Everett, Anna. 2002. "The Revolution Will Be Digitized. Afrocentricity and the Digital Public Sphere." *Social Text* 20, no. 2 (71): 125–46. https://doi.org/10.1215/01642472-20-2_71-125.

Farmer, Ashley. 2018. "Archiving While Black." *Chronicle of Higher Education* 64, no. 39.

Fineman, Martha. 1991. "Images of Mothers in Poverty Discourses." 1991 *Duke Law Journal*, 274–95.

Fish, John Hall. 1973. *Black Power/White Control*. Princeton, NJ: Princeton University Press.

Frazier, E. Franklin. 1957. *Black Bourgeoisie: The Rise of a New Middle Class in the United States*. New York: Free Press.

Frost, Jennifer. 2001. *"An Interracial Movement of the Poor:" Community Organizing and the New Left in the 1960s*. New York: NYU Press.

Fuentes, Marisa J. 2016. *Dispossessed Lives: Enslaved Women, Violence, and the Archive*. Philadelphia: University of Pennsylvania Press.

Galbraith, John Kenneth. 1998. *The Affluent Society*, 40th anniversary ed. New York: Houghton Mifflin.

Gans, Herbert. 1974. *Popular Culture and High Culture: An Analysis and Evaluation of Taste*. New York: Basic Books.

Gerstle, Gary. 1994. "The Protean Character of American Liberalism." *American Historical Review* 99, no. 4: 1043–73.

Gillborn, D., P. Warmington, and S. Demack. 2018. "QuantCrit: Education, Policy, 'Big Data' and Principles for a Critical Race Theory of Statistics." *Race, Ethnicity and Education* 21, no. 2: 158–79. https://doi.org/10.1080/13613324.2017.1377417.

Gilmore, Stephanie. 2008. *Feminist Coalitions: Historical Perspectives on Second-Wave Feminism in the United States*. Urbana: University of Illinois Press.

Glickman, Lawrence B. 1999. "Introduction: Born to Shop? Consumer History and American History." In *Consumer Society in American History: A Reader*, ed. Lawrence B. Glickman, 1–16. Ithaca, NY: Cornell University Press.

Goldberg, Gertrude Schaffner, and Eleanor Kremen. 1990. *The Feminization of Poverty: Only in America?* New York: Praeger.

Greenberg, Cheryl L. 1997. *Or Does It Explode?: Black Harlem in the Great Depression*. New York: Oxford University Press.

REFERENCES • 209

Guy, Roger. 2007. *From Diversity to Unity: Southern and Appalachian Migrants in Uptown Chicago, 1950–1970*. Lanham, MD: Lexington.

Hall, Stuart. 1990. "Cultural Identity and Diaspora." In *Identity: Community, Culture, Difference*, ed. J. Rutherford, 222–37. London: Lawrence & Wishart.

Hall, Stuart, David Morley, and Kuan-Hsing Chen. 1996. *Stuart Hall: Critical Dialogues in Cultural Studies*. London: Routledge.

Hancock, Ange-Marie. 2004. *The Politics of Disgust: The Public Identity of the Welfare Queen*. New York: NYU Press.

Harrington, Michael. 1997. *The Other America: Poverty in the United States*. First published 1962 by Macmillan. New York: Scribner.

Harris-Perry, Melissa. 2011. *Sister Citizen: Shame, Stereotypes, and Black Women in America*. New Haven, CT: Yale University Press.

Hartman, Saidiya. 2008. *Lose Your Mother: A Journey Along the Atlantic Slave Route*. New York: Farrar, Straus & Giroux.

Harvey, David. 2005. *A Brief History of Neoliberalism*. Oxford: Oxford University Press.

Iceland, John. 2006. *Poverty in America: A Handbook*, 2nd ed. Berkeley: University of California Press.

Jenkins, Richard. 2002. *Pierre Bourdieu*. New York: Routledge.

Jones, Arthur F. Jr., and Daniel H. Weinberg. 2000. "The Changing Shape of the Nation's Income Distribution: 1947–1998." Report no. P60-204, June 1, 2000. Washington, DC: U.S. Bureau of the Census. https://www.census .gov/library/publications/2000/demo/p60-204.html.

Jordan-Zachery, Julia. 2013. "Now You See Me, Now You Don't: My Political Fight Against the Invisibility of Black Women in Intersectionality Research." *Politics, Gender and Identities* 1, no. 1: 101–9.

Kornbluh, Felicia. 1991. "Subversive Potential, Coercive Intent: Women, Work, and Welfare in the 1990s." *Social Policy* 21, no. 4: 23–39.

——. 1997. "To Fulfill Their 'Rightly Needs': Consumerism and the National Welfare Rights Movement." *Radical History Review* 69: 76–113.

——. 2003. "Black Buying Power: Welfare Rights, Consumerism, and Northern Protest." In *Freedom North: Black Freedom Struggles Outside the South, 1940–1980*, ed. Jeanne Theoharis and Komozi Woodard. New York: Palgrave Macmillan.

——. 2007. *The Battle for Welfare Rights: Politics and Poverty in Modern America*. Philadelphia: University of Pennsylvania Press.

210 • REFERENCES

Lambert, Josiah Bartlett. 2019. *"If the Workers Took a Notion": The Right to Strike and American Political Development*. Ithaca, NY: Cornell University Press.

LeGates, Richard T., and Frederic Stout. 2011. *The City Reader*. London: Routledge.

Lorde, Audre. 1979. Comments at "The Personal and the Political" Panel, Second Sex Conference, October 29, 1979.

Marotta, Vince. 2000. "Zygmunt Bauman: Order, Strangerhood and Freedom." *Thesis Eleven* 70, no. 1: 36–51.

Massey, Douglas S., and Nancy A. Denton. 1993. *American Apartheid: Segregation and the Making of the Underclass*. Cambridge, MA: Harvard University Press.

Mead, Lawrence. 1986. *Beyond Entitlement*. New York: Free Press

Melamed, Jodi. 2006. "The Spirit of Neoliberalism: From Racial Liberalism to Neoliberal Multiculturalism." *Social Text* 24, no. 4 (89): 1–24.

Merriam, Ida C., Alfred M. Skolnik, and Sophie R. Dales. 1968. "Social Welfare Expenditures, 1967-68." *Social Security Bulletin*, December 1968. http://www.ssa.gov/policy/docs/ssb/v31n12/v31n12p14.pdf.

Milkman, Ruth. 2019. *Organizing Immigrants: The Challenge for Unions in Contemporary California*. Ithaca, NY: Cornell University Press.

Mingione, Enzo, ed. 1996. *Urban Poverty and the Underclass: A Reader*. Cambridge, MA: Blackwell.

Mohanty, Chandra Talpade. 1984. "Under Western Eyes: Feminist Scholarship and Colonial Discourses." *Boundary* 2 12, no. 3: 333. https://doi.org/10.2307/302821.

Moynihan, Daniel. 1973. *The Politics of a Guaranteed Income: The Nixon Administration and the Family Assistance Plan*. New York: Vintage.

Murray, Charles. 1984. *Losing Ground: American Social Policy, 1950–1980*. New York: Basic Books.

Nadasen, Premilla. 2005. *Welfare Warriors: The Welfare Rights Movement in the United States*. New York: Routledge.

Naples, Nancy A. 1998. *Grassroots Warriors: Activist Mothering, Community Work, and the War on Poverty*. New York: Routledge.

Obermiller, Phillip J., Thomas E. Wagner, and Edward Bruce Tucker. 2000. *Appalachian Odyssey: Historical Perspectives on the Great Migration*. Westport, CT: Praeger.

REFERENCES • 211

O'Connor, Alice. 2002. *Poverty Knowledge: Social Science, Social Policy, and the Poor in Twentieth-Century U.S. History.* Princeton, NJ: Princeton University Press.

O'Neil, Catherine. 2017. *Weapons of Math Destruction: How Big Data Increases Inequality and Threatens Democracy.* New York: Penguin.

Orleck, Annelise. 2005. *Storming Caesar's Palace: How Black Mothers Fought Their Own War on Poverty.* Boston: Beacon.

Pacyga, Dominic A. 2009. *Chicago: A Biography.* Chicago: University of Chicago Press.

Parker, Traci. 2019. *Department Stores and the Black Freedom Movement: Workers, Consumers, and Civil Rights from the 1930s to the 1980s.* Chapel Hill: University of North Carolina Press.

Pattillo-McCoy, Mary. 2000. *Black Picket Fences: Privilege and Peril Among the Black Middle Class*, 2nd ed. Chicago: University of Chicago Press.

Phillips, Kimberley. 1999. *AlabamaNorth: African-American Migrants, Community, and Working-Class Activism in Cleveland, 1915–45.* Urbana: University of Illinois Press.

Piven, Frances Fox, and Richard A. Cloward. 1977. "Dilemmas of Organization Building." *Radical America* 11: 39–60.

——. 1998. *The Breaking of the American Social Compact.* New York: New Press.

Prahalad, C. K. 2009. *The Fortune at the Bottom of the Pyramid: Eradicating Poverty Through Profits*, Upper Saddle River NJ: Wharton School Publishing.

Puar, Jasbir K. 2020. "'I Would Rather Be a Cyborg than a Goddess.'" In *Feminist Theory Reader: Local and Global Perspectives*, 5th ed., ed. Carole McCann, Seung-Kyung Kim, and Emek Ergun. New York: Routledge.

Pugh, Allison. 2009. *Longing and Belonging: Parents, Children, and Consumer Culture.* Berkeley: University of California Press

Reese, Ellen, and Garnett Newcombe. 2003. "Income Rights, Mothers' Rights, or Workers' Rights? Collective Action Frames, Organizational Ideologies, and the American Welfare Rights Movement." *Social Problems* 50, no. 2: 294–318.

Ritzer, George, ed. 2007. *The Blackwell Encyclopedia of Sociology*, vol. 2: Consumption. Malden, MA: Blackwell.

Russell, Legacy. 2020. *Glitch Feminism: A Manifesto.* New York: Verso.

212 • REFERENCES

Sharpe, Christina. 2016. *In the Wake: On Blackness and Being*. Durham, NC: Duke University Press.

Simmel, Georg, and Claire Jacobson. 1965. "The Poor." *Social Problems* 13: 118–40.

Smethurst, James Edward. 2005. *The Black Arts Movement: Literary Nationalism in the 1960s and 1970s*. Chapel Hill: University of North Carolina Press.

Spear, Allen. 1967. *Black Chicago: The Making of a Negro Ghetto (1890–1920)*. Chicago: University of Chicago Press.

Springer, Kimberly. 2005. *Living for the Revolution: Black Feminist Organizations, 1968–1980*. Durham, NC: Duke University Press.

Steele, Catherine Knight. 2021. *Digital Black Feminism*. New York: NYU Press.

Stein, Ronald. 1980. "The Consumer Movement in Higher Education: Past, Present and Future." *NASPA Journal* 18, no. 1: 8–14.

Tiemstra, John. 1992. "Education of the Consumer: A Review of Historical Developments, Theories of Regulation, and the History of Consumerism." *International Journal of Social Economics* 19, no. 6: 1–65.

Triece, Mary Eleanor. 2013. *Tell It Like It Is: Women in the National Welfare Rights Movement*. Columbia: University of South Carolina Press.

——. "The Great Migration, 1910–1970," September 13, 2012. https://www.census.gov/dataviz/visualizations/020/.

Weems, Robert E. 1998. *Desegregating the Dollar: African American Consumerism in the Twentieth Century*. New York: NYU Press.

——. 2009. "African American Consumers Since World War II." In *African American Urban History Since World War II*, ed. Kenneth Kusmer and Joe Trotter, 359–75. Chicago: University of Chicago Press.

Wilkenson, Isabel. 2011. *The Warmth of Other Suns: The Epic Story of America's Great Migration*. New York: Vintage.

Williams, Rhonda. 2006. "From Welfare to Workfare: The Unintended Consequences of Liberal Reform, 1945–1965." *Business History Review* 80, no. 2: 343–46.

Williamson, John B., and Kathryn M. Hyer. 1975. "The Measurement and Meaning of Poverty." *Social Problems* 22: 652–63.

Wilson, William Julius. 1987. *The Truly Disadvantaged: The Inner City, the Underclass, and Public Policy*. Chicago: University of Chicago Press.

——. 1997. *When Work Disappears: The World of the New Urban Poor*. New York: Vintage.

World Bank. 2015. "World Development Indicators" (table). http://data.worldbank.org/indicator/SI.POV.GINI?locations=US.

INDEX

Abernathy, Ralph, 74, 178n53
absolute income metrics, 138; GDP for, 136, 137; patriarchy relation to, 133
absolute poverty measures, 133–35, 146, 153, 160
abstract liberalism, 38
ACORN. *See* Association of Community Organizations for Reform Now
ACP. *See* Chicago Archdiocesan Committee on Poverty
ADC. *See* Aid to Dependent Children
Ad Hoc Committee for a Guaranteed Income, of University of Chicago, 12, 143–44
Advisory Council on Public Welfare, 119
AFDC. *See* Aid to Families with Dependent Children
affirmative action programs, 45
Affluent Society, The (Galbraith), 39
African Americans. *See specific topics*
Aid to Dependent Children (ADC), 126, 131, 139, 202n41

Aid to Families with Dependent Children (AFDC), 202n41
A & I State University, 100
AlabamaNorth (Phillips), 108
Alexander's Restaurant, 77
algorithmic assemblages, 3, 14–17, 51, 157, 162, 169n2; government protections and, 94–95; in leadership, 85–86, 87; materiality and, 84; power and, 144; stratification and, 160; of TWO, 86; in Uptown, 57; whiteness and, 82–83; in Woodlawn, 54
algorithms, 14, 170n1; absolute poverty measures and, 134–35; archives compared to, 21–22, 46; of poverty, 18–19, 124–25, 126, 131, 132, 140, 143, 146, 147; of the state, 169n2; welfare policies as, 152–53
Alinsky, Saul, 53–54, 55, 60, 67, 182n86, 191n164; Von Hoffman relation to, 65
anti-Blackness, 139–40, 157; ideology of, 162; of Roman Catholic Archdiocese, 54
antidiscrimination legislation, 41

214 • INDEX

Appalachia, 56
archives, 16, 46; erasure in, 5–6,
  21, 160; violence of, 5, 22, 156,
  163, 171n2; of welfare rights
  movement, 25
Associated Block Clubs of
  Woodlawn, 180n79
Association of Community
  Organizations for Reform Now
  (ACORN), 43, 172n17
Atlanta, 32
Automating Inequality (Eubanks),
  132
automation, 58; unemployment
  from, 141–42

Back of the Yards neighborhood,
  54, 75
Bailey, Moya, 171n8
Baudrillard, Jean, 35–36
Bauman, Zygmunt, 8, 47
BBB. *See* Better Business Bureau
"Being Poor Is Expensive," 113–15,
  116
Bell, Derrick, 192n163
Better Business Bureau (BBB), 96,
  196n18; consumer education by,
  99; Senate Bill 977 and, 104–5
"Beware" flier, 101, 103
bill 19H, 104
Black Apostolic Church of God, 74
Black female leadership, 49–50;
  demonization of, 140; erasure
  of, 131–32; IAF relation to, 65; of
  JOIN, 60–61, 86; of KOCO, 141;
  poor people relation to, 152–53; in
  Uptown, 85
Black feminism, 8, 47
Black feminist technology, 3, 90,
  163; consumer credit as, 91–92,

118, 119–20, 122–23; welfare rights
  movement and, 155
Black homeowners, 99
"Black Metropolis." *See* Southside,
  Chicago
#BlackOutBlackFriday, 100, 158
Black Panther Party, 51
Black patrons, 31, 77
Black women. *See specific topics*
Board of Arbitrations, 189n137
Bourdieu, Pierre, 8–9
boycott, 100, 173n5; consumerism
  relation to, 15; of Country
  Delight, 82; hiring practices
  relation to, 32; of Price Rite
  repair shop, 79–80; of Sears
  Corporation, 12–13, 88–89
Brazier, Arthur, 64, 74, 80–81
Brown, Millard, 70–71
Bureau of Labor Statistics, 127,
  145–46, 160
Butler, Octavia, 20

Cabrini-Green housing project, 51
CABS. *See* Consumer Action
  Bedford-Stuyvesant
capitalism, 16–17, 118–19, 125, 129,
  132, 134; citizenry rights and,
  12–13; consumer credit relation
  to, 97–98, 152; consumerism
  relation to, 95, 109; consumption
  relation to, 133; economic policies
  for, 11; liberation relation to, 15;
  materiality and, 84; middle-class
  whites and, 121–22; patriarchy
  relation to, 42, 68, 85; poverty
  relation to, 120, 150–52; power in,
  155; retail credit and, 18; TWO
  relation to, 78, 79; urban renewal
  and, 60

INDEX • 215

Carlson, Arthur B., 67, 76–77, 189n138
Carson Pirie Scott & Co., 198n40
Cavalcade of Fashions, of TWO, 49–50
CCC. *See* Civilian Conservation Corps
CCCO. *See* Coordinating Committee of Community Organizations
CCDPA. *See* Cook County Department of Public Aid
Census, 142–43, 176n29
Census Bureau, 160
Certified, 81
Chambers, Jason, 29
Chen, Kuan-Hsing, 36
Chicago. *See specific topics*
Chicago Archdiocesan Committee on Poverty (ACP), 115
Chicago Committee on Urban Opportunity, 76
Chicago Defender (newspaper), 49, 182n86
Chicago Dwelling Association, 188n132
Chicago Friends Welfare Rights Organization, 61
Chicago Housing Tenant Organization (CHTO), 51
Chicago Sun-Times (newspaper), 131
Chicago Tribune (newspaper), 131
Chicago Urban League (CUL), 100–101, 103, 128
Chicago Welfare Rights Organization (CWRO), 2, 82, 124, 157, 159, 161; in consumer rights movement, 15; erasure and, 21; at Sears Annual Fashion Show, 88–89
Christmas, 83–84

CHTO. *See* Chicago Housing Tenant Organization
Cincinnati, 13
citizen consumer, 193n173
citizenry rights: capitalism and, 12–13; consumer credit and, 17, 90–91, 111, 122–23; consumerism relation to, 2, 14, 28–29, 42, 159, 193n173; employment and, 163
citizenship, 44, 121; in consumerist society, 9, 94, 98; materiality relation to, 84
citizen shoppers, 189n137
City Plan Commission, 68
City-Wide Welfare Union (CWWU), 73
civil disobedience, 74
Civilian Conservation Corps (CCC), 95
Civil Rights Act (1964), 32
civil rights movement, 32
class, 7, 8; Cavalcade of Fashions relation to, 50; consumerism relation to, 47, 172n14. *See also* algorithmic assemblages
classism, 15, 94–95
Claytor, Cassi Pittman, 30
Cloward, Richard, 43
Cold War, 108
Coleman, Dovie "Big Dovie," 4, 61–64, 157, 163, 178n56; disciplining technology and, 86; NWRO and, 124
Collins, Patricia Hill, 9
"Comet, The" (Du Bois), 20
commodification, 133; GAI and, 154; power relation to, 29; of social lives, 125, 145–46, 147, 161
Commonwealth Edison, 71
communism, TWO relation to, 75, 76

216 • INDEX

community, 47; erasure relation to, 68; individualism compared to, 4–5; self-determination for, 49
Concerned Parents for Adequate Welfare, 115
Congress of Racial Equality (CORE), 58, 170n7
conservatism, 172n17; neoliberalism and, 44
Consumer Action Bedford-Stuyvesant (CABS), 112
Consumer Action Credit Union, 112
consumer advocacy, 4–5
Consumer Bill of Rights (1962), 101
consumer choice, 117, 153; inequity relation to, 123; liberalism and, 18, 121–22; as social justice, 115
consumer credit, 161; Black feminism and, 47; as Black feminist technology, 91–92, 118, 119–20, 122–23; capitalism relation to, 97–98, 152; citizenry rights and, 17, 90–91, 111, 122–23; education on, 97, 105–6, 113; exploitation relation to, 106; legitimacy and, 89–90, 103; NWRO relation to, 13–14, 111–12, 164, 194n4; for poor people, 17, 116–17, 160; from Sears Corporation, 3, 91, 101; social deprivation and, 121–22; as technology, 97–98, 108, 152, 162–63; Welfare Council of Metropolitan Chicago and, 50
"Consumer Credit and the Poor," 110–11
consumer education, 99, 105, 111, 159, 196n20
Consumer Education Curriculum Development Committee, 96

Consumer Education Plan, 96
Consumer Federation of America, 173n3
consumer identity, 10, 51, 96, 193n173
consumerism, 37–39, 46, 79, 158, 194n6; boycott relation to, 15; capitalism relation to, 95, 109; citizenry rights relation to, 2, 14, 28–29, 42, 159, 193n173; class relation to, 47, 172n14; democracy and, 35–36; economy relation to, 105, 142; employment relation to, 25; identity and, 104; ideology of, 22; legitimacy and, 8, 17, 48, 85, 147, 154, 156, 162; neoliberalism and, 11, 29–30, 90; politics and, 50–51, 117; power and, 9, 155–56; race relation to, 118–19; in welfare rights era, 10
consumerist society, 9, 94, 98, 108–9
consumer market, 26, 26–27
consumer protection, legislation for, 40, 93–94, 101
consumer republic, 193n173
consumer rights, 28–29; legislation for, 32, 102; whiteness and, 82–83
consumer rights movement: CWRO in, 15; parallel activism with, 33
consumers, 203n69; corporations relation to, 129; customers versus, 92–93; education of, 92, 96–97, 99, 102, 103–4, 105, 111; exploitation of, 148–49; industry relation to, 95; middle-class, 114–15, 116; poor people as, 109–10, 113–14; renters as, 70, 86; segregation of, 95–96
Consumer Society in American History (Glickman), 94

INDEX • 217

consumption, 3–4, 36; capitalism relation to, 133; neoliberalism relation to, 18; shielding, 194n3

Cook County, 62–63; Department of Public Aid of, 64, 117; food stamp programs in, 150–51

Cook County Department of Public Aid (CCDPA), 128

Coordinating Committee of Community Organizations (CCCO), 72, 81–82

CORE. *See* Congress of Racial Equality

corporations, 79, 129

Coser, Lewis, 133

Country Delight, 81–82

Countryman, Matthew, 30

Covelli, Daniel, 130–31

COVID-19 pandemic, 14, 158, 162

credit unions, 79, 113, 122; of CABS, 112; JOIN for, 86

crooked room, 37

Crusader, The (newspaper), 66–67

CUL. *See* Chicago Urban League

customers, 92–93, 100–101

Cuyahoga County relief administration, 108

CWRO. *See* Chicago Welfare Rights Organization

CWWU. *See* City-Wide Welfare Union

Daley, Richard J., 69, 149; Consumer Education Plan of, 96; JOIN relation to, 72–73; TWO relation to, 75

Dandridge, Catherine, 64, 163

Daniel, David, 64

DaVinci, of Country Delight, 81–82

democracy: consumerism and, 35–36; in marketplace, 29–30

Democratic Party, in Chicago, 73

democratic socialism, 86, 108

demonization: of Black female leadership, 140; of welfare rights movement, 43–44

Department of Agriculture, 145–46

Department of Public Aid, of Cook County, 64, 117

Departments of Labor and Health, Education, and Welfare, 120

deserving/underserving dichotomy, 134

dignity, 107, 164

disabilities, poor people with, 144

disciplining technology, 62, 86

discrimination, 53, 81–82, 96

Don't Buy campaigns, 31

Du Bois, W. E. B., 20

Dunne, George, 130

Du Sable, Jean Baptiste Point, 1

DuSable High School, 99

economic policies, 158; for capitalism, 11; neoliberalism as, 35–36, 47; of Nixon administration, 147–48; of Reagan, 44–45

Economic Research and Action Project (ERAP), 57

economy, 26; consumerism relation to, 105, 142; intersectionality in, 26–27; neoliberalism relation to, 35; poor people relation to, 150–52

education, 45, 111, 117; on consumer credit, 97, 105–6, 113; of consumers, 92, 96–97, 99, 102, 103–4, 105, 111; history, 104; neoliberalism in, 159

egalitarianism, 135, 138
Elementary and Secondary
  Education Act (ESEA), 129–30
employment, 161; citizenry rights
  and, 163; consumerism relation
  to, 25; labor and, 24, *24*, 25
encoding/decoding theory, 34
ERAP. *See* Economic Research and
  Action Project
erasure, 46, 67–68; in archives,
  5–6, 21, 160; of Black female
  leadership, 131–32
ESEA. *See* Elementary and
  Secondary Education Act
Eubanks, Virginia, 132
Evanston United Fund, 110
exploitation, 1–2, 66–67; consumer
  credit relation to, 106; of
  consumers, 148–49; of customers,
  93, 100–101; of labor, 36; white
  flight and, 53

fair wages, 94
Family Assistance Plan, 44, 200n23
Family Assistance Program (FAP),
  128–29, 200n23
Farmer, James, 149
Federal Credit Union Bureau, 112
federal guaranteed income, 41–42
Federal Trade Commission, 94
feminism, 8, 33, 47
feminization, of poverty, 10, 11,
  38–39, 46–47, 136, 142
Feminization of Poverty, The
  (Goldberg and Kremen), 42
Finney, Leon, 65
Firing Line, The (newsletter), 58,
  64, 78
FOL. *See* Future Outlook League
food-buying clubs, 122

food co-op, 78–79, 86, 116
food prices, 115
food stamp programs, 44; in Cook
  County, 150–51; JOIN relation to,
  191n150; stigma of, 79
Foucault, Michel, 34
From Welfare to Workfare (Williams),
  139
Fuentes, Marisa, 5
Future Outlook League (FOL), 76;
  TWO relation to, 77, 189n138,
  192n167

GAI. *See* guaranteed annual
  income
GAIN. See *Guaranteed Annual
  Income Newsletter*
Galbraith, John Kenneth, 39–40
Garvey, Amy, 33
GDP. *See* gross national product
gender: NWRO relation to, 13;
  as social location, 7, 8. *See also*
  algorithmic assemblages
Gibbs, Irene, 151–52
Gini coefficient, 137–38
Goldberg, Gertrude, 42
government protections, algorithmic
  assemblages and, 94–95
Great Society, 44, 45, 125
Greenberg, Cheryl, 29
Gregory, Dick, 149–51
gross national product (GDP), 136,
  137, *137*
guaranteed annual income (GAI),
  109, 114, 124–25, 161, 162;
  automation relation to, 141–42;
  commodification and, 154; JOIN
  for, 86; NWRO and, 134, 138, 141,
  144–46; University of Chicago
  for, 143–44

INDEX • 219

*Guaranteed Annual Income
Newsletter (GAIN)*, 143–44
Gutman, Max, 185n107

Hall, Stuart, 34, 36
Harlem Consumer Education, Inc.,
50–51
Harrington, Michael, 39–40
Harrison, L. Eugene, 180n79
Harris-Perry, Melissa, 37
Harry Truman College, 184n94
Hartman, Saidiya, 5
High-Low Foods Inc., 77
Hilliard, Raymond, 63, 73
hiring practices: boycott relation to,
32; discrimination in, 81–82, 96
history education, 104
homeowners, Black, 99
Honore, Henry, 103
Horn, Etta, 90–92, 110–11
Horvat, Paul, 115–16
housing, 69, 75
Housing and Planning Committee,
of TWO, 71
Hyer, Kathryn M., 146–47

IAF. *See* Industrial Areas
Foundation
identity, 93; consumer, 10, 51, 96,
193n173; consumerism and, 104;
neoliberal, 17; oppression relation
to, 117–18
ideology, 9, 18, 35–38, 153, 169n5;
of anti-Blackness, 162; of
consumerism, 22
Illinois, 97, 125–26, 130–31, 149–50;
consumer rights legislation in,
32; Senate Bill 977 of, 103–4
Illinois Retail Merchants
Association, 97

imperialism, 173n5
individualism, community
compared to, 4–5
Industrial Areas Foundation (IAF),
22, 156, 162, 182n83; Black female
leadership relation to, 65; erasure
and, 21; NORC relation to, 99;
TWO relation to, 53–54, 67–68,
180n79
industry, 26; consumers relation to,
95; intersectionality in, 26–27
inequity, 125; consumer choice
relation to, 123; consumerism
and, 119; in neoliberalism, 109,
172n12
interest convergence, 81, 192n163
intermediate reading, 25, 26,
171nn6–7
interracial collaborations, 195n16
intersectionality, 169n2, 203n69; in
economy, 26–27; social location
and, 8, 11
intersectional political consumerism.
See specific topics

Jackson, Jesse, 131–32
James, Hulbert, 107, 162
Jim Crow laws, 1
job security, 98
Jobs or Income Now (JOIN), 64,
178n56, 179n65, 185n107; Black
female leadership of, 60–61,
86; boycotts by, 79–80; food
co-op of, 78–79, 86; food stamp
programs relation to, 191n150;
KOCO and, 63; materiality
relation to, 83–84; NWRO
relation to, 58, 174n10; rent strikes
of, 51, 71–72; SCLC relation to,
72–73; socialism and, 58; TWO

220 • INDEX

Jobs or Income Now (JOIN)
(*continued*)
compared to, 16–17, 52, *59*, 60,
74, 77, 82–83, 85–87, 156–58;
in Uptown, 56–57; whiteness
relation to, 68
Johnson, Lorraine, 65
Johnson, Lyndon B., 45, 125–26
JOIN. *See* Jobs or Income Now
JOIN Community Union
(newsletter), 63
Jordan, June, 20
Jordan-Zachary, Julia, 21
JSTOR database, 23, 25, 155, 160,
171n3
June 30 demonstrations, 12

Kennedy, John F., 40
Kenwood Oakland Community
Organization (KOCO), 63, 73,
141
Kerner, Otto, 103–4
Kerner Commission, 36
King, Martin Luther, Jr., 61, 72, 178n53
Kiplinger Washington Letter
(publication), 147–48
KOCO. *See* Kenwood Oakland
Community Organization
Kornbluh, Felicia, 32, 42, 44
Kremen, Eleanor, 42
Kyros, George, 76–77, 80–81

labor: employment and, 24, *24*, 25;
exploitation of, 36
Lakeview-Uptown Community
Council, 69
Land Clearance Commission, 68
landlords, of low-income properties,
70
Lanier, Jonquil, 112

Lawndale Tenants Union, 51
leadership: algorithmic assemblages
in, 85–86, 87. *See also* Black
female leadership
League of Credit Unions, 112
legislation, 39; antidiscrimination,
41; for consumer protection, 40,
93–94, 101; for consumer rights,
32, *102*
legitimacy, 146; consumer credit and,
89–90, 103; consumerism and, 8,
17, 48, 85, 147, 154, 156, 162; power
relation to, 8
Leland Food Buying Club, 78–79
Lewis, Oscar, 39
liberalism: abstract, 38; consumer
choice and, 18, 121–22; in New
Deal, 134; poverty and, 138–39
liberation, 157; capitalism relation
to, 15
Lind, Earl, 96, 196n18
"Live on a Welfare Budget,"
120–21
local school boards, 130
Lorde, Audre, 20, 140
Losing Ground (Murray), 45–46
low-income properties, landlords
of, 70
Lutherans, 182n83

Mabry, Ruby, 131, 163
Mack, Ginger, 144, 163
maladaptive behaviors, poverty and,
39–40
male leaders, 4–5
Mallet, 173n4
March on Washington for Jobs and
Freedom, 57
Mark, Julius, 70
marketplace, 29–30, 198n40

INDEX • 221

Marshall Field's, Black employment at, 77
Martin, C. Virgil, 198n40
materiality, 18, 83–84, 164
McClure, Edward, 110
"Measurement and Meaning of Poverty, The" (Williamson and Hyer), 146–47
Michael Reese Hospital, 103
middle-class Black families, 53
middle-class consumers, 114–15, 116
middle-class whites, 30, 60, 108–9, 119; capitalism and, 121–22; materiality and, 18, 83–84; neoliberalism of, 17
misogynoir, 28, 153, 171n8; neoliberalism relation to, 47; in policies, 132
mobilization, organization relation to, 43
mom co-ops, 158
Montgomery Ward, 106
Moore, Ada, 65, 163
Morley, David, 36
Moynihan, Daniel Patrick, 40, 128, 172n17, 200n23
multinational businesses, 194n6
Murray, Charles, 45–46

National Association of Market Developers (NAMD), 100
National Consumer League, 173n3
National Coordinating Committee, 12
National Opinion Research Center (NORC), 99
National Tenants Organization (NTO), 141
National Urban League (NUL), 118, 148

National Welfare Rights Organization (NWRO), 2, 41–42, 149–50, 153–54, 159, 173n3; ACORN compared to, 43; "Being Poor Is Expensive" of, 113–15, 116; Coleman and, 61, 124, 178n56; consumer credit relation to, 13–14, 111–12, 164, 194n4; ESEA relation to, 129–30; FAP relation to, 128–29; GAI and, 134, 138, 141, 144–46; JOIN relation to, 58, 174n10; "Live on a Welfare Budget" of, 120–21; National Coordinating Committee and, 12; Nixon administration relation to, 125, 132; poor people relation to, 136; Sears Credit Campaign of, 18, 32, 88–89, 106–7, 122; social deprivation and, 119; SSA relation to, 147; Stamps relation to, 51–52; strategic action conference of, 182n86; unemployment relation to, 127; Ways and Means Committee of, 90–91
Near North, 51
neoliberalism, 135; conservatism and, 44; consumer credit and, 122–23; consumerism and, 11, 29–30, 90; consumption relation to, 18; as economic policies, 35–36, 47; in education, 159; inequity in, 109, 172n12; of middle-class whites, 17; poverty relation to, 37–38; power and, 35, 38; racism and, 36; social welfare programs relation to, 110; welfare policies and, 46
Newcombe, Garnett, 43
New Crusader (newspaper), 75
New Deal, 44, 95, 134

222 • INDEX

New Opportunities for Waterbury (NOW), 112–13
News of Welfare (NOW), 50
Newton, Huey, 58
New York City, 41
Nixon administration, 132, 133, 200n23; algorithms of poverty and, 124–25, 126; CUL relation to, 128; economic policies of, 147–48; Family Assistance Plan of, 44; Gini coefficient during, 137–38; welfare policies of, 18, 153
NORC. *See* National Opinion Research Center
#NotOneDime, 100, 158
NOW. *See* New Opportunities for Waterbury; News of Welfare
NTO. *See* National Tenants Organization
NUL. *See* National Urban League
NWRO. *See* National Welfare Rights Organization

objectivism, 28
Obligacion, Gaudencio, 113
Observer Printing and Publishing, 78
O'Connor, Alice, 139
Office of Economic Opportunity, 76
Ogilvie, Richard, 130–31, 133
Operation Breadbasket, of SCLC, 32, 81, 131–32
oppression, 84, 117–18
organization, mobilization relation to, 43
Other America, The (Harrington), 39
Outlook (magazine), 151

Page, Ray, 104, 196n18
Parable of the Sower (Butler), 20

parallel computing, 15, 32–33
Parker, Traci, 29
Partee, Cecil, 97–98
Pastor's Alliance, 67
paternalism, 108; poverty and, 161
patriarchy, 10, 134; absolute income metrics relation to, 133; capitalism relation to, 42, 68, 85; inequity and, 125; poverty and, 138; of TWO, 64–65, 85–86
Pattillo-McCoy, Mary, 30
Peterson, Esther, 118–19
Philadelphia, 13, 32, 107, 162
Phillips, Kimberley, 108
PIE-C. *See* Public Interest Economic Center
Pitts, Rosa, 65, 163
Piven, Frances Fox, 43
policies: economic, 11, 35–36, 44–45, 47, 147–48, 158; misogynoir in, 132; welfare, 18, 46, 152–53, 194n4
political economic action, 7
politics, 115–16; consumerism and, 50–51, 117; research relation to, 21–22
poor people, 39, 42, 83–84, 140; Black female leadership relation to, 152–53; consumer credit for, 17, 116–17, 160; as consumers, 109–10, 113–14; with disabilities, 144; economy relation to, 150–52; middle-class consumers compared to, 114–15; NWRO relation to, 136
Poor People's Campaign, 61, 178n53
Poor People's Organizing Convention, 63
Poor People's Platform, 141

INDEX • 223

poverty, 1–2, 36, 41, 159; absolute measures of, 133–35, 146, 153, 160; algorithms of, 18–19, 124–25, 126, 131, 132, 140, 143, 146, 147; capitalism relation to, 120, 150–52; feminization of, 10, 11, 38–39, 46–47, 136, 142; Great Society and, 125; liberalism and, 138–39; maladaptive behaviors and, 39–40; neoliberalism relation to, 37–38; paternalism and, 161; power relation to, 132–33, 154; social welfare programs relation to, 45, 119; in Uptown, 56
Poverty Level, 145
Poverty Rights/Action Center (PRAC), 12, 170n7
power, 8; algorithmic assemblages and, 144; in capitalism, 155; commodification relation to, 29; consumerism and, 9, 155–56; neoliberalism and, 35, 38; poverty relation to, 132–33, 154; social location and, 9, 47; in welfare rights movement, 48
PRAC. *See* Poverty Rights/Action Center
"Price of Credit" (filmstrip), 105
Price Rite repair shop, boycott of, 79–80
private businesses, 18
privilege, 169n3
Protestants, 182n83
Puar, Jasbir, 169n2
Public Interest Economic Center (PIE-C), 51
public schools, consumer education in, 105, 111, 159
Pure Food and Drug Act (1906), 93–94

race, 118–19; on Census, 142–43; as social location, 7, 8. *See also* algorithmic assemblages
racism, 15, 125, 134; neoliberalism and, 36; poverty relation to, 10, 133; whiteness relation to, 55
Reagan, Ronald, 35, 44–45, 131
Reese, Ellen, 43
regulation, 93–95
relative poverty measures, 135, 138, 153
rental housing market, 158
renters, as consumers, 70, 86
rent strikes, 51, 70–72, 86, 157–58
research, 27; politics relation to, 21–22; on poverty, 41
Resolution on Retail Trade, of TWO, 80
retail credit, capitalism and, 18
revolution, 136
Robinson, William, 63–64, 73
Roman Catholic Archdiocese, 182n83; anti-Blackness of, 54; IAF relation to, 67
Roosevelt, Franklin Delano, 95, 107–8
Roosevelt, Theodore, 12
Rustin, Bayard, 178n53

Sadlow, Constance, 112
Saving Our Lives Hear Our Truths (SOLHOT), 204n1
Schaibel, Walter, 67
School of Social Service Administration, of University of Chicago, 143–44
SCLC. *See* Southern Christian Leadership Conference
SDS. *See* Students for a Democratic Society

224 • INDEX

Sears Annual Fashion Show, 88–89, 119–20

Sears Corporation, 159; boycott of, 12–13, 88–89; consumer credit from, 3, 91, 101

Sears Credit Campaign, 18, 32, 88–89, 106–7, 122

segregation, 1, 76, 95–96, 182n83

selective patronage campaigns, 32

self-determination, 75–76; for community, 49; TWO and, 78

Self-Help Action Center (SHAC), 115

Senate Bill 977, of Illinois, 103–5

sexism, 15, 94–95

SHAC. *See* Self-Help Action Center

Sharpe, Christina, 5

Shavers, Dorothy, 4, 115, 116, 163

shielding consumption, 194n3

shopping centers, 110

Shriver, R. Sargent, 73

Sister Citizen (Harris-Perry), 37

SNCC. *See* Student Nonviolent Coordinating Committee

social deprivation: consumer credit and, 121–22; NWRO and, 119

socialism, 16–17; democratic, 86, 108; JOIN and, 58

social justice, 115, 192n163

social lives, commodification of, 125, 145–46, 147, 161

social location, 7, 29; intersectionality and, 8, 11; power and, 9, 47

Social Security Administration (SSA), 145–47

social support programs, 44

social unrest, 41

social welfare programs, 139; neoliberalism relation to, 110; poverty relation to, 45, 119

"Sociology of Poverty" (Coser), 133

SOLHOT. *See* Saving Our Lives Hear Our Truths

Solidarity Day, 61

South East Commission, 68

Southern Christian Leadership Conference (SCLC), 141; JOIN relation to, 72–73; Operation Breadbasket of, 32, 81, 131–32; TWO relation to, 74–75

Southside, Chicago, 1–2

speculative fiction, 20

Square Deal campaign, 77, 81, 117, 189n137

SSA. *See* Social Security Administration

Stamps, Marion, 51–52, 163

the state, 18, 39, 130; algorithms of, 169n2; disciplining technology of, 62; neoliberalism relation to, 35

State Jewelers and Clothiers, 103

state-sanctioned violence, 100

strategic action conference, of NWRO, 182n86

stratification, algorithmic assemblages and, 160

Student Nonviolent Coordinating Committee (SNCC), 32, 60

Students for a Democratic Society (SDS), 57, 78

Stulman, Harriet, 62

subprime lending, 163

subsidized income programs, 150

"Subversive Potential, Coercive Intent" (Kornbluh), 42

INDEX • 225

success, 164
Sullivan, Leon, 32

technology, 15, 20–21, 34, 132, 170n1; consumer credit as, 97–98, 108, 152, 162–63; disciplining, 62, 86. *See also* Black feminist technology
Temporary Woodlawn Organization. *See* The Woodlawn Organization
tenant unions, 158
Terry, Peggy, 58, 60–61, 79, 84
Thomas, Rose, 115
Thurman, Dovie "Little Dovie," 62–64, 163
Tillmon, Johnnie, 119, 173n3
Title I, 129–30
topic modeling, 23–24, *24*, 25, *26*
trickle-down economics, 44
Truth, Sojourner, 33
TWO. *See* The Woodlawn Organization
TWO-Hillmans shopping complex, 78

UAW. *See* United Auto Workers union
unemployment, 126–28, 151; from automation, 141–42
United Auto Workers union (UAW), 57
United Woodlawn Conference, 180n79
universal basic income, 14, 162
University of Chicago, 12, 55; for GAI, 143–44; Woodlawn relation to, 68–69, 81
Uptown, Chicago, 56–57, 69, 184n94; Black female leadership in, 85; rent strikes in, 71–72

Urban Coalition, 173n3
urban renewal, 60, 75–76, 81

Victory Mutual Life Insurance, 71
violence, 16; of archives, 5, 22, 156, 163, 171n2; state-sanctioned, 100
Vivian, C. T., 74
Von Hoffman, Nicholas, 65
voting rights, 94
Voting Rights Act (1965), 32

wage garnishments, 101, 103
wage process, 109
Walker, Ruth, 141
Washington, D.C., 147
Washington, Harold, 51
Washington Post (newspaper), 119
Waterbury, Connecticut, 112–13
Ways and Means Committee, of NWRO, 90–91
WBMA. *See* Woodlawn Business Men's Association
wealthy people, 136
Weems, Robert, 29
welfare. *See* social welfare programs
Welfare Council of Metropolitan Chicago, 50, 109–10
welfare policies, 18, 42–43, 194n4; as algorithms, 152–53; neoliberalism and, 46
Welfare Recipients Demand Action (WRDA), 62, 178n56
Welfare Rehabilitation Service Center, 64
welfare rights era, 6, 10, 14, *137*
welfare rights movement, 20–21, 108, 157; archives of, 25; Black feminist technology and, 155; demonization of, 43–44; neoliberalism relation to, 35, 135;

226 • INDEX

welfare rights movement (*continued*)
parallel activism with, 33; power
in, 48. *See specific topics*
welfare rights organizations
(WROs). *See specific topics*
Wells-Barnett, Ida, 33
West Side, Chicago, 127–28, 148
West Side Organization (WSO),
141
Westside Recipients Action Group
(WRAGS), 64
West Woodlawn Woman's
Community Club (WWWCC),
65–66, 67–68
white establishments, Black patrons
relation to, 31
white flight, 53, 81, 182n83
whiteness, 17, 169n3; consumer rights
and, 82–83; JOIN relation to, 68;
racism relation to, 55
white-owned businesses, Black
employment at, 76–77
white savior narratives, 67–68
white supremacy, 172n12
white women, Black women
compared to, 143
Wilde, Oscar, 84
Wiley, George, 12, 52, 110–11, 141,
170n7
Williams, Rhonda, 139
Williamson, John B., 146–47
Willis, Nezzie, 124, 163
Wilson, William Julius, 172n17
Wood, Arthur, 91
Woodlawn, Chicago, 52–55, 67,
76–77, 99, 176n29, 191n164;
University of Chicago relation
to, 68–69, 81

Woodlawn Booster (newsletter),
80–81
Woodlawn Business Men's
Association (WBMA), 77, 80–81,
99
Woodlawn Community
Rehabilitation Center, 68–69
Woodlawn Conference, erasure of,
67–68
Woodlawn Observer, The
(newsletter), 78
The Woodlawn Organization
(TWO), 66, 159, 182n86, 183n92,
189n137; capitalism relation to,
78, 79; Cavalcade of Fashions
of, 49–50; Chicago Dwelling
Association and, 188n132;
communism relation to, 75, 76;
Country Delight and, 81–82;
FOL relation to, 77, 189n138,
192n167; Housing and Planning
Committee of, 71; IAF relation
to, 53–54, 67–68, 180n79; JOIN
compared to, 16–17, 52, 59, 60,
74, 77, 82–83, 85–87, 156–58;
patriarchy of, 64–65, 85–86;
rent strikes of, 51, 70–71; SCLC
relation to, 74–75; WBMA
relation to, 80–81
WRAGS. *See* Westside Recipients
Action Group
WRDA. *See* Welfare Recipients
Demand Action
WROs. *See* welfare rights
organizations
WSO. *See* West Side Organization
WWWCC. *See* West Woodlawn
Woman's Community Club

Printed and bound by CPI Group (UK) Ltd, Croydon, CR0 4YY

19/11/2024

14595385-0001